Architecture In Use

An Introduction to the Programming, Design and Evaluation of Buildings

Theo JM van der Voordt
Herman BR van Wegen

AMSTERDAM • BOSTON • HEIDELBERG • LONDON • NEW YORK • OXFORD
PARIS • SAN DIEGO • SAN FRANCISCO • SINGAPORE • SYDNEY • TOKYO

Architectural Press is an imprint of Elsevier

ELSEVIER

Architectural
Press

Architectural Press
An imprint of Elsevier
Linacre House, Jordan Hill, Oxford OX2 8DP
30 Corporate Drive, Burlington, MA 01803

Published by arrangement with THOTH Publishers, Bussum, the Netherlands

First published in English, 2005

This publication is a co-product of the Departments of Architecture and Real Estate & Housing of the Faculty of Architecture at the Delft University of Technology, Berlageweg 1, 2628 CR Delft, the Netherlands

National referees
Hans Cornelissen, Prof. Leen van Duin, Maarten Korpershoek, Dr Otakar Macel, Dick Vrielink and Dr Pieter van Wesemael, all present or former colleagues at the Faculty of Architecture

International referees
Prof. Dr Halina Dunin-Woyseth, Oslo School of Architecture, Norway; Prof. Richard Foqué, Henry van de Velde Instituut, Antwerpen, Belgium; Prof. Juhani Katainen, Tampere University of Technology, Department of Architecture, Finland; Prof. Dr Sheila Ornstein, School of Architecture and Urban Planning, University of Sao Paulo, Brazil; Prof. Necdet Teymur, METU, Faculty of Architecture, Ankara, Turkey

Translation
Arthur Payman

Photography
Authors, photographic service Faculty of Architecture and P. van Dooyeweert, unless otherwise mentioned

Graphic design
Johannes Niemeijer, Delft

British Library Cataloguing in Publication Data
A catalogue record for this book is available from the British Library

ISBN 0 7506 6457 6

For information on all Architectural Press publications visit our website at: http://books.elsevier.com

Printed and bound in United Kingdom

Contents

Preface   *vii*
List of Tables   *ix*
Figure Credits   *xi*

Chapter 1: Architectonic and functional quality of buildings   **1**
1.1. Functions of a building   1
1.2. Functional quality   3
1.3. Architectonic quality   4
1.4. Phases of the building process   8
1.5. Conclusion   10
Bibliography   11

Chapter 2: Function and form   **13**
2.1. The search for form   13
2.2. Functional and constructional efficiency   14
2.3. Development of functionalist ideas   19
2.4. Flexibility and multifunctionality   32
2.5. Context   37
2.6. Autonomy of form   46
2.7. Conclusion   66
Bibliography   68

Chapter 3: Programme of requirements   **71**
3.1. Introduction   71
3.2. The role of programming in the building process   73
3.3. Contents of the programme of requirements   83
3.4. Steps leading to a programme of requirements   96
Bibliography   105

Chapter 4: From brief to design   **109**
4.1. Introduction   109
4.2. What is design?   110
4.3. Design methodology   112
4.4. Design processes   118
4.5. Design methods   124
4.6. Quality control   132
Bibliography   135

Contents

Chapter 5: Evaluating buildings   **141**
    5.1. Introduction   141
    5.2. Product and process, ex ante and ex post   142
    5.3. Why evaluate?   142
    5.4. Quality assessment   149
    5.5. An integrated approach   164
    Bibliography   166

Chapter 6: Quality assessment: methods of measurement   **169**
    6.1. Criteria for functional quality   169
    6.2. Methods of measurement   205
    6.3. Checklists and assessment scales   208
    Bibliography   219

Name index   **227**
Subject index   **233**

Preface

Architecture is often thought of as a synthesis of form, function and technology, subject to specified conditions such as time, money and regulations. This tripartite quality of architecture goes back more than 2000 years to the time when Vitruvius distinguished three components of architecture: *utilitas* (functionality or utility value: the social dimension), *firmitas* (strength and rigidity: the technological dimension) and *venustas* (beauty: the artistic or aesthetic dimension). There seems therefore to be a permanent consensus on the importance of functional quality in architectonic design.

The aim of this book is to show how the concept of functional quality can be made measurable and expressed in concrete terms, with particular reference to the design of buildings. After a short introduction dealing with the functions performed by a building and the relationship between functional quality and architectonic quality, the book moves on to give a bird's-eye view of the history of architecture. The main question is how different architectural schools of thought deal with the relationship between function and form. This is followed by a discussion on how the desired functional quality can be expressed in a programme of requirements or brief and put into practice in a design. The next chapter deals with the evaluation of a design or completed building. Here a distinction is made between process- and product-directed evaluations and ex ante (before construction of the building) versus ex post (after realisation). Particular attention is paid to those aspects which can be important and the way in which a design or building can be examined to see whether it provides the desired quality of use. In the last chapter the concept of functional quality is analysed into nine different aspects. For each aspect an indication is given of its spatial implications and how it can be translated into concrete programmatic requirements and design principles. The chapter also discusses the criteria that are available to examine designs and completed buildings for functionality. Each chapter ends with a survey of the literature consulted, partly in acknowledgement and partly as a guide to further reading.

The book is primarily intended for students of architecture at establishments of higher education, though it is hoped that it will find its way also into architectural design practice.

Preface

Note to the English edition
This book is an English translation and update of the Dutch publication 'Architectuur en Gebruikswaarde'. The character of a book is always coloured by the background of its authors. Although this book has an international focus, much attention is paid to the way people at the Faculty of Architecture in Delft think about quality of use as an integral component of architectural design. Many illustrations are drawn from Dutch architecture. But the thinking behind them is universal, and is supported internationally in professional literature. We would like to thank Karen Rodrigues for her support in translating all schemes and Noëlle Huijgen for supporting us in our search for new international research findings and references.

Theo van der Voordt
Herman van Wegen

List of Tables

3.1. Example of a space table for an office building   94

5.1. Sample questions for the evaluation of buildings   143

5.2. Comparison of supply and demand   156

5.3. Example allocation of weighting factors   160

6.1. Conceptual framework for flexibility of buildings in the use phase   180

6.2. Examples of design techniques for incorporating flexibility   182

6.3. Environmental effects on health and well-being   196

6.4. Instruments for measuring building quality   216

Figure Credits

Every effort has been made to trace the owners of copyright material but the publishers would be glad to hear from any copyright owners of material produced in this book whose copyright has unwittingly been infringed.

Photography: Authors, photographic service.

2.1. Courtesy of Chicago Historical Soceity	15
2.6. Courtesy of Sainsbury Centre for Visual Arts	21
2.7. Courtesy of Richard Bryant	22
2.8. Courtesy of Suzuki, Hisao	23
2.21. Courtesy of Jeff Goldberg/Esto	43
2.22. Courtesy of www.arcadata.com; www.earthcam.com; www.daniel-libeskind.com	44
2.26. Courtesy of Paul Rocheleau, Museum of Modern Art, New York	52
2.36. Courtesy of www.archrecord.com	64
2.37. Courtesy www.noarch.com	65
6.11. Courtesy of Architekton/Dieter Leistner	203

CHAPTER 1

Architectonic and functional quality of buildings

1.1 Functions of a building

In psychology the term 'function' is defined as 'ability' or 'power'. The dictionary amplifies this definition by adding 'special kind of activity' or 'mode of action'. Various authors have devoted their considerations to the functions of a building. In the 1960s De Bruijn, one of the founders of functional analysis as a discipline at Delft's Faculty of Architecture, distinguished four different functions (Zeeman, 1980):

- *Protective function*: protection of people and property against harmful influences and dangers, e.g. wind and rain, inquisitive onlookers, interference.
- *Domain or territorial function*: buildings make it possible to operate in a place of one's own, without disturbance from others. Key words are privacy, safety and security.

■ *Social function*: buildings create spaces and places in which people can carry on their activities optimally. Primary elements here are health, welfare, communication and quality of life.

■ *Cultural function*: a building must also satisfy requirements relating to the form and character of the spatial environment. The cultural function involves aesthetic, architectonic, urban design, planning and environmental factors. Culture also includes the notion of civilisation, one of whose implications are that buildings and the activities they accommodate should not be nuisance or cause damage to the environment.

The architecture critics Hillier and Leaman (1976) also distinguish four main functions of a building, but divide them up differently:

■ *Spatial organisation of activities*
A building needs to provide optimum support for the activities desired by properly arranging the available space: for example, by siting related activities next to one another and providing efficient communication between them, and by separating activities that are likely to conflict with one another.

■ *Climate regulation*
A building must provide an optimum interior climate for the user, his activities and his property. This necessitates a protective 'filter', separating the inside from the outside, and efficient plant. Inside the building, elements which separate and connect and the equipment of the different rooms must make it possible to adjust the interior climate of each room to suit its own particular use.

■ *Symbolic function*
A building can be seen as the material embodiment of the specific ideas and expectations not just of its designer but also of the client and the users. This makes it a cultural object, an object with social and symbolic significance and meaning.

■ *Economic function*
A building requires investment. It gives added value to raw materials. Maintenance and management form part of the exploitation cost, and must be set against income from rental or sale. It follows that a building, whether property or an investment object, has economic value and so an economic function.

The first functions named in the above lists can be summarised as *utility functions*. The last two functions refer to *cultural functions*. This division corresponds closely to the functions distinguished by the architect Norberg-Schulz (1965). A building creates an artificial climate, protecting people against the influence of weather, insects, wild animals, enemies and other environmental hazards. The building also provides a functional framework, within which human activities can be carried out. These activities are socially determined, and so give buildings a social meaning. A building can also represent something cultural – perhaps something religious or philosophical. Norberg-Schulz refers to the combination of a building as a piece of social environment and its cultural symbolism as a 'symbolic environment'.

Delft University of Technology's Professor Dirken (1972), head of the product ergonomics department of the industrial design faculty, uses the terms *primary* and *secondary* functionality. Primary functionality means the utility value or effectiveness of a product. Secondary functionality is concerned with function as a bearer of meanings, as for example a building as a means of expressing status, evoking a sense of beauty or representing the kind of experiential values that are described in terms such as 'pleasant', 'pleasing' or 'attractive'. Ekambi-Schmidt (1972) calls this 'affective functionality'. Others call the function of form to evoke a sense of beauty as the 'aesthetic' function.

1.2 Functional quality

Quality is the extent to which a product fulfils the requirements set for it. 'Functional' refers to the function or functions performed by something, in this case a building. Thus, the functional quality of a building means its ability to fulfil the functions envisaged for it. Van Dale's Dutch dictionary defines *functioneel* [related to the English 'functional'] as 'suitable for its purpose' and mentions functional design as an example. Here the term is mainly used in connection with making possible and providing spatial support for the use envisaged. *Webster's Dictionary* provides a similar definition, defining functional as '. . . connected with, used to contribute to the development or maintenance of a larger whole, designed or developed chiefly from the point of view of use'. Thus, functional quality can be defined as the extent to which the building and the constructional means applied make possible and provide a proper level of support for the utility function or the activities envisaged.

The functionality of a building does, however, also depend on the extent to which its spatial and physical qualities support the other three functions listed by Hillier and Leaman – the climatologic function, the cultural function and the economic function. A climatologically unsatisfactory building is not user-friendly. A high cultural value can increase a building's utility value. A building is only functional when resources (ground, construction and materials) are used efficiently and the building is arranged effectively and efficiently. In a wider sense, therefore, the functional quality of a building can be defined as the extent to which it provides a proper level of support to the desired activities, creates a pleasing interior climate, has a positive symbolic or cultural meaning and contributes to a favourable economic return and an optimum price–performance ratio.

In practice, however, it is usual for the expression 'functional quality' to concentrate on the first of these functions. If a building is being discussed as a climate regulator it is much more usual to talk of the quality of the building technology or building physics. Symbolic value is generally considered to fall under architectonic quality or be treated as aesthetic quality. Experiential value falls under the same heading. The relationship between quality and cost is often treated as a functional aspect (efficiency of design), or as an economic issue.

Summarising, it can be concluded that functional quality refers primarily to a building's efficiency, practical usability or utility value, taking into accounts the financial means available. Functional quality requires a building to have good accessibility ('access for all'), to provide sufficient space, to be arranged efficiently and comprehensibly, to be sufficiently flexible and to provide spatial and physical conditions that will ensure a safe, healthy and pleasant environment. More details are given in Chapter 6.

1.3   Architectonic quality

The term 'architectonic quality' is used both in a narrow sense and in a wider sense. In architectural journals and discussions on architecture, architectonic quality is generally linked primarily with visual and compositional qualities and symbolic or cultural meaning, so that it comes to be seen as complementing or sometimes even contrasting with functional quality. Take, for example, an observation like, 'Functionally the building is well thought out, but architectonically it is poor'. According to Delft University of Technology's Professor Carel Weeber, quoted by Van Dijk and De Graaf (1990), a building can be perfectly sound even if it lacks architectonic interest. A building's architectonic quality is not determined by the professionalism with which it was built, but by the part it plays in architectural discussion. A building only becomes architecture when it is discussed; i.e. when it plays a part in cultural discussion. Weeber believes that the fact that a building is well thought out professionally is not enough to make it a piece of architecture. It remains unclear whether the converse might also be true – whether one can speak of architectonic quality in cases where the user requirements are satisfied insufficiently or not at all, and the workmanship is unsound. Tjeerd Dijkstra, former government architect, is very explicit on this point. In a paper on architectural policy entitled *Architectonische Kwaliteit* (Architectonic quality), dating from 1985 and adapted in 2001, he explicitly links architectonic quality with utility value. In his view it is essential that the form of a building is derived from the user requirements and the possibility of achieving efficient construction with available materials and techniques and taking into account the urban design context. And this should be done in a way that is both stimulating and appealing (Box 1.1).

Similar to Dijkstra's view is the opinion of Van Rossum and De Wildt (1996). These authors studied the relationship between the way a commission is awarded and the architectonic quality achieved. With the help of four groups of questions, three architecture critics judged the architectonic quality of 18 buildings. They also emphasise the relationship between form, function and construction, consistency and context (Box 1.2).

Box 1.1 Components of architectonic quality, according to a former government architect

■ Utility value: the extent to which the building is suitable for the use envisaged suggests this use and gives it an extra dimension.
■ Clarity and complexity: the composition of the building should structure the way it is perceived, making it clear, comprehensible, recognisable and, in due course, familiar. At the same time the building should be stimulating, which requires a degree of complexity. Complexity exists when a composition combines a number of different themes: for example when the structure of the building derives not just from its function but also from its urban design context.
■ Object and context: internally, this refers to such things as the treatment of the transition between public and private, between collective use and individual use; externally, it refers to the contribution the building makes to (and the influence it exerts on) the quality of public open space.
■ The way in which use is made of architectonic resources such as size ratios, materials, texture, colour and light.
■ Associative meanings.

Source: Dijkstra, 1985/2001.

Box 1.2 Components of architectonic quality, according to a number of architecture critics

1. *Building, function and context*
What was the context in which the project had to be completed? What was the nature of the site? Did the site have special qualities? Did it impose special requirements, tacitly or not? Was there any conflict between programme and site? Does the building add quality to the site or has it damaged its original quality? Does the building as realised satisfy its intended function? Is it a faithful translation of that function? Or is it more than that; does it add something, because of its expressiveness and spatial quality? Does it elevate the required functions to a more poetic level, so creating new associations and meanings?

(*Continued*)

---

2. *Internal consistency*

How is the building's function reflected in its spatial organisation? Does it conform to a particular typology or does it raise questions about a particular typology? How is the spatial quality of the building perceived? Is the visitor 'led' through the building by a consistent spatial configuration? Is there a 'story', a 'thread' running through the development of the interior space: introduction, development, tension, gradual transition, in-between, contrast, climax, surprise? Do important rooms perform important functions?

3. *Form, function and meaning*

Is the form a translation or expression of the internal spatial structure? Can the internal structure be deduced from the exterior? Or does the external form live a life of its own, independent of what goes on inside? Does the form say anything about the content? Does the building as a whole display a consistent form? Is the chosen formal vocabulary worked out consistently in all its components?

What part is played by the constructional technique? Does it determine the form or serve it? Is it emphasised or hidden away? Does it use its own metaphors, based on its own logic, and if so does it evoke some relevant meaning?

Does its form give the building a meaning that is legible to all? Does the form express what it is: a house, a theatre, a church, a factory, an office, a government building? What is the meaning of the building in its context, particularly in its urban context? How does the building relate to the buildings which surround it? Does it act in this relationship as subordinate or coordinator? Does it allow itself to dominate or does it fit in discreetly? Does all this tie in with the meaning of its function in the given context? Does the building express different meanings at the same time? Does it achieve a synthesis of complex content with clear expressive form, a simple form in which complexity is nonetheless perceptible?

4. *Special factors for government buildings*

How does government use architecture to present itself? How does it use buildings to present itself or its services to the population at large? Should it be dominant, neutral or self-effacing, haughty, stand-offish, receptive or friendly, firm, confidence-inspiring or provisional, ephemeral? What means, what metaphors will allow a building to express these different characteristics?

How does the building relate to public space? Does it contribute to the determination, arrangement or character of public space? Does the building express a particular view of culture or society? Does it make a statement about how society works or how it ought to work? Has the building sufficient poetic quality or is it sufficiently innovative to serve as an example?

Source: Van Rossum and de Wildt, 1996.

The paper *Ruimte voor Architectuur* [Space for Architecture] (WVC/VROM, 1991), prepared jointly by the Ministry of Culture and the Ministry of Housing, Spatial Planning and Environment, uses the terms cultural value, utility value and future value. Utility value refers to the extent to which a building or space serves the desired potential uses. Cultural value refers to criteria such as originality, expressiveness, relationship with the environment, value as a piece of cultural history, design quality and experiential quality. Future value relates to the sustainability of the building and its surroundings and also to such matters as suitability for other purposes (flexibility) and value over time (value as a piece of cultural history).

According to Cold (1993), a lecturer in architecture in Sweden, quality cannot be treated as a static, objective, rational or logical concept. Experience of quality originates in the confrontation between the individual and the object, building or place. It concerns the characteristics of the individual, the object and the situation. Architectural history, with its various and changing aesthetic expressions and styles, does not offer unambiguous answers to the question, 'What is quality?' We should therefore concentrate more seriously on the authenticity of our own time and not just imitate architectural expression in order to solve the current longing for more significant and aesthetically stimulating architecture. To this end, Cold offers three recommendations. We should:

- sharpen our awareness and study the message of time, place and quality in architecture, so that contextual understanding can inspire us to work creatively;
- train our sensitivity and develop 'a refinement of the senses', so as to experience, try out and create a new cognition; and
- learn about the relationship between people and the environment, so as to widen our knowledge and understanding of 'the purpose of architecture'.

Cold (2001) refers to Stokols (1988), who distinguishes three fundamental approaches to architecture:

1. Minimalist – building as protection against climate, enemies etc.
2. Instrumental – architecture as an instrument to achieve behavioural and economic efficiency.
3. Spiritual – physical settings are viewed not as tools, but as ends in themselves, as contexts in which important human values can be cultivated. This third approach requires empathy and an understanding of general human needs, the concept of place (physical, social and symbolic), the technical and economic premises relevant to the realisation of the design concept and the cultural and artistic courage needed to create spiritual architecture.

All these opinions make clear that architectonic quality is an umbrella term, covering various aspects of quality. It is more than just aesthetic quality or cultural value. Although quality of use can be studied and defined on its own, this component is an inseparable part of architectonic quality in a wider sense.

1.4 Phases of the building process

To ensure that the building will actually support the desired activities, proper attention needs to be paid to the utility value in all phases of the building process (Fig. 1.1). The following sections take a brief look at these phases.

a. Exploratory phase

The first exploration of the building task takes place in this phase. Why is there a need for housing (or re-housing)? Is the task one of building a new building or rebuilding or extending an existing building? What is the level of ambition and to what extent can this ambition be achieved within the available budget? It often happens that the first ideas are developed in this phase, based on anticipated use. For example, a hospital might suggest a comb-shaped structure, because of the flexibility (extensibility) that such a shape provides. A much-used metaphor for a psychiatric establishment is a small village, because of its homeliness and smallness of scale. The final result of this phase is a paper setting down basic principles, including information about organisation, the main requirements and a feasibility study.

b. Programme of requirements or brief

In the programme of requirements the housing need is worked out in more detail, in the form of performance requirements for the location, the building, the rooms,

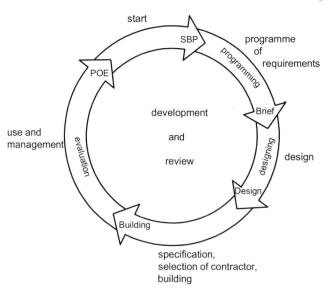

Figure 1.1 Phases in the building process. SBP = Start of the Building Process, POE = Post-Occupancy Evaluation.

the components of the building and the facilities to be provided in the building itself and in the grounds. The programme needs to be supported by a careful analysis of the organisation, the activities to be housed and the necessary or desirable special conditions – in short a functional analysis. This subject is discussed in more detail in Chapter 3.

c. Design

If everything has gone well, the desired quality of use will have been carefully defined in the programme of requirements. If there is no detailed programme of requirements, a functional analysis still needs to be carried out. There is generally a great gap between programme and design. Often all kinds of design variants are possible, each satisfying the programme of requirements but leading to a radically different quality of use. Important activities in this phase include the study of reference projects (precedents), analysis of the urban design context, consideration of the implications of that context for the design, and checking design proposals against the programme of requirements and other measures of quality of use. A more detailed treatment is given in Chapters 4 and 5.

d. Specification, selection of contractors and building

The materialisation and detailing of the design mainly takes place in the design phase and is then finished off in the specification phase. It is extremely important that the effect of the choice of materials and detailing on quality of use is properly checked. Considerations of quality of use play a less emphatic role in the selection of contractors and during the execution phase. Nonetheless, care must be taken to avoid errors made during execution that may cause problems later on in using the building.

e. Use and management

When the design has been realised, it is important to check whether the resulting building comes up to expectations. A careful analysis of how well the building functions is a useful way of identifying possible bottlenecks. This applies not just to the period immediately after the building has been handed over but also to the medium and long term. An evaluation of the building in the use phase (Post-Occupancy Evaluation or POE) can be used in making adjustments to the building itself and to assist design processes elsewhere. This can lead to well thought out guidelines for programmes of requirements and designs for related buildings, particularly when several buildings are involved in the evaluation. For a more detailed approach, see Chapters 5 and 6.

1.5 Conclusion

As this chapter makes clear, the functional quality of a building can be under-stood in different ways. In the narrowest sense, it refers merely to the building's utility value: the extent to which the building makes possible and supports the use envisaged for it. In a wider sense, it involves the ability of the building to perform all kinds of different functions: utilitarian, climatologic, cultural, symbolic, aes-thetic, economic and so on. The same holds true for the concept of architectonic quality. In the narrowest sense it primarily refers to perceptual qualities, cultural values and symbolic meanings. In a wider sense it is the extent to which an original, stimulating, efficient and cost-effective synthesis is achieved of form, function and technique (Fig. 1.2). As a consequence, the architectonic quality of a building in its widest sense includes the following sub-qualities (Van der Voordt and Vrielink, 1987):

■ *Functional quality or utility value*
The usability of the building in practice: the extent to which the building is suitable for the activities that have to be able to take place inside.
■ *Aesthetic quality*
The extent to which the building is perceived as beautiful, stimulating or original; the way it is experienced, whether as pleasant, cosy, spacious, homely or simply

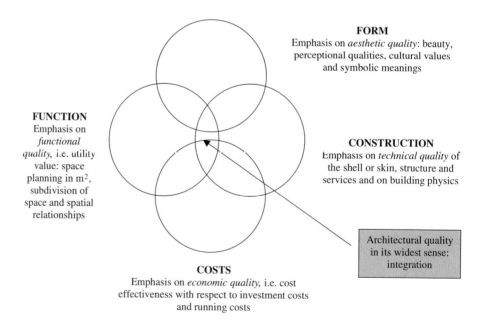

Figure 1.2 Architectural quality as an integration of functional, formal, technical and economic issues.

commercial; the extent to which it is seen as a piece of culture, e.g. whether it is representative of a particular style or period of building; and the extent to which the building evokes different meanings.

■ *Technical quality*
The extent to which the foundations, the load-bearing structure, the shell, the infill kit and the technical services satisfy technical requirements relating to such matters as strength, rigidity, stability, sustainability and limited need for maintenance. An important component is physical quality, the extent to which the building is capable of achieving an attractive, safe and healthy interior climate, measured in terms of temperature, humidity, illumination, natural lighting and acoustics, in an environmentally friendly and energy-saving way.

■ *Economic quality*
The extent to which financial resources are applied effectively and efficiently, i.e. the price–performance ratio. If the building is viewed as an investment object, its economic quality also depends on the level of return achieved.

The chapter has also made a preliminary exploration of the part played by functional quality in the different phases of the building process. It has made clear that attention to functional quality is an important part of every phase of the building process. Because careful programming, design and evaluation are so important, they are each treated in detail in a separate chapter. The aim is to assist the reader to work methodically, systematically and in a properly thought out way, using instruments that are suitable to the task, e.g. design guidelines derived from experience with existing buildings, checklists, itemised procedures and quality standards.

Bibliography

Cold, B. (1993), Quality in architecture. In: B. Farmer and H. Louw (eds), *Companion to contemporary architectural thought*. Routledge, London.

Cold, B. (ed.) (2001), *Aesthetics, well-being and health*. Essays within architecture and environmental aesthetics. Ashgate, Aldershot.

Dijk, H. van, R. de Graaf (1990), *Vormgeving is amoreel. Een gesprek met Carel Weeber* [Design is amoral. A conversation with Carel Weeber] Archis no. 1, 28–31.

Dijkstra (1985; 2001), *Architectonische kwaliteit* [Architectonic quality]. Policy note prepared by the government architect. The Hague.

Dirken, J.M. (1972), *Overeenkomst tussen ontwerpen, produkt en konsument* [Correspondence between designs, product and consumer]. Delft University of Technology.

Ekambi-Schmidt, J. (1972), *La perception de l'habitat*. Editions Universitaire, Paris.

Hillier, B., A. Leaman (1976), Architecture as a discipline. *Journal of Architectural Research*, Vol. 5, No. 1.

Ministerie van WVC [Ministry of Welfare, Health and Cultural Affairs] (1991), *Ruimte voor architectuur* [Space for architecture]. Rijswijk.

Norberg-Schulz, C. (1965), *Intentions in architecture*. MIT Press, Cambridge, Mass.

Rossum, H. van, R. de Wildt (1996), *Rijkshuisvesting in ontwikkeling* [Governmental building in progress]. NAI Publishers, Rotterdam.

Semper, G. (1989), *The four elements of architecture and other writings*. Cambridge University Press.

Voordt, D.J.M. van der, D. Vrielink (1987), *Kosten-kwaliteit van wijkwelzijnsaccommodaties* [Cost-quality ratio for local welfare premises]. Publications office, Faculty of Architecture, Delft University of Technology.

Zeeman, J. (1980), *Funktionele analyse. Voorbereiding en methodiek bij het ontwerpen van gebouwen* [Functional analysis. Preparation and methodology for the design of buildings]. Lectures by W.N. de Bruijn. Faculty of Architecture, Delft University of Technology.

CHAPTER 2

Function and form

2.1 The search for form

How does a designer arrive at his choice of form? What are the factors that influence the spatial image, size, scale and rhythm of the building mass, the spatial arrangement, the choice of colour and materials? And most of all, in the context of the subject of this book, to what extent does form follow from the requirements imposed by the intended use? Many different answers have been given to this question over the course of time, some based on theoretical considerations – often also based on a personal attitude and influenced by the spirit of the age. This chapter reviews a number of ideas about the relationship between function and form, with reference to different movements in architecture. It takes a rapid journey through history and presents the views of a number of different architects. It will emerge that the final form of a building is the result of a complex decision-making process in which many factors play a part. It is almost universally agreed that the form of a building must be sufficiently well suited to the building's anticipated use. It would be horrible to live in a room that is 2 metres wide and 20 metres long, and very unpleasant to have to work in a building with no natural light. Some people even argue that form is completely determined by function: i.e. *form follows function*. However, the context in which the building takes place also plays an important role in the choice of form. The qualities of the location, the time of construction, social conditions, fashion, economic and legal restrictions, etc., all individually influence the design. A building put up in a city will be different from one put up in a village; a building in China will be different from one in Belgium; the 21st century produces architecture different from the architecture of the Middle Ages. Further, a building must not only perform the functions required by its use; it has climatologic, cultural and economic functions. All this adds complexity to the relationship between function and form.

Experiential value, conveyance of meaning, visual quality, aesthetics and symbolism are also just as important. People sometimes talk about form having a degree of autonomy, distinct from its utility function. Two former professors of architecture in Delft, Van den Broek (1898–1978) and Bakema (1914–1981), spoke of 'the function of the form' (Ibelings, 1999). Finally, building is a human activity. The personal opinions, preferences and characters of the client, designer and everyone else involved also have their influence. Many clients give priority to utility value. Quantity surveyors are often concerned mainly with whether the designer is keeping within time and budget. Designers generally attach a good deal of value to expressiveness and originality; they want 'their' building to make them distinctive. Some go so far as to choose the form primarily on the basis of artistic considerations, a metaphor or a desire to propagate particular ideals or meanings. Only later they do the best they can to fit the required functions into the chosen form: for them, *function follows form*. But if function is too much subordinate to form, utility value suffers. Architecture is a regulated art. Form is never totally free. An attractive and stimulating design is only one of the rocks on which good architecture stands; others include functional efficiency, technical quality and affordability. Generally, and not surprisingly, function and form interact: on the one hand, a suitable form is sought on the basis of function; on the other hand, an attractive form is sought in the light of considerations other than those derived directly from function and then examined to see whether it will permit and support the use envisaged. The commission and the programme (demand side), the quality of the designer, the consultants and builders who are to do the work (supply side) and the means available ultimately determine whether the building manages to achieve a successful synthesis of form, function, technology and cost.

2.2 Functional and constructional efficiency

For many architects the design is to a significant extent determined by the effort to achieve *functional efficiency*. The building's form and arrangement must provide effective and efficient support for the activities it houses. The word generally used when the primary motive for the design is functional efficiency is *functionalism* (Whittick, 1953; Leuthäuser and Gössel, 1990). Functionalist designers are of course well aware of the importance of aesthetics and meaning, but these qualities are more or less considered to derive from purpose and convenience. According to the American architect Louis Henri Sullivan (1856–1924), every function has a single most appropriate form: witness the efficient design of tools and machines. This led him at the beginning of the 20th century to coin the well-known motto *form follows function* (Sullivan, 1924). At the same time Sullivan found that beauty was not the prior result of a form derived from function (Figure 2.1). Thus, form is also influenced by the need to experience beauty. Well-known buildings in the Netherlands dating from the beginning of the age of functionalism include Duiker and Bijvoet's sanatorium De Zonnestraal in Hilversum (Figure 2.2), and Brinkman and Van der Vlugt's Van Nelle factory in Rotterdam (Molema and Casciato, 1996;

(a)

Figure 2.1   (a) The overall view and (b) the façade of the Carson Pirie Scott Department Store, Chicago. Design by Louis Sullivan (1899–1906). This building marked the high point of the functional tradition in the Chicago School and is a striking example of the transformation of utility and structure into powerful architecture. The great cellular screens along the streets are derived directly from the steel cage behind them.

Figure 2.1 Continued.

Barbieri et al., 1999; Van Dijk, 1999). Functionalism remains an important force in architecture to this day (Figure 2.3).

The effort to achieve *constructional efficiency* implies trying to deal efficiently with constructional elements and materials, e.g. by not using more material than necessary. Wherever possible, materials are used in a way that takes account of their properties. The drive to achieve constructional efficiency means that form is largely determined by the logical way that constructional elements are combined, and is often accompanied by a drive to achieve 'constructional honesty'. Construction and detailing must not contradict one another. According to this view, constructions added purely for show, e.g. the addition of a non-load-bearing column purely for the sake of symmetry, should be avoided. 'Truth' is thought of as vitally important. Constructional elements and pipe work are often left visible. This approach was already evident in the work of the Russian constructivists at the beginning of the 1900s, e.g. Vladimir Tatlin's design for a memorial to the Third International (1919). Tatlin, a painter, was one of the most important representatives of constructivism. His design for a monument to and a headquarters for the Third International was generally seen as the first architectural project to make a complete break with tradition. Whether Tatlin's

Figure 2.2 De Zonnestraal, Hilversum. Design by Duiker and Bijvoet (1926–1931). Jan Duiker was a member of De 8, a group of architects opposed to the excessively emphatic concern with design typical of, for example, the expressionism of the Amsterdam School and the architecture of De Stijl. The group's main concern was with functional and constructional efficiency.

project can pass as real architecture is doubtful: 'It is much more a monument than the headquarters building of offices and meeting rooms to which it pretends' (Kopp, 1985). Other examples of Russian constructivism include Alexander and Victor Vesnin's office building for Leningrad-Pravda (1924) and El. Lissitzky's 'Wolkenbügels' (1925) in Moscow (Van Heuvel and Verbrugge, 1996). The preferred arrangement was for lifts to move up and down on the outside of the building. In England in the 1960s, *Archigram*, a group of young architects, again gave technology pride of place as the starting point for architecture. The group favoured large-scale load-bearing systems into which prefabricated elements could later be inserted to produce the required dwellings or business accommodation. Such buildings were often referred to as *high-tech*, because of their emphasis on technology. Well-known examples include Renzo Piano and Richard Rogers' Pompidou Centre in Paris (Figure 2.4), Norman Foster's Sainsbury Centre for Visual Arts in Norwich (Figure 2.6) and Richard Rogers' head office for Lloyd's of London (Figure 2.7). Jan Benthem and Mels Crouwel are well-known representatives of High-Tech in the Netherlands (Figure 2.5).

Figure 2.3 Building for Nationale Nederlanden, Rotterdam. Design by A. Bonnema
(1987). This design was selected from five competing entries, not so
much for its appealing quality but rather on the basis of programmatic
considerations. The deciding factors were the advantages offered in
terms of possible arrangement of office space, a high net to gross
ratio, an efficient work environment and other usability features.
According to Bonnema, the form of the building derived from its function. In his view, whatever architectonic movements may arise in future,
functionalism will go on forever.

Of course, when the search for form is also steered primarily by constructional efficiency, function and art play an important role, too. The teamwork of
Helmut Jahn (architect) and Werner Sobek (engineer) is an example of an integrated design method. They are convinced that it is necessary that 'the engineer
thinks like an architect and the architect – in turn – thinks like an engineer' in
order to have a good cooperation. If so, the result can be termed 'Archi-Neering'
(Anna, 1999). From scratch, Jahn and Sobek gather around the table to get the
best results. Santiago Calatrava considers engineering the art of the possible.
Binding as technical demands may be, there remains a margin of sufficient
freedom to show the personality of the creator of a work. This allows that his
creation, even in its strict technical obedience, become a real and true work of
art, as can be seen in Calatrava's work (Figure 2.8).

Figure 2.4 The Pompidou Centre, Paris. Design by Piano and Rogers (1972–
1977). Visible constructional elements and pipe work dominate the
form. Different functions are emphasised by colours: blue represents
water, red represents traffic and green represents electricity.

2.3 Development of functionalist ideas

The effort to achieve functional and constructional efficiency is as old as man-
kind. Even the most primitive hut has a functional and constructional basis.
Nonetheless, concentration on programme and construction means breaking
with the past, when the emphasis lay much more on principles of form going
back to classical antiquity. The effort to achieve functional and constructional
efficiency has its philosophical roots in rationalism. In 1637 René Descartes
wrote his *Discours de la méthode*, in which he formulated rules for scientific
thought that essentially dealt with following a particular system of reasoning
and understanding qualities like beauty, truth and goodness. The acquisition
and application of knowledge call for rational thought and empirical testing.
Rationalism came to full flower during the Enlightenment (18th century). The
metaphysical worldview increasingly gave way to reason. This body of thought
has had a great influence on people's thinking about architecture.

Figure 2.5 Malietoren, The Hague. Design by Benthem Crouwel Architects (1996). Because of its special situation – over a tunnel – this high-rise office block was constructed in the form of a steel and concrete bridge. The wind bracing on three levels shows how forces are offloaded on to the two side elevations.

The early functionalists

One of the first functionalists was Auguste Durand (1760–1834), professor at the Ecole Polytechnique in Paris at the beginning of the 19th century. In his view, science and technology are more important than artistic ambition. In his *Leçons d'Architecture* (1809) Durand stressed the importance of convenience ('convenance') and efficiency ('economie'). A building must support its intended use and contribute to health and welfare, making optimum use of capital, labour and material. For Durand, functional and constructional efficiency determine design. Another early supporter of functional and constructional efficiency was Viollet-le-Duc (1814–1879), professor of the history of art at the Ecole des Beaux Arts in Paris, known for example for his book *Entretiens sur l'architecture* (1863). In his books Viollet-le-Duc called emphatically for the honest use of materials and decoration based on rationalist theory. Although mainly known for his restorations of medieval churches and other monuments, as long ago as 1864 he designed a hall with a steel roof construction (Van Heuvel and Verbrugge, 1996). Horatio Greenhough, a contemporary, pointed out the correspondence

Figure 2.6 (a) Exterior and (b) interior views of, the Sainsbury Centre for Visual Arts, Norwich. Design by Norman Foster (1974–1978). The different functions are grouped within a single, clear-span structure, glazed at both ends, and lit from above. The internal space is covered by a double layer of the walls and roof, which houses service and ancillaries and also provides access for lighting and installations.

Figure 2.7 (a) Exterior and (b) interior views of, the Lloyd's of London, London. Design by Richard Rogers (1978–1986). All normal fixed obstructions, i.e. toilets, stairs, entrances, lifts and columns, are placed outside the building in six vertical towers clad in stainless steel. Another important aspect is the building's flexibility.

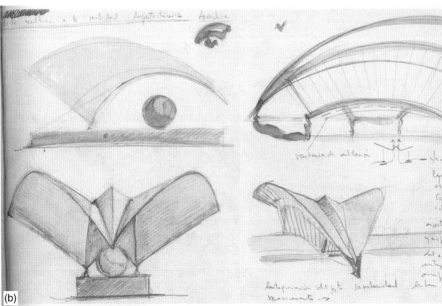

Figure 2.8 (a–c) Lyon-Satolas TGV Station, Lyon, France. Design by Santiago Calatrava (1989–1994). The bridge connects the station to the terminal of the airport. The form of the central hall's structure derives from one of Calatrava's sculptures: a balanced shape resembling a bird at the point of flight.

Figure 2.8 Continued.

between constructional function and form in animal skeletons, where function and form virtually coincide (Mees, 1984).

Beauty through functionality

The Austrian Adolf Loos (1870–1933) was another architect who found usability an important criterion for architecture, calling for pure architecture and simple forms suited to practical usability. In his *Ornament und Verbrechen*, written in 1908, he vehemently rejected the use of ornamentation for purely decorative purposes. He viewed decorations as 'tattooed architecture', and thought it impossible for anything impractical to be beautiful. This sounds very much like the words of the philosopher David Hume almost 200 years earlier in *A treatise of human nature* (1739), in which he identified beauty with utility. Efficiency generates beauty. The real beauty of a house lies in its convenience, an opinion shared by Frank Lloyd Wright (1869–1959). If the inside of a house is convenient and properly arranged to suit the needs of its occupiers, its exterior will be attractive too. That's why Wright omitted the friezes and cornices that were usual in his day, and based his designs for houses on the function for which they were to be used. What he wanted to achieve was 'organic architecture': a house must grow from people's needs and from the character of the land, like a living organism. Then 'form and function are one', just as in nature.

The modern movement

In the first half of the 20th century functionalism developed into one of the most important movements in architecture. On the analogy of Frederick Taylor's work-process analyses, architects of the modern movement analysed social activities to enable them to arrange floor plans as efficiently as possible. In the Netherlands of the 1920s a number of architects grouped together in the Amsterdam architect's association 'De 8' [The eight] and in the Rotterdam group 'De Opbouw' [(up)building] (Mattie and Derwig, 1995). According to 'De 8, 'the construction of beautiful buildings is not ruled out, but it is better to build ugly and functional buildings than to erect show-piece architecture for bad ground plans'. Well-known representatives of the Dutch modern movement are J.A. Brinkman (1902–1949), L.C. van der Vlugt (1894–1936), J. Duiker (1890–1935), J.J.P. Oud (1890–1963), G. Rietveld (1888–1964), J.B. van Loghum (1881–1941), M. Stam (1899–1986) and W. van Tijen (1894–1974). These architects built mainly in steel, glass and concrete, but brick was also used. The structure was formed by a steel skeleton, such as in the Bergpolder gallery flats in Rotterdam, designed by W. van Tijen in 1932, or by a concrete skeleton comprising floor slabs and columns, such as in the Van Nelle Factory by Brinkman and Van der Vlugt. The skeletons were open structures. Load-bearing walls were not necessary, so that the ground plan could be arranged freely, or be designed as a transformable space with sliding doors. In Germany, Hugo Häring (1882–1958) spoke of *Formfindung* based on an analysis of activities. According to him, design is not a separate issue. Conformity between function and form is essential. A design must provide each activity with its own separate space. Architects should express in the form the essential function of the building. The total form, the *Gestalt*, must be a response to the function. Häring believed that the way that form expresses something is tied to a particular place, time and group of individuals. In the Bauhaus programme for 1926, the then director Walter Gropius (1893–1969) used a similar basic assumption. Two years later his successor, Hannes Meyer, expressed the view that a building that is suitable for its purpose is a good building, regardless of its form (Mumford, 1952, quoted in Arnheim, 1966). According to Meyer, every architectural problem can be solved by scientific analysis. Significantly, the artistically charged term 'architecture' was replaced by the much more commercial term 'building'.[1] Many designers thought that this was going too far. They were perfectly prepared to accept functionality as an important basis for architecture but not as the only or most important basis for form. Nonetheless, in the course of time, the rational approach enjoyed a boom, providing a basis for mass production, prefabrication,

---

[1] In this connection it is striking that in 1997 the then Dean Cees Dam attempted to change the name of the Faculteit Bouwkunde [literally 'Faculty of Building Science'] into Faculteit Architectuur [Faculty of Architecture]!

standardisation and normalisation. Design began to be influenced more and more by production processes and ease of assembly. Leading international figures in the modern movement such as Walter Gropius (1883–1971) and Le Corbusier (1887–1965) allowed themselves to be expressly inspired by what they saw as the great beauty of technical perfection. Significantly, the metaphor that Le Corbusier used for his housing designs was 'machines to live in'. Mies van der Rohe (1886–1969) was a technical perfectionist as well. For him, true beauty came forward from minimalism. His office building designs are based on concepts such as 'less is more', 'God is in the details' and 'the building is almost nothing'. According to Mies van der Rohe, technology is far more than a method. It is a world in itself. Whenever technology reaches its real fulfilment, it transcends into architecture. It is true that architecture depends on facts, but its real field of activity is in the realm of significance. Mies' buildings look like glass-and-steel boxes and are very characteristic for modern architecture (Figure 2.9).

Figure 2.9 Seagram Building, New York. Design by Mies van der Rohe (1954–1958). This building has been regarded as the ultimate expression of the International Style. The design is based on the production of components and, as such, is anchored to the industrial process. I-beams were used in different kinds of length and function, load bearing and representative as well. The beams formed the skeleton of the building but also articulated the façade in segments.

Architects of the modern movement met regularly at the international congresses held from 1928 onwards under the name *Congrès Internationale d'Architecture Moderne (CIAM)*. At the first congress in Sarraz, Switzerland, a joint declaration was presented at its close, saying that architects should show they are a child of their time and not introduce elements from earlier times. Architects should focus on the new materials, constructional and production techniques, on standardisation and on internationalisation. With regard to town planning, the declaration stated that town planning is not aesthetically, but functionally, determined. Urban functions should be grouped according to dwellings, work, transportation and recreation. People should be brought up with good architecture and be imbued with the wholesome ideal of light, air, sun and hygiene. In 1933, CIAM proclaimed the 'Charter of Athens', in which the authors declared that, in the interests of hygiene and health, modern urban design must provide for the separation of the functions. The congresses went on until the early 1950s.

Visual functionalism and adjustment to suit human dimensions

Many architects are critical of a one-sided functionalist approach. At the end of the 1960s the Dutch architect Jaap Bakema introduced the term *visual functionalism*, to make clear that function is not the only determinant of form. Architecture must also appeal to the imagination (Figure 2.10). J.J. Oud (1890–1963) expressed the same thought some decades earlier. Despite his connection

Figure 2.10   The Great Hall, Delft University of Technology. Design by Van den Broek and Bakema (1962–1965). The main outlines of the auditorium are clearly recognisable in the exterior. The fact that the ground floor is kept open on the side containing the entrance means that the main entrance stands on the same building line as the adjoining buildings. The huge cantilevers, the expressive stairways and the split-level floors all contribute to the building's fascinating visual quality.

Figure 2.11 Houses on the Scheepmakerstraat, Hook of Holland. Design by J.J.P. Oud, 1924. This monument to the modern movement was declared a national monument in 1984. The complex is characterised by intelligent floor plans and a disciplined, modern exterior. The intention was to strike a balance between tradition and experiment.

with the ideas of De Stijl (see Section 2.6), this Rotterdam architect was constantly searching for a synthesis between rationalism and aesthetics. One example of a successful balance between technology and art was the design for a row of working-class houses on the Scheepvaartstraat in Hook of Holland, built in 1926. Oud himself used the term *poetic functionalism* (Figure 2.11). The houses in question were particularly spacious and comfortable for their time and, with their disciplined elevations and rounded ends, became a well-known monument to the so-called 'Nieuwe Bouwen' movement. The complex was thoroughly renovated in 1984. The design was partly inspired by the location. According to Oud, Hook of Holland is neither a village nor a town. The horizontal lines and wide windows referred to the breadth and limitless nature of the countryside. The disciplined exterior and the perfection of the details referred to the extra refinement that distinguishes a town from a village. The pale gold colour was inspired by the nearby sand dunes.

In 1959, *Forum* magazine, edited by Aldo van Eyck, Herman Hertzberger, Jaap Bakema and Joop Hardy, published the 'story of another idea' (Van Eyck,

1959). The so-called Forum group criticised the largeness of scale and monotony of post-war building and the separation of functions called for by CIAM. What they wanted was to enrich functionalism by adjusting home and work environments to suit specific human needs. They strongly believed in the possibility of changing the nature of society, and attempted to devise an architectonic language which would have something to say about human behaviour, and meaningful structures with a wealth of transitions, including most importantly transitions between interior and exterior. Largeness of scale was not thought of as wrong in itself; the main thing that they were reacting against was absence of scale. In the words of Hertzberger, 'Things may only be big when they consist of multiples of units which are themselves small; excessive size easily leads to dissociation. Big in the sense of multiple implies an increase in complexity and so an enrichment of possible interpretations'. The same criticism was also expressed at the CIAM Congress in Otterloo (1959), at which Van Eyck, Hertzberger and Bakema represented the Netherlands. Significantly, a proposal was made by Team X to change CIAM's name to *Groupe de Recherches des Interrelations Sociales et Plastiques*. However, placing a heavy emphasis on utility value does not immediately lead to a particular style. As Hertzberger said, there is no such thing as humanist architecture, unless one means a fundamental attitude based on a respect for people, their values and their dignity.

According to the architect Carel Weeber, architecture is not a means of improving society. In his view, the drive in the 1960s and 1970s to achieve habitability and encourage social contacts led to an excessive fixation on smallness of scale (Figure 2.12). He characterised the architecture of the day as 'the new dowdiness' and spoke derisively of 'railway accidents', a reference to the lavish use of wooden sleepers in newly built modern estates. What was missing was any large-scale organisation. This, according to Herman de Kovel, explains the revival of the modern movement and why there is so much interest in the work of Duiker, Le Corbusier and the Russian constructivists. De Kovel rejected functionalism as lacking formal basic principles and too little discussed, arguing that today the visual qualities of architecture take priority. Architects want to return to designing: witness the work of Rem Koolhaas and Daniel Libeskind.

Rather than focusing on form and facade, Franck and Lepori (2000) argue that architecture should take its character from the human body, which is a moving, animated structure that relies on its inner geography for optimum experience. When designed from the inside out, buildings will offer spatial sensations that connect with people and evoke a comforting ambiance, joyful spirit and feelings of support. With the contemporary interest in architecture as idea and image and a strong emphasis of clients on financially profitable products, there is a loss of attention to content and process. Being an environmental psychologist and a practising architect, respectively, Franck and Lepori plea for an alternative approach that places human life and experience as well as materiality at the centre of design. Design should not be seen as a project, but as a process,

Figure 2.12 (a) De Tanthof housing estate, Delft. (b) The Zwarte Madonna (Black Madonna) residential block, The Hague. Carel Weeber typified the smallness of scale and the large number of different roof styles in the districts newly built in the 1970s and 1980s as 'the new drabness'. His own designs were characterised by a strongly rationalistic streak. The form of the Zwarte Madonna represents a longing for the purification of decorative architectonic and ideological elements.

evolving from inside out: from the desires and activities of people, from site and context, and from a dialogue between architect and client. This requires an attitude to architecture that recognises the value of people and matter as the very reasons for its existence.

Functionalism without dogma

Although functionalism has by now been succeeded by many other ideas about architecture, the aim of achieving functional and constructional efficiency remains to this day an important motive in the production of 'good' architecture. In *Hoe modern is de Nederlandse architectuur* [How modern is Dutch architecture] (Leupen et al., 1990), Mels Crouwel writes that the achievement of optimum usability must be the most important aim of any building. The materials and constructions used must be selected purely for their suitability to achieve this aim. Beauty is a product of the direct relationship between building and purpose and from natural characteristics. At the same time it can be observed that a functionalist approach can form a good accompaniment to expressive design, as for example in Delft University of Technology's university library (Figure 2.13).

Leen van Duin, current professor of form and function in the Faculty of Architecture at Delft University of Technology, advocates combining the engineering approach (with its emphasis on the quantitative analysis of functions and constructional requirements) with a more architectonic approach. In other words, what he would like to see is a synthesis of art and science. The publication *Architectonische studies*, produced under his editorship, consists of descriptions, classification and reworking of existing buildings – 'precedents' – making it possible for architectonic approaches to be reconstructed. Knowledge so gained can subsequently be applied to new design tasks. Van Duin defines functional design as the generation of designs satisfying a set of accepted norms. Achieving a functionally efficient building requires a thorough analysis of the programme of requirements. According to van Duin, the functional analysis of buildings must involve three elements:

- A description and identification of social needs, activities and dependencies and their relationships with one another.
- An explanation of the way in which the form influences the function.
- An analysis of the relationship between form, function and norm.

All this must be done in conjunction with a study of building methods and commercial and managerial considerations. Analysis of the desired use enables one to deduce the quantity of space required by a particular combination of activities and how this quantity of space can be distributed over the building. But quantity does not determine quality. Establishing the form of a building requires reference to earlier solutions to related problems. According to Van Duin (1996), knowledge of typology and imaginative power play an important

Figure 2.13 Library of the Delft University of Technology. Design by Mecanoo Architects (1995). Functionalism without dogma: the effort of achieving conceptual clarity and functional efficiency is accompanied by huge delight in the design and an attractive end result.

part in all this. Thus, the relationship between function and form is not unambiguous. There is a constant tension between form and function that cannot be resolved by logical procedures.

2.4 Flexibility and multifunctionality

Just as a tailor-made suit only fits one wearer, so a space designed to suit only one function is often rather badly suited to other functions. However, both use and users change with time. This is why many architects try to produce structures that are suitable for multiple use, allowing individual interpretations and interventions. In an article on the reciprocal nature of form and programme in 1963, Hertzberger wrote:

To be able to stand up to change, forms must be built to allow a multitude of different interpretations. They must be able to take on several meanings and then abandon them again without harming their own identity. This means searching for primary forms which can not only accept a programme but also liberate it. Form and programme inspire one another. The impossibility of creating an individual environment to suit everyone makes it necessary to allow individual interpretation by designing things in such a way that they are indeed capable of interpretation.

A characteristic feature of many of Hertzberger's designs is the way that the interior is deliberately left unfinished, so challenging users to make the space their own ('appropriation of space'). A certain amount of over-dimensioning is required if space is to be used multifunctionally. This same idea can be found in the work of Mies van der Rohe, whose designs were strongly influenced by the effort to achieve a degree of independence from function, location and climate (Mees, 1984). Mies believed that good architecture can accommodate a variety of different functions, as can be seen from the way his designs provide simple, generous spaces which can be equipped and used by the users to suit their needs in any way they think proper.

Structuralism

Structuralism, a movement in architecture that pays much attention to changing user functions, came about in reaction to the functionalism of post-war Dutch architecture (Van Heuvel, 1992). The movement was characterised by the use of modules as components in a larger coherent whole capable of accommodating changing functions. Other characteristics included the application of space-structuring constructions ('honest' use of materials, a visible skeleton), special attention to transitions between outside and inside, great emphasis on encounters, identity (individual recognisability of an individual's own living or working space), liveability, flexibility and extensibility. The spatial configuration was composed of a large number of basic elements that could be moved relative to one another to create a high level of spatial richness. A frequently chosen constructional plan included a skeleton of columns, beams, parapets and walls, all visible throughout the building. Examples in the Netherlands include the library building for the University of Leiden (designed by Joop van Stigt and Bart van Kasteel), the Burgerweeshuis (Orphanage) in Amsterdam, designed by Aldo van Eyck (Figure 2.14), the Drie Hoven Home for the Elderly in Amsterdam, designed by Herman Hertzberger (Figure 2.15), and the Ministries of Foreign Affairs (Dick Apon, 1984), Education and Sciences (Philip Rosdorff, 1985, Figure 2.16) and Social Affairs and Employment (Herman Hertzberger, 1990). Well-known examples outside the Netherlands include Louis Kahn's Medical Research Building, Philadelphia (1957) and Ottokar Uhl and Jos Weber's 1976 housing projects. Structuralist principles can also be applied to urban design; examples include a study for a plan for an urban grid in Apeldoorn (de Boer, Mol, Parvin, Reijenga, 1968) and an urban design sketch for New York by Yona Friedman (1964).

Figure 2.14 Burgerweeshuis, Amsterdam. Design by Aldo van Eyck (1960). According to Aldo van Eyck, concepts such as open/closed, small/ large, inside/outside are completely neutralised by the stark style of building produced by the modern movement. Large glass walls provide continuity of space, but destroy the balance between open and closed, so neutralising space. The design of the Burgerweeshuis (an orphanage) attempts to reconcile opposites like movement/rest or inside/ outside and to create places for people to be.

Structuralism in architecture is related to structuralism in the social sciences, and was partly inspired by the work of the social anthropologist Lévy-Straus. Just as the sounds and rules of language take on meaning in a structure, building elements too form part of a larger structure. In fact people build structures, within which everything is possible. The same principle can be found in Nico Habraken's book *De drager en de mensen* [Load-bearers

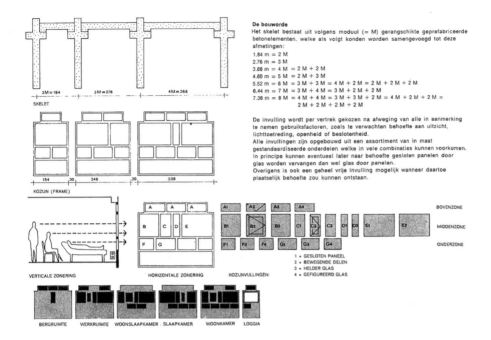

Figure 2.15   De Drie Hoven, Amsterdam. Design by Herman Hertzberger (1975). The consistent application of prefabricated concrete elements set in modules allows a great variety of different interpretations, permitting different uses without losing the coherence of the whole. The choice of load-bearing structure should simplify any later rebuilding.

and people] (1961). In it the author warns against excessive development of mass-produced housing concerned only with technology, organisation and economics. People must be able to take charge of their own environment. Habraken therefore called for a distinction between load-bearers and in-built units and between the functions of load-bearing and space-dividing. Load-bearers should be skilfully designed to allow an infinite variety of forms, within which residents are able to make choices to suit themselves (see also Bosma et al., 2000).

Function-neutral buildings

During his lectures, Carel Weeber, former professor of architectural design at Delft University of Technology, is always pointing out that functional analysis does not define design. The form of a building has several potential uses and must be capable of accommodating constantly changing activities. There is always room for compromise between fitting precisely, unchangeable, typical of one specific activity, and flexible, allowing a range of different activities.

Figure 2.16 Ministry of Education and Sciences, Zoetemeer. Design by Philip Rosdorff (1976–1985). The way the rooms are arranged was determined by the wish to create individually recognisable units for different parts of the organisation, with short lines of communication between functions needing much contact with one another. The constructional plan was based on the metaphor of the city and contains a city centre (ministers and secretaries, senior civil servants, large conference rooms, etc.), a district community centre (directorates, small conference rooms, etc.), local community centres (lifts, toilet facilities, coffee machines) and housing (workrooms for staff). The original idea of an inward-looking building form comprising nine identical quadrangles was abandoned in favour of L-shaped blocks so that everyone would have an outside view. Differences in colour and material reinforce the recognisability of separate components.

Activities should be so grouped as to create a balance between space specific to a single activity and space that can be used for all conceivable activities. The increasing frequency with which designs are prepared for an unknown user means a rapid decrease in the demand for buildings to be used in one specific way. Neutral forms, less directly linked to one particular function, can overcome this objection. As Weeber sees it, there is a demand for function-neutral buildings. This view seems to complete the circle. In former times functional efficiency was rejected as the primary justification for a building's form. Then the advance of functional specialisation led to the development of specific types of building. Now that functions are changing more and more rapidly, it is becoming more and more necessary to design buildings that can accommodate a range of very different functions.

2.5 Context

Besides functional and constructional efficiency, context also plays an important part in the choice of form, and on a number of different levels. Many architects are prepared to make some adjustment to the size, scale, rhythm, mass, use of colour and materials in the elevation, etc., to fit in with surrounding buildings and ensure the degree of harmony and continuity often required by the local design review committee. Sometimes a deliberate choice is made in favour of contrast, either to increase recognisability or because of a need to mark a break with the past. Movements in architecture that emphasise the link between design and the socio-cultural, historical and spatial context include traditionalism, critical regionalism and neo-rationalism.

Traditionally minded architects attach great value to local traditions and to preserving a culture of craftsmanship. They prefer sacral arrangement, security and calm and reject pretentiousness and artificiality. Their building carries on traces left behind by the past; they move forward by looking backward, as it was (Barbieri et al., 1999). A well-known Dutch representative in the first half of the 20th century was Grandpré Molière (1883–1972). He was for years associated as professor with the Faculty of Architecture at Delft University of Technology. Molière strove on philosophical and theological grounds to achieve a harmonious unity between the spontaneous inspiration of the artist, tradition and the laws of nature, i.e. those immortal truths laid down by the Creator. The characteristic features of his architecture and that of the *Delft School* included a strong preference for sloping roofs, building in brick, simple geometrical shapes and small windows creating an enclosed, homely atmosphere. Farm buildings often inspired housing designs (Figure 2.17). This is not to say that functional and constructional efficiency meant nothing to the traditionalists, but their forms were based primarily on a traditional vocabulary of form. There was little liking for the abstract visual vocabulary of the functionalists.

Figure 2.17   Vreewijk, Rotterdam. Design by Grandpré Molière et al. (1916). An example of traditionalist architecture, designed to fit in with the immediate environment.

Critical regionalism also tried to find a design to suit the identity and potential of the site, the *genius loci*, but was not prepared to fall back on a nostalgic preference for traditional architecture (Lefaivre and Tzonis, 2003). The main concern of the movement's members was to oppose universalism and inhumane, technocratic architecture (Speaks, 1996). Their aim was to produce a form which would bring out whatever made the site different from all others. Elements of local architecture were analysed and schematised, and then applied in an updated form. Kelbaugh (1997) summarised the movement's main characteristics as follows:

- A preference for local building materials and building methods and the use of local vegetation ('sense of place') (Figure 2.18).
- A concentration on ecological and sustainable building ('sense of nature').
- The analysis, transformation and application of principles of form derived from historical types such as the basilica, the campanile, the palazzo and the galleria ('sense of history').
- The use of local traditional knowledge and skills ('sense of craft'). The movement deplored the disappearance of skilled craftsmanship brought about by

Figure 2.18   The Alvaro Siza project in Schilderswijk, The Hague. The work of the Portuguese architect Alvaro Siza Viera exhibits various elements of critical regionalism. Siza makes use of local materials such as brick and stucco and access principles like the gateway, typical of The Hague, all in a style of his own.

progressively industrialised methods of production, while realising that it was probably unavoidable for economic reasons.

- Recognisable forms and boundaries ('sense of limits'). While modernists considered space to be abstract, neutral and continuous, critical regionalists called for human scale and psychological demarcation.

Because of its emphasis on individual character, regionalism has come to be associated with conservatism, chauvinism, a predilection for folklore and sometimes even with *Blut und Boden* [blood and soil] (Jongert et al., 1995). Its characteristic feature, however, is its attempt to apply local elements in a new, different way, free of sentimental associations. This explains the later addition of the adjective 'critical'.

Representatives of Italian *neo-rationalism*, some of whom came together in the Tendenza movement, attach a good deal of value to historical references and the use of historic architectonic elements. One example is the public library in Groningen, designed by Giorgio Grassi (1992) (Figure 2.19). Another good

Figure 2.19 Public library, Groningen. Design by Giorgio Grassi (1990–1992). Here the patterned brick elevation, composed of standardised elements and typical of Grassi's work, is adjusted to suit inner-city conditions.

illustration is provided by Aldo Rossi's ideas for the Kop van Zuid in Rotterdam (Figure 2.20). Rossi argues that by analysing cities over time we can understand those elements that either support or obstruct the interests of the 'collective will' (Rossi, 1982). In the Kop van Zuid district the original structure consisted of large harbours separated by isolated urban districts. The main features of the harbour – its basins, roads, warehouses and industrial buildings – determined the arrangement of these districts. The houses are a combination of traditional Dutch housing types: small brick houses often terraced. Rossi found that even today historical continuity and the use of sound materials give these houses a special beauty that needs to be recaptured in the new plans.

Socio-cultural and economic context

Besides the spatial and historical context, the relationship between function and form is strongly influenced by both socio-cultural and economic factors. Rogers (1991) calls 'form follows profit' the very aesthetic principle of our times. Thus, design skills are measured today by the architect's ability to build

Figure 2.20 Aldo Rossi's plan for the Kop van Zuid, Rotterdam. Rossi bases his designs on morphological analyses and typological research. He is strongly attracted to formal architecture – architecture that shows respect for historical references.

the largest possible enclosure for the smallest investment in the quickest time. The strong influence of investment policies led the famous Dutch architect Rem Koolhaas to found a second office, in addition to OMA, called AMO. Its main objective is to think about the interaction between architecture, politics, and cultural and economic developments. Apart from economic factors, many other contextual factors affect the final form of a building, as Juriaan van Meel (2000) has shown. Van Meel was struck by the fact that organisations with comparable administrative functions are housed in widely different office buildings, whereas 'form follows function' would lead one to expect much less variation. In his PhD thesis, Van Meel sought to explain international differences in mass, floor plan and layout of the workspace. He therefore studied office designs in Great Britain, Germany, Sweden, Italy and the Netherlands. Typical differences relate to the context in which the designing and building take place, in particular:

■ The urban design context: the urban structure and planning principles.
■ Market conditions: market relationships and rent levels.
■ Labour relationships, in particular the part employees play in decision-making.

- Culture: norms and values relating to hierarchy, privacy, personal space and interaction.
- Legislation and regulations affecting working conditions.

Van Meel explained the fact that none of the countries have any real tradition of building high-rise office blocks, by reference to the prevailing urban design structures, and rents that are much lower than those found in such cities as New York and Hong Kong. London, Frankfurt and Rotterdam are exceptions. London's metropolitan role means that market rents are quite high. Frankfurt aims to present itself as a world-class financial centre. And of course in Frankfurt, as in Rotterdam, the original urban structure was destroyed during the Second World War, providing an opportunity to break with the past. Floor plans in Great Britain are very different from those in mainland Europe. In Great Britain offices are often long, open plan and high-density, with workplaces which can be as much as 14–16 metres from an outside wall. Most workplaces in the other countries investigated were situated against an outside wall. Van Meel believed this can be traced back to differences in the balance of power within organisations and in the office market. Employees in mainland Europe have considerably more power than in Great Britain, which means that much more account is taken of their wishes for such things as an outside view and natural lighting and ventilation. These wishes are also reflected in local legislation and regulations. Moreover, project developers and investors who, according to Van Meel, are by nature mainly interested in efficiency and flexibility, dominate the British market. The Netherlands has its Occupational Health and Safety Act (Arbeidsomstandighedenwet or ARBO), which lays down rules to put into effect a policy of maximum safety, health and welfare in the workplace.

As a consequence of ongoing globalisation, one might wonder what the influence of the cultural or historical context will be in the future. According to many sociologists and architects, globalisation will lead to homogenisation. An example is the fast food chains with rather similar buildings and interior design all over the world. As a consequence of a growing mobility, the world is becoming characterised by short and fast experiences, so that people's perceptions are coloured more and more by information from the media (Ibelings, 2002). The airport is an attractive model for the kind of existence that is nowadays associated with globalisation. But although one can observe international styles again, at the same time local circumstances still strongly affect the search for form. An example is the design of the Petronas Towers in Kuala Lumpur (Figure 2.21), that responds to the dominant Islamic culture of Malaysia (Pearson Clifford, 1999). Another striking example is Ground Zero in New York (Figure 2.22). The way Libeskind included references to death and life in his design for a follow-up for the twin towers of the World Trade Center was one of the reasons why he won the design contest for this very particular site (Box 2.1).

Figure 2.21 Petronas Towers, Kuala Lumpur, Malaysia. Design by Cesar Pelli (1998). The towers are the tallest buildings in the world with a height of 452 metres (1483 feet). The towers are a symbol of Malaysia's modernisation and rising profile on the international scene. The towers break with modernist orthodoxy by being symmetrically arranged on the site and figurative in design. The design of the towers responds to formal characteristics of the dominant Islamic culture. By studying Islamic architecture, Pelli learned, that repetitive geometries are keys to understanding buildings in predominantly Muslim countries. The towers represent a landmark and a gateway to an important new development.

Box 2.1 Ground Zero Memorial

In the World Trade Center Site Memorial Competition, the Memory Foundation designed by Studio Daniel Libeskind has been the selected design for Ground Zero. The aim was to deliver a design for a single memorial that remembers and honours all loss of life on September 11, 2001. Therefore, the design of Libeskind is filled with symbolism. Libeskind perceived the great slurry wall as the most dramatic element that survived the attack. The Memory Foundation's design leaves portions of the slurry wall exposed as a symbol of the strength and endurance of American democracy, while reserving a majestic setting for the memorial and museum in the area known as the bathtub. The memorial site is sunk 30 feet and is a quiet, meditative and spiritual space. This site represents the story of the tragedy but also reveals the dimensions of life. The museum of the event, of memory and hope, is in the epicentre of Ground Zero.

Figure 2.22 (a and b) Destruction of World Trade Center, New York. (c) The Wedge of Light, Ground Zero, The Memory Foundation.

(Continued)

In remembrance of September 11, Libeskind developed the Wedge of Light. This is a large public place on ground level where the sun will shine without shadow, in perpetual tribute to the altruism and courage displayed on September 11 between the hours of 8:46 a.m., when the first airplane hit, and 10:28 a.m., when the second tower collapsed. The design jury was pleased that skyline was maintained. The Antenna Tower reaches a height of 1776 feet (541 metres) in height, a number that is a tribute to the year of the United States' Declaration of Independence. The top floor of the tower houses gardens, because 'gardens are a constant affirmation of life'. With this tower, the design is signalling the rebirth of Lower Manhattan and its iconic skyline and honours those who were lost while affirming the victory of life.

Figure 2.22 Continued.

(Continued)

Figure 2.22 Continued.

2.6 Autonomy of form

The form of a building is of course not only determined by functional and constructional efficiency and the context within which the design and building take place but also by a striving to achieve beauty and cultural meaning. This means that form is in some sense autonomous. According to Cees Dam, architect and former Dean of the Faculty of Architecture, Delft University of Technology, this fact receives too little recognition. Dogma, legislation and regulation imprison today's architect. The gross/net ratio, the 30% glazing rule, prescribed roof slopes, building process management and user requirements limit the profession's scope and opportunities. 'The architect lives in an atmosphere of fear produced by constant demands for efficiency and economy' (Dam, quoted in Leupen et al., 1990). People are much too ready to assume that in essence anything that is not quantifiable is unnecessary. Dam argues for a closer relationship between architecture and the arts. This means that people will have to learn to look, both in a technical and professional sense (learning to recognise and measure dimensional ratios, rhythm, structure, materials, light and colour) and in a cultural sense (to build up a mental stock of images, associations and interpretations). So a search for form should also be steered by principles such as 'form follows aesthetics' and 'form follows meaning'. Symbolism is a combination of perception and cognition. People's perceptions, expectations and interpretations are influenced by earlier aesthetic experiences, their knowledge and understanding of the built environment, how they feel at the present moment, and by the link between utility value and historical and cultural value (Hill, 1999; Jencks, 1985). In the past centuries, a number of architectural styles and views have passed the review, showing different connections between cultural issues and form.

Classicism and neo-styles

The emphasis on beauty, experiential value and the creation of meaning recurs constantly throughout the history of architecture: e.g. in Greek and Roman architecture, Romance architecture, Gothic architecture, Renaissance architecture, classicism, and different neo-styles until the present days (Smith, 1956; Pevsner, 1960; Van Heuvel and Verbrugge, 1996; Barrie, 1996). Although utility value and technology always play some part in design, the main emphasis is on composition. Building is above all an art. Symmetry, dimensional ratios (e.g. the application of the golden mean) and decoration are all used to evoke a sense of beauty. Principles of form are laid down in manuals of 'good' design. Form, more particularly in public sector buildings like churches, theatres, museums, town halls and other government buildings, often also expresses some underlying meaning or, put differently, has a secondary functionality or symbolic function. Thus, church buildings have always been characterised by verticality. The pointed arches, high vaulting and flying buttresses of Gothic churches make the walls seem lighter and higher; the design supports the function of meditating on God and uplifting the human soul. It was usual for medieval churches and cathedrals to have a floor plan shaped like a Latin cross, a reference to Christ's Passion. Renaissance churches of the 15th and 16th centuries often chose a centralised structure based on squares and circles or polygonal figures derived from them. These geometrical figures were regarded as 'pure' and so 'suited' to the function of a church and expressed an effort to achieve lasting value. There was, however, much discussion about the proper placing of the altar. Some people argued for a position against the outside wall, symbolising the distance between God and man. Others argued that it should be placed centrally, because the centre is unique and absolute. This is not to say that the form was determined exclusively by the wish to convey this kind of meaning. For example, the dimensions of these churches were determined in part by the desired capacity, which is one aspect of primary functionality.

The effort to achieve beauty and convey meaning can also be seen in the castles of the baroque period (late 16th and 17th century). The architecture of the baroque was characterised by excessive spatial effects and sensory experiences (Figure 2.23). Ornament, sculpture, painting and building were combined to form a single whole. On the other hand, the arrangement of the

(a)

Figure 2.23   The Residenz, Würzburg. (a and b) The location and dimensions of the staircase were only partly derived from functional considerations and were mainly determined by a wish to convey meaning. The stairs were where the status of the prince – and others – was declared publicly. The etiquette of the day laid down precisely how far down the host should go to meet his guests: whether to the foot of the stairs or halfway down, or whether he should remain at the top.

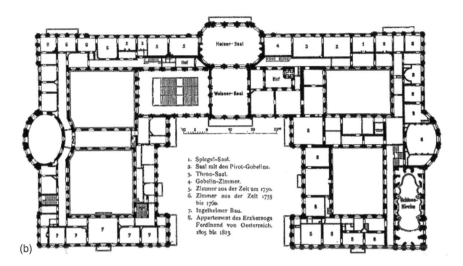

(b)

Figure 2.23 Continued.

rooms was primarily determined by ceremonial customs, by who was allowed to go where (Macel, 1981). So, for example, the staircase of the Residenz in Würzburg should not simply be seen as an architectonic solution, a particular treatment of space. The staircase could be recognised in the external shape of the building and took up more space than the hall of audience. This was not so much a consequence of the function of the staircase, as a connection between different floors, but of the function of the staircase in a regularly recurring ceremony. The staircase was where the staff stood to await the arrival of a prince and to welcome guests.

The 19th century indulged in large-scale elaboration of the classical vocabulary of form. This led to all kinds of neo-styles, many of which can still be found today. A contemporary example is the 'industrial classicism' of the Spanish architect Ricardo Bofill (Figure 2.24). A well-known supporter of classical forms is Prince Charles, whose book *A vision of Britain; a personal view of architecture* is violently opposed to what he sees as excessive discipline and the rejection of history. On the other hand, many architects are reluctant to accept any return to classical forms. Their reluctance is partly ideological, because they believe that such a return would mean architecture being reduced to copying historical examples, and is partly based on functional considerations. Temples have sometimes been copied to provide accommodation for parliaments! Henri Labrouste (1801–1875) was an early critic. He originally favoured the study of Roman buildings but later he set up a private school of architecture in which he allowed himself to be guided mainly by functional and constructional considerations (Mees, 1984).

Figure 2.24 Le Théâtre, Paris. Design by Ricardo Bofill (1980). In the 1970s and 1980s Bofill and his Barcelona-based firm Taller de Arquitectura designed various large housing complexes in and around Paris, characterised by classical pilasters and arcades. The concrete elements used in the elevations incorporated coloured additives. In fact, the arrangement of the houses was subordinated to the historic décor.

Expressionism

The principal characteristic of expressionist architecture is the use of an attractive design to contribute to the creation of an ideal community in which everyone can feel at home. Architecture is primarily viewed as a social and moral problem, to which the designer must give an individual form (Barbieri et al., 1999).

Figure 2.25 Housing in Spaarndammerbuurt, Amsterdam. Design by Michel de Klerk (1914). The architecture of the Amsterdam School was characterised by expressive design, with much attention to colour, materials, rhythm and detailing.

A building must have something personal to tell its users, and so convey meaning to the neighbourhood and the city. No strict rules were followed for the design itself. Expressionist architects used both organic forms and geometrical proportional systems. An artist has no need to justify himself historically or scientifically. What matters is the cogency of the design and its involvement in society. An obvious example is Mendelssohn's expressionist design for the Potsdam Observatory (1917–1921). A well-known Dutch example is the expressionist brick architecture of the Amsterdam School in the 1920s, with Van der Mey, De Klerk and Kramer as its most important architects (Figure 2.25). They emphasised individual artistic endeavour and the integration of crafts under the hegemony of architecture and reached back to the symbolic iconography of the fin de siecle (Van Dijk, 1999). A modern variant is the organic architecture, based on an anthroposophical view of life.

Organic architecture

The term organic architecture embraces a colourful variety of architectural approaches and expressions that developed in different places at the beginning of the 20th century. Organic architecture is a reinterpretation of nature's principles, which are implemented in the relationship between form and function, and between force and construction. This often led to free and expressive forms, not as an imitation of nature, but to support people as living and creative beings. For example Frank Lloyd Wright's organic architecture takes on a new meaning. He states that organic architecture is a reinterpretation of nature's principles as they are filtered through the intellectual minds of men and women, who can then build forms that are more natural than nature itself. Within the organic movement, architecture is not only seen as an expression of culture and society but also as something that influences the inner and outer lives of people. Human beings are perceived as physical, psychological

Figure 2.26 Falling Water, Bear Run, Pennsylvania, USA. Design by Frank Lloyd Wright (1935–1939). (a and b) The building achieves the placement of man in relation to nature. Wright put the occupants in a close relationship to the glen, the trees, the foliage and the wild flowers. The glory of the natural surroundings is accentuated, brought in, and made a component of daily life. The vertical elements of the house are constructed in native stone. Horizontal elements are poured concrete.

Figure 2.26 Continued.

and spiritual entities connected to their surroundings at all these levels. In response to architecture that is largely dominated by economics, technical possibilities and regulations, organic architecture strives for an integral approach, including ecological aspects, cultural meaning and spirituality. Whereas the modern focus on progressive economy often leads to regressive ecology, organic architecture seeks to ameliorate this situation with new technologies and 'green architecture' (Jencks, 2002). It emphasises respect for the properties of the materials, the harmonious relationship between form and function of the building and the relationship between man and nature (Figure 2.26). Pioneers such as Frank Lloyd Wright in the USA, Antonio Gaudí in Spain and Rudolf Steiner in Germany interpreted organic architecture in different ways. Wright focused on the relationship between buildings and their environment, the continuity between inner and outer space, the coherence of parts of the building and the whole, and respect for building materials. Gaudí worked with plastic design that would make the building mass alive. Construction according to nature's principles was a very important aspect of Gaudí's design. The altar space of the crypt of the Sagrada Familia looks like a cave. All pillars are different, such as trees in nature. The staircase in Parc Guëll was designed around an old pine tree, because building a staircase is a fast job, but growing up of a tree takes a long time, as Gaudi explained. Being

Figure 2.27 Headquarters building for Gasunie, Groningen. Design by Ton Alberts and Max van Huut. An example of (neo)-organic architecture, incorporating free expressive spatial forms. The design was strongly influenced by the desire to achieve a particular visual and spatial effect. For example, the rhythm of the windows is completely independent of specific inside rooms. The office space behind the windows is standard.

the founder of anthroposophy, Rudolf Steiner emphasised the importance of education and spiritual growth. In 1913 he designed the Goetheanum, the first meeting centre of his movement in Basel, Swiss. The floor plan looks like a mother's uterus.

Organic architecture seemed to have expired after a couple of decades, but in the 1950s and 1960s it underwent an unexpected revival. Remarkably, some of the pioneers of the modern movement brought about this revival, transforming its initially rigid geometrical character into a lively, organic direction. An example is the Notre-Dame-du-Haut in Ronchamp, which is an interesting turn in the design work of Le Corbusier. In the work of Alvar Aalto and Hans Scharoun, a more gradual development occurred. This modern organic architecture used local building traditions, new techniques and new creative impulses. A new diversity of approaches and forms of expression originated worldwide. Calatrava, who is strongly inspired by Gaudí, is in the same way inspired by

Figure 2.28 Sydney Opera House, Sydney. Design by Jørn Utzon (1973). This striking building has put Sydney firmly on the world map. The shape suggests billowing sails, a reference to its waterside location. Other associations are with seagulls, shark fins and white shells. Utzon is fond of using organic metaphors in his work. The enormous cost overrun brought about the architect's premature dismissal.

natural constructions. Well-known Dutch representatives are Alberts and van Huut, who designed the office building for Gasunie in Groningen and many other 'organic' buildings (Figure 2.27). Organic metaphors are also included in Jørn Utzon's Sydney Opera House (Figure 2.28).

The modern movement

The 1920s and 1930s saw the beginning of a new movement in the field of art and culture that also extended into architecture. Within this modern movement (In Dutch: 'Het Nieuwe Bouwen', literally New Building, or 'Nieuwe Zakelijkheid', New Objectivity) a new vocabulary of form was developed, influenced by cubism and the ideas of Le Corbusier expressed in the journal *L'Esprit Nouveau*. In the Netherlands a number of architects, including Theo van Doesburg (1883–1931), Gerrit Rietveld (1888–1964) and J.J.P. Oud (1890–1963), combined to form De Stijl. According to Theo van Doesburg, the optical-aesthetic needs of man are satisfied by the angular townscape rather than by the irregular forms of nature (Mattie and Derwig, 1995). The patterned elevation and primary colours of the Café de Unie in Rotterdam, a replica of

Figure 2.29   Rietveld-Schröder house, Utrecht. Design by Gerrit Rietveld (1924). The surfaces of the elevations are finished in white, broken white and four shades of grey. Window frames and pillars are painted red, yellow, blue and black.

one of Oud's designs, refers to the paintings of Piet Mondriaan (1872–1944). A high point in the architecture of De Stijl was the Rietveld-Schröder house in Utrecht, designed by Gerrit Rietveld (Figure 2.29). The space inside this house is not enclosed by elevations with window openings but by vertical and horizontal surfaces separated by glass partitions. Functional considerations also played a part in the design. The use of sliding doors enabled the house to be used in different ways. The absence of window posts in the windows at the corners on the first floor ensured a smooth transition between interior and exterior space. Later on, architect Oud took distance from the quite dogmatic principles of De Stijl (Figure 2.30).

Although many designers of the modern movement have a strongly functional mindset, there is no doubt that they also allow themselves to be guided by aesthetic considerations. In their book *The international style* (1932), Henry-Russell Hitchcock and Philip Johnson clearly demonstrate that there is such a thing as a common style. Space is seen as volume bounded by surfaces, not a hollowed-out mass. Important principles of arrangement include modular regularity and non-axial symmetry. Random ornamentation is rejected. White surfaces and geometrical forms are much in evidence. The authors do, however, return to this subject in the preface to the reissue of *The international style,* which they describe as more a series of different and almost personal styles. For instance, as a reaction to the light constructions of International Style with their

Figure 2.30 Former headquarters for Shell, The Hague. Design by J.J. Oud (1942). This design was characterised by a combination of strict symmetry and ornamentation in stone and coloured majolica. Oud had previously taken a very negative view of the application of ornament. For example, in 1921 he wrote, 'Ornament is the universal cure for architectural impotence'. Not surprisingly, he was much criticised for his Shell building design by those involved in modern building. His about-turn was seen as a betrayal of *Het Nieuwe Bouwen* [New Building].

plain, smooth wall surfaces, representatives of so-called Brutalism, such as Peter and Alison Smithson and Goldfinger, designed monolithic concrete erections of great mass. It was an attempt to redefine modern architecture using a look and aura that is cold and dour. The use of raw concrete was perceived as a quick and easy way of constructing durable buildings. This shows that an effort to achieve functional efficiency can be consistent with very different designs. According to Summerson (1957), the objectivity sought for by functionalist theory is conflicting with the subjectivity of the personal expression achieved by buildings realised in practice.

One example of an architect who undoubtedly designed functionally but rejected functionalism in its strictest form (function determines form) is Le Corbusier. He held that the layout of the interior is indeed strongly determined by functional considerations, but that the external form must have some representative quality and so must be primarily determined by aesthetic considerations. In this context, Mees (1984) talks of introverted functionalism, as the counterpart to the extroverted functionalism of such architects as Hugo

Häring (1882–1958), who believed that the exterior form must also express the essence of the functions, or at least the main functions. In his book *Vers une architecture* (1923), Le Corbusier wrote that the essence of architecture lies in the power of form to arouse special emotions. Utility and intelligent construction are basic requirements for good architecture, but a building only becomes architecture when the aesthetic dimension transcends both.

Partly in reaction to the modernists, Italian morphological research in the early 1980s led to renewed interest in the autonomy of form. Even the concept of typology reappeared. A well-known representative of the morphological or typological approach was Aldo Rossi (1931–1999). This Italian architect and theorist attached little value to statistical analyses and population forecasts. Disputing the idea that form must follow function, he looked for an architecture of form that made no reference to possible use. As he saw it, a design must in principle allow any sort of use, but it is up to the user to make the possible actual.

Postmodernism

A recent movement that paid much attention to the function of form was postmodernism. The name derived from literary theory and was first applied in the field of architecture by Charles Jencks (1977) in the mid 1970s. Many postmodernists were opposed to the disciplined design of modern post-war high-rise. Their criticism was directed towards the monotony, semantic impoverishment and one-sided emphasis on functionalist and economic principles. Functionality was not seen as the basis of form. Architecture needs to convey symbolic meaning. Irregularity is more important than symmetry. The Italian architect Manfredo Tafuri went so far as to describe the modernism of the 1920s and 1930s as the enemy of joy, saying that it should be replaced by architecture of pleasure ('form follows fun'). Architecture must get back to appealing to the imagination, as Robert Venturi and Denise Scott Brown wrote in their book *Learning from Las Vegas* (1972). Peter and Tony Mackertich (2001) show a similar view in their photographic reassessment of fun in architecture.

Postmodernism expressed itself in a multitude of different styles and lavish detailing, harking back once more to classical forms. Jencks described this as radical eclecticism, a new form of classicism aiming to unite old and new. One example was Philip Johnson and John Burgee's AT&T building in New York (designed in 1976), a modern skyscraper whose roof refers to the triangular gable of antiquity. Other examples include Michael Graves' Portland Building (1980), Sjoerd Soeters' Circus in Zandvoort (1986–1991) and De Resident in The Hague (Figure 2.31), a combination of housing, shops and offices design by Sjoerd Soeters and Michael Graves (1990), with the urban design by Rob Krier. Here the form is quite autonomous. The first thing to be

Figure 2.31 De Resident, The Hague. Design by Michael Graves and Sjoerd Soeters. A clearly recognisable feature of Michael Graves' design is the metaphor of the Dutch house, with its two narrow elevations and high gabled roofs. So far the space under these roofs remains empty, which means that their sole function is to contribute to the form.

developed was the general shape of the building. Only later were functions worked in to satisfy the requirements of the market. An emphasis on symbolic meaning can also be found in the work of Daniel Libeskind (Figure 2.32).

Deconstructivism

Some postmodernists were unable to feel comfortable with eclecticism and went off in search of a theoretical framework for their designs. Architects like Peter Eisenman and Frank Gehry found their way to the philosophical works of Lévi-Strauss, Foucault and Derrida. Architects who appeal to these particular philosophers are often referred to as deconstructivists (Johnson and Wigley, 1988; Wigley, 1993). According to Bolle (1989), deconstructivism rests on two supports: one in the history of art, harking back to Russian constructivism, and one philosophical, mainly based on the philosophy of Jacques Derrida. A characteristic feature of deconstructivism is the creation of space for absence. Fragments are accepted as autonomous. Tschumi replaces a model based on

Figure 2.32 The Jewish Museum, Berlin. Design by Daniel Libeskind. This design attempts to express the oppressive atmosphere of the holocaust. There is hardly any programme that can be expressed in terms of square metres and spatial relationships. The main aim is to convey meaning. A broken Star of David, the absence of doors, corridors leading nowhere and a black ceiling call up associations with a nuclear bomb shelter and the total dislocation of a culture. At the time of the opening in 1999 there was still no collection to display, but the building still attracted 140,000 visitors in the first year alone.

units and totality by one based on dispersion and schizophrenia,' wrote Bolle. At the same time, Tschumi calls the events in space as equally important as the space itself. As such, form does not follow function, and function does not follow form, but function and form interact (Noever and Himmelblau, 1991). Most deconstructivist architecture is characterised by whimsical forms (Figure 2.34). But according to Peter Eisenman, deconstructivism must be judged primarily on ideological grounds and not on style. Ghirardo (1996), on the other hand, claimed that the underlying ideology was unclear. According to Ghirardo, the works of Peter Eisenman, Frank Gehry and Rem Koolhaas never led to any new theory of architecture or to new ideas about the role of the architect. Koolhaas himself is sceptical about deconstructivism. As he sees it, deconstructivism is really just decoration. He finds the analogy between irregular design and a fragmented world in which values are no longer firmly rooted, 'frankly trivial'. Nowadays, symbolic meaning or philosophical ideas are less used to steer the

Figure 2.33   Louvre pyramid, Paris. Design by Ieoh Ming Pei (1989). I.M. Pei's proposal was to create the desired extension to the Louvre below the Cour Napoleon. The decision to create a monumental entrance in the form of a glass pyramid arose from the need to create a pure architectural form. The decision to use glass was inspired by a wish to provide ample daylight and to preserve the view of the historic Louvre. The pyramid is a lightweight construction and was one of former President Mitterand's Grands Projects.

search for form. Whereas symbolism was fundamental to both postmodernism and deconstructivism – with postmodernist architecture being a vehicle for symbolic messages and deconstructivist architecture a metaphor for non-architectural concepts – recent architecture reflects a declining interest in accommodating a symbolic cargo or rendering a sometimes only half-understood philosophical or scientific idea. Architecture is primarily perceived as art again, with form as a result (Ibelings, 2002). A search for a pure form was also one of the drivers behind the Louvre pyramid (Figure 2.33).

Blobism

The blob buildings that appear more and more nowadays represent a new movement in architecture that is not yet really defined. Its basic ideas go back to the complexity theories of Jacobs, Venturi, Ungers and many others, and the postmodern movement in science. But above all it was steered by computer design and production (Jencks, 2002). Being one of the protagonists of this

Figure 2.34 The Groningen Museum. Design by Alessandro Mendini, Philippe Stark, Coop Himmelblau and Michelle de Luchi (1994). The pavilion designed by Coop Himmelblau is a typical piece of deconstructivism. The roof, with its steel plates laid out at random, symbolises the breakthrough of fossilised systems.

movement, Peter Eisenman envisioned an electronic or digital architecture. Philosophically, blob architecture is linked with the theory of *Le Pli* (Deleuze, 1988, 1993), which concerns folding and is as much metaphysical as physical – the way the mind is joined to the body in seamless continuity (Jencks, 2002). Architects wanted to warp floor, wall and ceiling into a continuous and seamless surface. Computer-aided design (CAD) was already available throughout the 1980s, but it did not become a tool to create radical architecture until the 1990s. The fish-shaped pavilion in Barcelona by Frank Gehry was the first building built that was really computer generated. Eisenman also developed buildings that were a co-creating between designer and software. The Guggenheim museum in Bilbao (Figure 2.35) was the spin off of the new movement, that the magazine *Any* (1995) called *blobitecture*. Using computer software it is now possible, by manipulating vectors and grids, to create forms that are more flexible, amorphous, supple, fluid, incomplete, non-ideal and pliable than ever before. Blobitecture brings us closer to organic shapes. Vitruvius and the Greeks called the body 'the measure of all things' and made it the standard for architecture. With blobitecture, this is becoming a more realistic idea. According to Charles Jencks, the blob is a complex sphere and our bodies are evolved blobs (Jencks, 2002). Blobism is architecture of art, which

Figure 2.35 The Guggenheim Museum, Bilbao. Design by Frank Gehry (1993). Bilbao is undergoing a process of transformation, changing from an industrial harbour city to a centre for trade and culture. The museum was partly intended to put Bilbao on the world map. The design was the result of an intuitive search for an appealing form. Dozens of scale models were made during the search for the right form. The form was then scanned in three dimensions and input into an advanced computer program, CATIA, which allowed the titanium facing plates to be made to the exact size.

wants to upgrade the experience of architecture and to achieve an ecstatic feeling. According to Paul Viriolio, this does not mean that the question of function and need disappears but rather that these issues are basic architectural obligations that have to be normatively resolved (Jencks, 1999).

Until 20 years ago blob buildings were impossible to build and so were thought of as fantasies. But although cyberspace is still an unreal world, new developments are taking place in its architecture. Blobism implies a dynamic architecture, although the buildings remain static. Cyberspace is an artificial world that is not subject to the usual laws of physics. Within a cyber environment, architecture can be completely 'liquid': as Marcus Novak puts it, 'It is an architecture that is no longer satisfied with only space and form and light and all the aspects of the real world. It is an architecture of fluctuating relations between abstract elements' (Jencks, 1999).

Representatives working on innovative shapes and theories on the relationships between architecture, bodies and cyberspaces are, among many others, Peter Eisenman (Figure 2.36), Greg Lynn, Jeff Kipnis, Zaha Hadid, Enric

Miralles, Coop Himmelblau, and in the Netherlands Kas Oosterhuis, Lars Spuybroek and Ben van Berkel. The first truly interactive blob in the Netherlands is the Fresh Water Pavilion of Neeltje Jans in Holland, designed by Lars Spuybroek (Figure 2.37). According to the website of NOX, the pavilion's architecture was developed simultaneously with a highly innovative interior that fully involved all senses in the visitor's experience. In this pavilion people can interact with light, sound, freezing of a wall, the spraying of mist, etc. The Dutch architect and lecturer at Delft Faculty of Architecture Kas Oosterhuis developed a theory on hyperbodies. A hyperbody is a programmable building body that changes its shape and content in real time with changes in use and with changing conditions. As such, architecture would become dynamic. One result of Oosterhuis' search for this kind of 'liquid' architecture is the E-Motive Architecture. E-Motive Architecture is the art of building transaction spaces The term refers to:

- *Electronically*: the living environment will be electrified; it has sensors and detects everything around it. This is data-driven architecture.
- *Motive*: using kinetic structures, the building will be able to react on the inputs it gets.
- *Emotions*: the building will behave as a complex organism with emotions.

E-Motive Architecture is based on the idea that buildings take in information, process it and pass it on in a different form. The programmability of form and

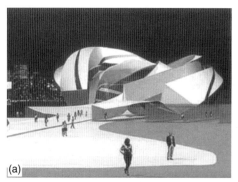

(a)   (b)

Figure 2.36   (a and b) Staten Island Institute for Fine Arts and Sciences. Design by Peter Eisenman (1999). Eisenman's continual interest in opposition, displacement, event, grid, mathematics, multiple geometric orders, the torquing of space, and the folding of form back upon itself seems ideally suited for exploration with computer-assisted design (CAD). White spirals of translucent glass and steel flow over a dense traffic intersection of boats, pedestrians and buses. According to Jencks, the spatial experience becomes an incomplete narrative, a destination without an end; his desire is to destabilize perception, blur categories, and challenge the existing space-time regime (Jencks, 1999).

information content allows the construction to become a lean and flexible vehicle for a variety of different uses (Oosterhuis, 2002; www.oosterhuis.nl). Its architecture can be changed in a few seconds, by reprogramming its form to suit a different function. Perhaps this architecture will lead to the replacement of Sullivan's 'Form follows function' by 'Form allows function'.

Figure 2.37 (a–c) Fresh Water Pavilion Neeltje Jans, Vrouwenpolder, Holland. Design by Lars Spuybroek (1993–1997). In this pavilion people can interact with light, sound, freezing of a wall, the spraying of mist, etc. The blob is made of 14 elliptical frames that vary in dimension, over which splines of stainless steel are braid.

Figure 2.37 Continued.

2.7 Conclusion

It should be clear from the above summary that at different times, or indeed at the same time, major differences of opinion could exist about the relationship between function and form (Figure 2.38). Broadly speaking, it is possible to distinguish three main lines of thought.

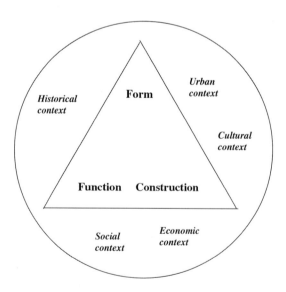

Figure 2.38 Factors influencing form.

Form is determined by functional and constructional efficiency

Pithy one-liners expressing this view include the well-known *form follows function* – with the variant *form follows behaviour* – and *form follows construction*. According to the first of these principles, a design must be based primarily on utility value and the wants and needs of the users. Geometrical principles of form not derived from users' requirements are seen as artificial. The building should primarily express its purpose and the activities, or at least the main activities, which take place within it. There should be no need for additional aids such as signs to indicate function. The load-bearing structure, materials and technical services should also be recognisable. The motto *form and function are identical* goes one step further. Here, the underlying thought is that functionality automatically leads to beauty. According to the second principle, 'form follows construction', form follows from the construction and the materials, both of which should be used 'honestly' and not for example be tucked away behind non-constructional additions. The architect is first and foremost a constructional designer. Constructions have a beauty of their own.

Form follows context

According to this approach, form is mainly determined by context. Factors that exert a significant influence include the site's architectonic and urban design characteristics, its geographical situation (including its distance from the city centre), its socio-cultural context, historical context, legal context (legislation and regulations) and economic context. The importance of this last factor is expressed in the motto *form follows economics* or *form follows profit.* Here the design is guided by an effort to achieve effective and efficient utilisation of the available means, both in the design process (e.g. by applying rational design methods) and in the design itself. A related motto, *form follows fiasco*, indicates that the choice of form can also be based on negative experiences with earlier design variants.

Form is autonomous

According to this approach, form is not primarily derived from users or construction but rather from principles of form, possibly geometrical, and the perceptual experiences that such principles evoke. Mottos can be *form follows aesthetics*, *form follows meaning* or *form follows fun*, in which 'fun' refers both to the pleasure experienced by the designer and the pleasure that the observer or user gets from the building. Yet another motto is *form precedes function* (Handler, 1970), reflecting the rejection of a purely functional approach.

Although some designers and designs can be recognised as belonging clearly to one or another of these approaches, most designers follow an approach somewhere in the middle. They see functionality as important but not the only motive. Function, form and construction all affect one another. Context also has its effect. Thus, the achievement of a satisfactory form requires a balance to be struck between the many factors that influence that form.

Bibliography

Anna, S. (1999), *Archi-neering; Helmut Jahn Werner Sobek*. Hatje Cantz, Ostfildern.

Arnheim, R. (1966), From function to expression. In: *Towards a psychology of art*. Faber and Faber, London, 192–211.

Barbieri, S.U., L. van Duin (ed.) (1998), *Ontwerpstrategieën* [Design strategies]. Publications Office, Faculty of Architecture, Delft University of Technology.

Barbieri, S.U., L. van Duin, J. de Jong, P. van Wesemael, W.W. Floet (1999), *Honderd jaar Nederlandse architectuur 1901–2000* [A hundred years of Dutch architecture 1901–2000]. SUN, Nijmegen.

Barrie, T. (1996), *Spiritual path, sacred place; myth, ritual, and meaning in architecture*. Shambala, Boston.

Benton, T., C. Benton (1975), *Form and function. A sourcebook for the history of architecture and design 1890–1938*. Crosby Lockwood Staples, London.

Bolle, E. (1989), *De filosofische wortels van het deconstructivisme* [The philosophical roots of deconstructivism]. *De Architect*, April 1989, 71–75.

Bosma, K., D. van Hoogstraten, M. Vos (2000), *Housing for the millions. John Habraken and the SAR (1960–2000)*. NAi Publishers, Rotterdam.

Charles, Prince of Wales (1989), *A vision of Britain; a personal view of architecture*. Doubleday, London.

Deleuze, G. (1993), *The fold, Leibnitz and the baroque*. University of Minnesota Press, Minneapolis. [Translation of Le Pli by Tom Conley.]

Dijk, H. van (1999), *Twentieth-century architecture in the Netherlands*. 010 Publishers, Rotterdam.

Duin, L. van (1996), *Vorm en functie* [Form and function]. Inaugural lecture, Faculty of Architecture, Delft University of Technology.

Eyck, A.E. van (1959), *Het verhaal van een andere gedachte* [The story of a different thought]. *Forum* No. 7.

Frampton, K. (1992), *Modern architecture. A critical history*, 3rd edn. Thames and Hudson, London.

Franck, K.A., R.B. Lepori (2000), *Architecture inside out*. Wiley-Academy, Chichester, UK.

Ghirardo, D. (1996), *Architecture after modernism*. Thames and Hudson, London.

Habraken, N.J. (1961), *De dragers en de mensen. Het einde van de massawoningbouw* [Load-bearers and people. The end of mass-produced housing]. Amsterdam.

Handler, A.B. (1970), *Systems approach to architecture*. American Elsevier, New York.

Heuvel, W. van (1992), *Structuralism in Dutch architecture*. 010 Publishers, Rotterdam.

Heuvel, W.J. van, B.D. Verbrugge (1996), *Geschiedenis van de bouwkunst* [A history of architecture]. SMD, Leiden.

Hill, R. (1999), *Designs and their consequences: architecture and aesthetics.* Yale University Press, New Haven.

Hitchcock, H.R., P. Johnson (1932), *The international style. Architecture since 1922.* New York.

Ibelings, H. (1999), *De functie van de vorm* [The function of form]. Van den Broek and Bakema, architecture and urban design. NAi Publishers, Rotterdam.

Ibelings, H. (2002), *Supermodernism. Architecture in the age of globalization.* NAi Publishers, Rotterdam.

Jencks, C. (1977), *The language of postmodern architecture.* Academy Editions, London.

Jencks, C. (1985), *Towards a symbolic architecture: the thematic house.* Academy, London.

Jencks, C. (1999), *Ecstatic architecture: the surprising link.* Academy, London.

Jencks, C. (2002), *The new paradigm in architecture: the language of post-modernism.* Yale University Press, New Haven.

Jodidio, P. (1998), Santiago Calatrava. Taschen, Cologne.

Johnson, P., M. Wigley (1988), *Deconstructivist architecture.* New York Graphic Society, New York.

Jongert, J., M. van Ouwerkerk, J. de Haan (1995), *Kritisch regionalisme* [Critical regionalism]. In: The critical landscape. *De Omslag*, No. 15, March 1995, 43–45.

Kelbaugh, D. (1997), *Common place. Toward neighbourhood and regional design.* University of Washington Press, Seattle.

Kopp, A. (1985), *Constructivistic architecture in the USSR.* Academy, London.

Lefaivre, L., A. Tzonis (2003), *Critical regionalism: architecture and identity in a globalizing world.* Prestel, Munich.

Leupen, B., W. Deen, C. Grafe (1990), *Hoe modern is de Nederlandse architectuur* [How modern is Dutch architecture]. 010 Publishers, Rotterdam.

Leupen, B., C. Grafe, N. Körning, M. Lampe, P. de Zeeuw (1997), *Design and analysis.* 010 Publishers, Rotterdam.

Leuthäuser, G., P. Gössel (1990), *Functional architecture: the International Style 1925–1940.* Taschen, Cologne.

Macel, O. (1981), *Barok architectuur* [Baroque architecture]. Faculty of Architecture, Delft University of Technology.

Mackertich, P., T. Mackertich (2001), *Architectural expressions: a photographic reassessment of fun in architecture.* Wiley, Chichester.

Mattie, E., J. Derwig (1995), *Functionalisme in Nederland* [Functionalism in the Netherlands]. Architectura en Natura, Amsterdam.

Meel, J. van (2000), *The European Office. Office design and national context.* 010 Publishers, Rotterdam.

Mees, F.M.L. (1984), *Architectuurideologieën. Studie en kritiek der grondbeginselen* [Architectural ideologies. A critical study of basic principles]. PhD thesis, Faculty of Architecture, Delft University of Technology.

Molema, J., M. Casciato (1996), *The New Movement in the Netherlands 1924–1933.* 010 Publishers, Rotterdam.

Mumford, L. (ed.) (1952), *Roots of contemporary American architecture.* Grove Press, New York.

Noever, P., C. Himmelblau (1991), *Architecture in transition: between deconstruction and new modernism*. Prestel, Munich.

Oosterhuis, K. (2002), *E-motive Architecture*. 010 Publishers, Rotterdam.

Pearson Clifford, A. (1999), Other than their status as world's tallest buildings, what else do Cesar Pelli's Petronas Towers have going for them? *Architectural Record* 1, 93–99.

Pevsner, N. (1960), *An outline of European architecture*. Penguin, Harmondsworth; 1960.

Rogers, R. (1991), *Architecture: a modern view*. Thames and Hudson, London.

Rossi, A. (1982) [1967], *The architecture of the city*. MIT Press, Cambridge, Mass.

Smith, E.B. (1978) [1956], *Architectural symbolism of Imperial Rome and the Middle Ages*. Hacker, New York.

Speaks, M. (ed.) (1996), *The critical landscape*. 010 Publishers, Rotterdam.

Sullivan, L. (1924), *The autobiography of an idea*. New York.

Summerson, J. (1957), The case for a theory of modern architecture. *RIBA Journal*, June 1957, 307–313.

Venturi, R., D. Scott Brown (1972), *Learning from Las Vegas*. MIT Press, Cambridge, Mass.

Whittick, A. (1953), *European architecture in the twentieth century*. Vol. 2, Part 3, The era of Functionalism 1924–1933. Lockwood, London.

Wigley, M. (1993), *The architecture of deconstruction: Derrida's haunt*. MIT Press, Cambridge, Mass.

CHAPTER 3

Programme of requirements

3.1. Introduction

If a building is to provide the proper level of support to its use, the design must be preceded by an understanding of the client and future users' point of view, aims and desires and the spatial consequences. What activities will need to take place in the building? How much floor space will be required, in all and per room? What requirements have been set for accessibility, security and flexibility? What kind of interior climate is required? Any cultural, aesthetic, economic or legal requirements and expectations must be clearly understood. Every requirement that the building has to satisfy must be carefully recorded, to avoid later disappointment, enable alternatives to be compared and make it possible to see whether what is wanted is compatible with what is possible. It hardly ever happens that everything that is wanted can be achieved with the time and money available. Laws and regulations currently in force also limit the number of possibilities. All this means that priorities must be set and choices made. Recording requirements, wishes and limiting conditions as part of the building process is known as *programming* or *briefing*. The present chapter discusses how programming is done and the ways in which programming and design affect one another. It also deals

Box 3.1   Terms and definitions

Programming is generally viewed as an information processing system setting out design directions that will accommodate the needs of the user, the client, the designer, or the developer.

Sanoff (1992)

A programme of requirements is an ordered collection of data expressing housing needs, on the basis of which one or more buildings will be evaluated or a design for a rebuilding or new building will be prepared and checked and the project will be carried on until the relevant specifications come into use.

Dutch Standards Institution [NEN] (1993a)

The programme of requirements is a summary of the limiting conditions and requirements, quantitative and qualitative, which need to be satisfied by the solution to a particular housing requirement.

Government Buildings Agency [Rijksgebouwendienst] (1995)

A programme of requirements is a document which serves to incorporate into the design process communication between client and the future users of the building on the one hand and architect and consultants on the other, in line with basic assumptions and taking account of the conditions to be satisfied, the needs, requirements, wishes and expectations of the client and future users, by means of a coherent set of activities, designed to achieve the complete and unambiguous collection, processing, evaluation, and transmission of information, in phases from global to detailed.

Building Research Foundation, Rotterdam (1996)

A programme of requirements is an ordered collection of data about an organisation's housing needs and the performance required in respect of the site, building, rooms, parts of the building and facilities in the building and on the site.

Van der Voordt et al. (1999)

Briefing is an evolutionary process of understanding an organisation's needs and resources, and matching these to its objectives and its mission. It is about problem formulation and problem solving. It is also about managing change. Ideas evolve, are analysed, tested and gradually refined into specific requirements. ... Briefing is the process by which options are reviewed and requirements articulated, whereas a brief is the product of this process.

Blyth and Worthington (2001)

briefly with a number of forms of contract, with different ways of assigning responsibility for programming, design, execution and management. The form of contract partly determines who is to set up the programme. Finally, the chapter discusses a number of aids to finding out wants and requirements and recording the findings in a document, *the programme of requirements* or *brief*.

Definitions of 'programme of requirements' often show content and purpose as related (Box 3.1). In essence, the programme records in documentary form the requirements the building must satisfy. Its task is to define the client's objectives in terms of utility, function, quality, time and cost and to define the required performance. It can be sensible to distinguish between requirements, which must be satisfied regardless, and wishes, which are less imperative. Requirements may be expressed quantitatively or qualitatively, and will refer to such things as location, building, rooms, parts of the building and facilities.

3.2   The role of programming in the building process

Programming and recording the results in a programme of requirements or brief is an essential step in the careful development of a plan. Care must be taken to avoid grasping too quickly at solutions which may well have been suitable elsewhere but which are not tailor-made to satisfy the specific wishes and requirements of the organisation concerned. If solutions are thought about too early, the programming phase often becomes a weak link in the building process. The decision to prepare an explicit statement of the requirements and conditions to be satisfied is sometimes only taken at a later stage, after the proposed solutions have been discussed, so making extra work and wasting time. Other drawbacks to taking insufficient care in writing a brief in the programme include:

- Insufficient benefit is gained from users' experience.
- The designer needs to spend a great deal of time collecting and analysing information.
- The feasibility of the project can only be established much later on, with the help of the first design sketch.
- The design will need to be changed more often and more radically. This will cost time and money, and will often mean irritating the parties involved.
- Insufficient time and attention are given to alternative solutions.
- The result of the design process is a building which is less suitable or more expensive.

3.2.1   Functions of the programme of requirements

It is therefore vitally important to have a carefully prepared programme of requirements. Depending on the phase in the process and the position of those involved, the programme of requirements can be expected to perform some combination of the following functions:

a. Reflection

The explicit formulation of basic assumptions, aims, requirements and wishes forces the client and the future users to give deliberate consideration to their organisation, the way it functions today and the way it will need to function in future. When the building is not being built for the client's own use, the preparation of a brief forces those responsible for the project to give careful thought to potential end-uses.

b. Information and communication

The brief is an important medium for transmitting information between the various people involved, in particular between client and designer, but also for example between client, users and consultants or official bodies. It provides the basis for the architectural and technical design. The characteristics of the organisation to be housed, its activities, basic assumptions, aims, wishes and expectations are an important source of inspiration to the designer, the more so when the document contains graphic material rather than being merely a dry compilation of words and figures.

c. Examination

For the client or his consultants the brief provides a way of checking the feasibility of the project at an early stage, making it possible to compare alternatives such as rebuilding, new building or the reuse of an existing building. Designers and consultants use the brief mainly to enable them to check the cost and quality of alternative locations, design variants, the final design and the specification against the desires and requirements of the client.

d. Budgeting

The brief makes it possible to establish a budget for building, investment and exploitation, allowing costs to be monitored. Conversely, the brief can be checked against the available budget when the sum available for investment and exploitation is fixed in advance. The Building Research Foundation [Stichting Bouwresearch] recommends including the budget in the programme as an internally imposed condition, so avoiding any delay in signalling budget overruns (SBR 258, Building Research Foundation, 1996).

e. Contracting

Because it sets down the characteristics required of the building, the brief can form part of the contract between the client and the designer, builder or tenderer of a product. But if the brief is a static document on which the designer no longer has any influence, then positive interaction between brief and design becomes almost impossible. It is therefore becoming more and more usual these days for programme development to continue right up to the specification phase.

3.2.2 Interaction between briefing and design

Programming, designing and building are the three main activities involved in the building process. Figure 3.1 is a schematic representation of the place of programming in a traditional building process. To keep the diagram simple it is assumed that the client is also the owner and acts on behalf of the future users of the building. Again, for the sake of simplicity, the diagram also ignores

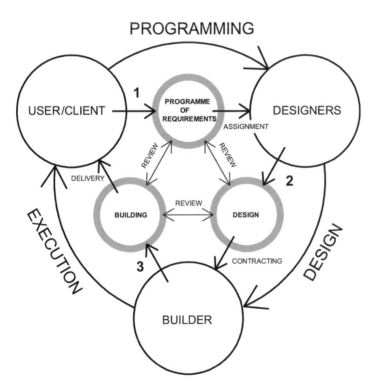

Figure 3.1   Part played by the programme of requirements in the traditional building process. Source: Vrielink (1991).

the fact that the client, owner and users are often supported by consultants, subcontractors and suppliers. The arrows connecting the products (programme, design and building) indicate that they are or should always be checked against one another, so giving the process a cyclical nature. For example, if the design fails to satisfy the programme, this can mean either adjusting the design or amending the programme. The fact remains that in the traditional building process, in principle, the end of the briefing phase is marked by the production of a definitive programme, and only then does the designer start work. This approach makes the brief a rather static document. Later developments mainly concern technical matters, and hardly involve anything spatial or functional. That is why Dutch standard NEN 2658 only refers to 'the' programme of requirements in general terms.

Even in building processes with modern forms of organisation such as design and build, general contracting, build-operate-transfer (BOT) and performance-based contracting out, the brief remains a rather static document (see the previous paragraph). First the programme is developed, then a single party or a building team is made responsible for design and execution. BOT implies that this party is also responsible for management, temporarily or permanently.

The advantage of a separate briefing phase, more or less distinct from the design phase, is that time and attention are explicitly devoted to formulating the requirements clearly without immediately starting to think about solutions. Once the results have been recorded in a brief, everybody involved knows what he is doing. On the other hand, the effort of translating the brief into pictures and rough plans often leads to new insights and so to other wishes. A designer can come up with solutions which were not called for by the brief and may even be in conflict with it, but which nonetheless represent a significant improvement to the plan, e.g. by designing to take advantage of the nature of the surroundings. It is also conceivable that the brief will contain requirements which are contradictory or mutually inconsistent, and that this only comes to light during the design. All this goes to support the view that the brief should not be treated as a static document. After all, programming and designing interact. It is up to the client to assess any divergences between programme and design and to accept or refuse them. This means that there is a growing need for information provided 'just in time', and in no greater quantity than is needed at the time. This is why the Building Research Foundation, Rotterdam recommends that the programme of requirements be developed gradually, from global to detailed, interactively with the development of the plan (Figure 3.2).

3.2.3 Authors of the brief

The responsibility for producing a usable brief rests with the client. That does not mean that the client has to prepare the programme himself. Generally, he will call

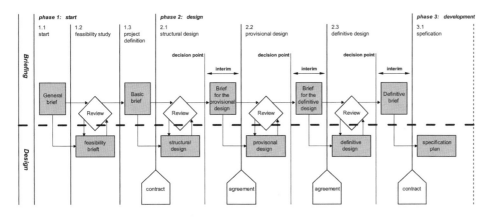

Figure 3.2 Interaction between the programme of requirements and development of the plan. Terms signify functions, not individuals. Source: SBR 258, 3rd revised edition, Building Research Foundation, 1996.

on the services of a programme consultant. Another option is for the architect to prepare the programme. It also sometimes happens that the company tendering the building determines the programme. The different variations are discussed below.

a.   Client

It is up to the client to decide what he wants, which makes him responsible for the brief. However, most clients have little experience of the building process, let alone the preparation of a brief. What they generally do understand very well is their own aim, organisation and activities. This is why many clients contract out the work of preparing the brief but still play an active role in the preparation. Of course some clients have a great deal of experience in the building process, e.g. the building departments of large companies, the Government Buildings Agency and larger local authorities, and so are often well able to prepare the brief themselves, yet even they will call in specialised consultants to advise on more complex projects.

b.   Specialist

Certain management consultants and other consultancies have built up expertise in the preparation of programmes of requirements and so can support the initiator of the project in this stage of the development. Some organisations specialise in particular types of buildings or functions, e.g. for schools, social or cultural activities, sports, libraries or hospitals. Besides preparing the brief, these organisations are generally geared up to check designs and coordinate the building process.

c. Designer

It still quite regularly happens that the architect develops the brief, in close consultation with the client. In such cases the architect's proposal generally takes the form of sketches showing various ideas and possible designs. The client simply provides a global indication of his desires and requirements, sometimes only verbally, and it is left to the architect to decide what actually gets put down on paper. In such cases the design sketch is in fact a brief presented in graphic form. The preparation of the brief is not a standard part of an architect's work. The standard Dutch conditions defining the legal relationship between client and architect prescribe that the client should provide the architect with the brief. If the architect has to do extra work on the brief, this should be charged separately. Some firms of architects specialise in this part of the building process.

The preparation of the brief by the architect has distinct supporters and opponents amongst professional practitioners, including architects, for the following reasons:

- The preparation of a brief requires an analytical approach. An architect is more concerned with synthesis and so is less suitable for the task of preparing a brief.
- The quality of the programme and the design is improved by polarising rather than combining different interests. If the designer sets the standards against which his designs are judged this can lead to deviations from the brief being approved after the event, so limiting the chance of any objective examination of design alternatives.
- A good programme and design benefit from an intensive dialogue between client and designer during the whole of the design process. Contact with client and users provides a designer with much information which is impossible to transfer, or to transfer well, by indirect means (i.e. by means of a written programme).
- The static character of the brief as a document that precedes design is outdated. When an external adviser prepares the brief, much of the interaction between programme and design is lost.

d. Tenderer

When project developers 'build for the market', the user is often 'unknown'. Examples include the development of office space or dwellings for sale or rental. In fact in such cases the tenderer is the person mainly responsible for establishing the programme, based on his knowledge of the market. To reduce risk, building often only starts when a certain percentage has been rented or sold in advance, so making it possible to discuss with the intended user what adjustments are desirable or possible before building starts. A good deal of attention needs to be paid to flexibility if adjustments are to be possible after the event, when the building is complete. Another option, mainly applied to office building, is to deliver the building unfinished and leave it to the user to decide on the built-in units.

3.2.4 Types of contract

As already indicated, significant changes are taking place in the organisation of the building process. Although the traditional form still occurs quite often, complex building tasks in particular often make use of new forms of project organisation and new types of contract, differing mainly in the extent to which responsibilities for design and execution are kept separate. Separation of responsibilities is found in traditional building processes, working with a building team and performance-related work. In general contracting, design and build, BOT and brochure plans, design and execution are handled by the same organisation. Because this can affect the part played by the programme of requirements in the building process, a brief account of the most important types of organisation is given below.

a.   Traditional building process

The traditional building process is characterised by a triangular relationship between the client, the designer and the contractor. The client provides the brief and hires an architect to prepare a design based on that brief. The architect seeks assistance from consultants. The architect and his consultants work out the technical details of the design and the design process is completed by the preparation of a specification and working drawings. Responsibility for materials,

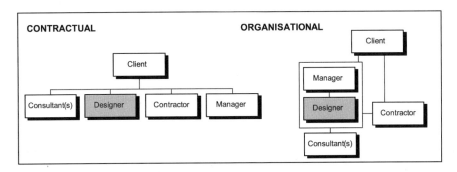

Figure 3.3 Schematic representation of the partners in a traditional building
process. Source: Van de Laarschot, 1998.

79

products and constructional features remains with the architect. The design is put out to contract (often publicly) and executed by the contractor. In the original triangular relationship the function of management remained with the architect. Today a building management firm often performs this role (Figure 3.3).

b.   Building team

The building team approach involves setting up a cooperative arrangement at an early stage between the people responsible for the design and the people responsible for the execution. The client, the designer, the consultants and the contractor are all members of a team that assumes total responsibility for the building being developed (Figure 3.4). In most cases the team's execution expert handles the execution. In some cases the building firm is required to sign a waiver, giving up any unquestioned right to carry out the work. Contractual relationships are much the same as those in the traditional building process. Each party enters into a separate contract with the client. The involvement of the party responsible for execution at such an early stage in the development of the plan makes it possible to take advantage of relevant skills in the field of execution and costs during the design phase. Two disadvantages are that competition is virtually eliminated and the contract amount may well be calculated less precisely.

c.   Performance concept

Here too, as in the traditional building process, the client is responsible for the programme. In this approach, developed by the Government Buildings Agency, the programme consists of as complete as possible a summary of functional and aesthetic performance specifications, supported by a spatial plan or structural design (Ang, 1995; Building Research Foundation, Rotterdam, particularly SBR reports 219, 296, 296a, 420 and 447). The spatial plan indicates the shape and

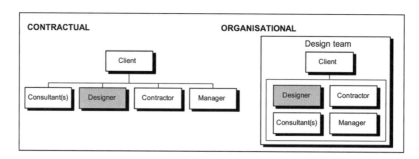

Figure 3.4   Schematic representation of the process of working with a building team. Source: Van de Laarschot, 1998.

arrangement of floor plans, elevations and roofs. Performance requirements and drawings do not prescribe materials, products or constructional elements. The demand specification also contains general project information, such as information about soundings, start and delivery dates, payment instalments and application procedure. The package of requirements, written and drawn, is put out to tender to a number of building firms, each of which then works out a plan, in conjunction with a designer, often its own, to produce a complete tender (Figure 3.5). The client then makes his choice based on a comparison of the different price/quality ratios. One advantage claimed for this method is that it encourages the contractor to come up with creative and innovative solutions. The best possible use can be made of his expertise and knowledge of suitable materials, products and constructional elements. One disadvantage is that the client has little influence on the choice of architects or the architecture (Ang, 1995). Not all types of performance can be measured objectively. This applies particularly to things like architectonic quality, which is difficult to measure. Moreover, each potential tenderer has to provide a complete design, which means that putting work out to public tender involves a good deal of extra work (Vrielink, 1991). Not surprisingly, in practice a number of different variations are found in the contracting phase and the type of contract. The contract can be entered into solely on the basis of the required performance or on the basis of

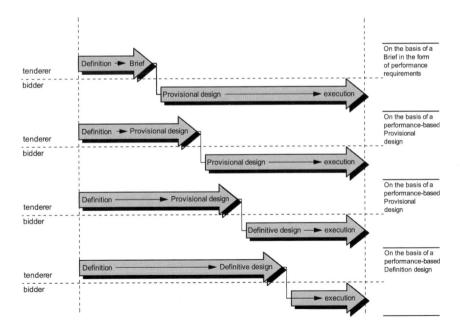

Figure 3.5 Times at which instructions are given to tenderers. Source: Building Research Foundation, Rotterdam, 1995 (SBR 348).

performance and an outline, provisional or definitive design. Different contract forms include the contracting out variant, where the definition phase ends with a fixed specification of requirements, and the consultation variant, where a preliminary specification of requirements is used to select a potential tenderer who is then consulted during the preparation of the definitive specification of requirements.

d. General contracting

In this form of organisation, coordination of the building process is left in the hands of the general contractor, who takes over responsibility for design and execution from the client (Figure 3.6). The client retains the right to intervene. The general contractor is generally a company specialising in complex building processes, e.g. a building management firm or project developer. The general contractor comes between the client and the other participants, whom he selects and with whom he contracts himself. Sometimes the general contractor even takes the financial risk. In this form the contribution made by the architect depends on the general contractor.

e. Design and build (D & B)

Here a single organisation is responsible for design and execution. The client has a single point of contact (one organisation, a joint venture or a group of different companies) with which he enters into a single agreement covering the entire project and to which he hands over complete responsibility. Unlike the situation with general contracting, the client has less opportunity to intervene.

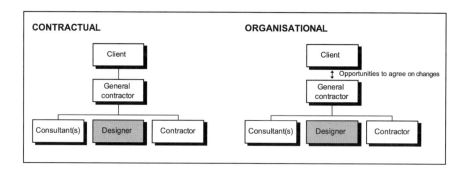

Figure 3.6 Schematic representation of the general contracting process. Source: Van de Laarschot, 1998.

f. Build-operate-transfer (BOT)

In this form of contract the tenderer is not only limited to designing and building a piece of real estate but is also responsible for exploitation, management and maintenance (Huijbrechts, 1997). A BOT project typically involves cooperation between the public sector and the private sector. Government grants a concession to a concessionaire to build a public facility and to own and exploit it for a predetermined period. The investor is responsible for expertise, finance, building and exploitation of the facility. During the life of the concession the investor will attempt to recover the cost of the development plus a margin of profit. At the end of the concession the concessionaire transfers ownership of the facility to the government at no further cost. The BOT form is often used for major infrastructural projects such as the Channel Tunnel or the Northumberland Bridge in Canada.

g. Brochure plans

Brochures contain standard building plans, unrelated to any particular project or location (Van de Laarschot, 1998). The plans are for more or less off-the-shelf products, and are put on the market as such. This explains the use of the term 'catalogue building'. Account can be taken of the wishes of the customer within the margins of the product. As in the case of design and build, catalogue building is a turnkey formula. The client enters into a contract with a single supplier. The performance delivered (the building) is based on the plan in the brochure, adjusted wherever possible to suit the programme of requirements set by the client. Turnkey contracts are really only suitable for routine projects put on the market by the contractor himself.

3.3 Contents of the programme of requirements

To ensure that the designer and others involved in the building process have sufficient support to work with, the programme should go as completely as possible into the requirements and wishes of the client and any other conditions which the building will need to satisfy. The number of requirements can be considerable, depending on the size of the building and the complexity of the task. It is therefore important to set out the requirements in an orderly way. In practice a number of different arrangements are used. This section will limit itself to considering the arrangements prescribed by the Dutch Standards Institution (NEN 2658, the current standard) and the Building Research Foundation (SBR 258, much applied in building practice).

3.3.1 The Dutch standard NEN 2568

According to *NEN 2658, Programmes of requirements for buildings and associated project procedure*, (Dutch Standards Institution,1993a), a programme of requirements or brief should consist of three sections:

1. Limiting conditions (prerequisites), in particular applicable laws and regulations, technical issues and financial issues.
2. Characteristics of the target group or groups to be housed. This section of the programme should describe the aims of the organisation, the users and their activities, the services or products to be delivered, organisational, economic, functional and ecological issues and future expectations.
3. Requirements relating to the object: the site, the building as a whole, the subdivision of space, i.e. the spatial configuration, particular aspects of spaces, building components and on-site facilities.

The next thing to be laid down is the *project procedure*, consisting of two sections:

1. Identification of the project (type of building, purpose, situation, overall dimensions and building volume, costs and financing arrangements, relevant documents and participants, etc.) (Box 3.2).
2. Description of the task (tasks and responsibilities of the various parties involved), process description and timetable.

Box 3.2 Examples of items to be included in the project identification

1. Code and name of project
2. Type and purpose of the building
3. Registered office and site characteristics
4. Main reasons for the project
5. Size, expressed in units relevant to the intended use (e.g. number of beds in a nursing home)
6. Overall dimensions or building volume (or both)
7. Maximum cost of investment (with 'as at' date)
8. Method of financing
9. Acceptable cost of exploitation or expected return (or both)
10. Present stage or phase of the project
11. List of documents relating to the programme and project procedure
12. Names and addresses of participants
13. If the building already exists: names of designers, constructional engineers, building firm and contractors involved in the past, with date of delivery.

Source: NEN 2658 (Dutch Standards Institution, 1993a).

Although cost estimates and budgets can often be prepared separately, financial information (including references to cost estimates and budgets) can often be included in various sections of the programme, such as limiting conditions, project identification and requirements for the object.

A number of practical guidelines, the Dutch Practice Guidelines [Nederlandse Praktijkrichtlijnen – NPRs] have been developed to assist in preparing a programme. The checklists included in these guidelines give a good idea of the subjects to be covered by the programme (Box 3.3). NEN 2658 is less clear about the content of the requirements, the conceptual framework and the phased development of the requirements.

3.3.2 SBR 258

The Building Research Foundation, Rotterdam, has carried out further research into the conceptual framework and the phased approach. In 1996 the third

---

Box 3.3 Examples of items to be included in requirements imposed on a building

- Occupancy
- Orientation (sun, wind, surroundings)
- Area of ground to be built on
- Required floor areas, per room and in total (gross and net, divided between useful, traffic and technical services)
- Building volume, number of storeys and desired ceiling height
- Wishes relating to design, colour and structure of the elevations, general lay-out and organisability
- Replaceability, movability, adjustability, extensibility
- Accessibility
- Signing
- Clarity (entrances, internal traffic)
- Transport (people, goods) and walking distances

- Waste removal
- Security (fire, burglary, vandalism)
- Health and comfort
- Efficiency
- Environment control (e.g. daylight)
- Floor loading and horizontal forces
- Energy requirement
- Indoor climate control
- Communication systems
- Technical maintenance
- Cleaning
- Rentability
- Sustainability and life span
- Future utility value
- Building method, load-bearing construction, dimensional grid

Source: NPR 3401 (Dutch Standards Institution, 1993b).

edition appeared of *SBR 258, Programme of requirements. An instrument for quality control* [Programma van eisen. Instrument voor kwaliteitsbeheersing]. Besides giving a clear account of the conceptual framework, this publication contains directions on how to put together a project-related programme of requirements. SBR 258 uses a five-part arrangement:

- User requirements
- Functions and performance
- Expected visual quality
- Internally imposed conditions
- Externally imposed requirements and conditions.

a.   User requirements

These are the requirements and wishes relating to all or part of the accommodation required to support the intended use. A description should be provided of the organisation to be housed, specifying its nature, size, organisational structure and its present and future pattern of activities.

b.   Functions and performance

The characteristics of the organisation to be housed need to be translated into spatial and building needs and desires relating to the location (accessibility, facilities in the neighbourhood, possibility of extension, etc.) and needs and desires relating to the building. Relevant items include the space required in the building as a whole and per room, the desired level of environmental control (temperature, lighting, humidity, sound and view), security and flexibility.

c.   Expected visual quality

Although the creation of visual quality falls within the competence of the designer, the client would be well advised to make his own wishes in this field as clear as possible. Does he want the building to give an impression of luxury, or should it aim to appear sober and efficient? Is he thinking of a traditional style building or something more high-tech? Should the building say anything about its function or the organisation's corporate identity?

d.   Internally imposed conditions

This section will in any event deal with the financial and economic conditions which need to be satisfied (possible investment and exploitation costs and any limitations applying to those costs) and conditions to be satisfied relating to time (delivery date, lapsed time taken by the housing process). Other internally imposed conditions include specific requirements relating to sustainable building.

Box 3.4 Extract from a brief on the subject of flexibility

The expected growth in and changeability of the business to be carried on necessitates a high degree of flexibility. It is important that the business should have available a good basic arrangement in terms of both load-bearing structure and design. Separating the load-bearers (the main load-bearing structure) from the in-built units will make a substantial contribution to flexibility. The following features must be included in the design and be both recognisable and usable:

- *Expansion.* It must be possible to extend the accommodation at some later date.
- *Arrangement.* It must be possible to change the way space is arranged within the building to suit changing space requirements. Such changes should be easy to make and should not involve high costs or disturbing the primary function of the business.
- *Function.* It must be possible to use rooms for different functions or for multiple functions without requiring any radical changes. This should in principle apply to all office space related in any way to production. It should not be a problem to convert office space into additional factory space or vice versa.
- *Over-dimensioning.* Extra space must be provided in advance (during the preparation of the accommodation) to cope with future growth in line with the forecast requirement. In the first instance, effort devoted to environmental control in this extra space should be kept to a minimum.

One important factor leading to the achievement of a flexible building is the choice of a suitable building pattern, one that will make it possible and relatively simple to change or extend the building at some later stage. It is important that elevations, ceilings, floors, furniture and technical services are dimensioned consistently, in accordance with a fixed module size. Current module sizes are 1800 and 3600 mm.

Source: Programme of requirements for commercial premises [Programma van eisen voor bedrijfshuisvesting] (DHV AIB, 1995).

---

e. Externally imposed requirements and conditions

This section deals with requirements imposed by spatial planning and other laws and regulations. Examples include a zoning scheme, requirements imposed to protect the appearance of a town, building regulations, fire protection regulations, the Licensing Act, the Hotel and Catering Act, the Food and Drug Act, the Environmental Protection Act, the Occupational Health and Safety Act (Arbo) and by-laws.

Box 3.5   Extract from a brief on the subject of acoustics

To ensure that speech is satisfactorily intelligible, desirable reverberation times or 'echo' times in the mid-frequency range (125–4000 Hz) are as follows:

- Offices   0.5–0.7 sec
- Conference rooms   0.5–0.7 sec
- Corridors and halls   1.0 sec
- Workshops (production floor)   0.8–1.0 sec
- Canteen   1.0–1.5 sec
- Telemarketing rooms   0.5 sec

Noise of technical services
Maximum acceptable background level:

- Conference rooms, consulting rooms, etc.   35 dB(A)
- Rooms for directors and management   35 dB(A)
- Offices   40 dB(A)
- Large offices   45 dB(A)
- Production floor   55 dB(A)
- Rooms for computer equipment   60 dB(A)
- Canteen, corridors   45 dB(A)

Source: Programme of requirements for commercial premises (DHV AIB, 1995).

Box 3.6 Extract from a brief on the subject of visual quality

The new building must be clearly recognisable as a public building with a social function, enjoying a special status within the university. Since the building also has a national task and will receive visitors from outside Delft, its design and positioning must be such as to create an impressive frontage on to Schoemakerstraat. The character of the back of the building, at present rather untidy and adding little to the impression given by the area behind the Great Hall, needs to be improved.

Source: Programme of requirements for a university library for Delft University of Technology (1995).

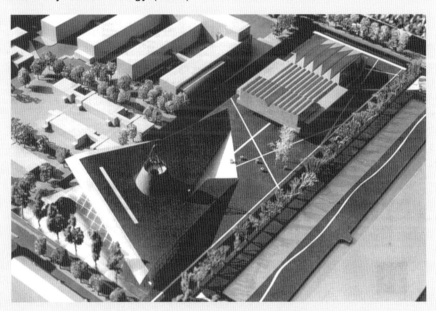

Figure 3.7 Model of the new Delft University of Technology library.

Box 3.7 Extract from a brief on the subject of externally imposed conditions

The programme assumes that the building will at least satisfy any require-ments that may be laid down by or on behalf of government or public utilities.

(Continued)

It is also assumed that use will be made of the current state of knowledge and technology as laid down for example by the Dutch Standards Institution in its standards current 3 months prior to the signing of the contract based on this programme of requirements.

Zoning scheme
A zoning scheme is in force for the Apeldoorn North Industrial Estate.

Provision of access
The building must be accessible by the handicapped and must conform with the guidelines laid down by the Council of the Dutch Handicapped Federation (Provision of access [Geboden Toegang], 11th edition, 1993) (now replaced by the Manual for Accessibility [Handboek voor Toegankelijkheid].

Environmental Protection Act
The company claims not to need to go through any elaborate procedure in connection with the Environmental Protection Act (the length of the procedure is 6 months).

Source: Programme of requirements for commercial premises (DHV/AIB, 1995).

3.3.3 Development from rough to detailed

People's ideas about requirements and wishes are not fixed all at once. It often takes a long time to collect information, clarify wishes and expectations and reach a consensus. It would not be efficient to delay the development of the plan until every last bit of information is available. Moreover, not all the information is required at once. In practice, therefore, it is not surprising that the programme of requirements is developed in phases, working from coarse to fine, from rough to detailed. SBR 258 distinguishes five versions:

- Global brief
- Basic brief to support the structural design
- Brief to support the provisional design
- Brief to support the definitive design
- Definitive brief, as the basis for the specification.

The Government Buildings Agency (1995) finds that three kinds of a brief are sufficient: global, basic and detailed. This corresponds more closely to what is done in practice and is therefore used in what follows.

a. Rough programme of requirements

A global programme is necessary to allow the feasibility of the project to be checked against the budgeted investment costs and exploitation expenses in the initial phase of a building project or, conversely, to determine the budget required and to see whether the project can be financed. A global programme is also necessary to determine what is required of the site and to allow the suitability of other sites to be checked.

The global programme contains at the very least an account of the basic aims and principles, a global survey of the functions and activities to be housed and an estimate of the amount of floor space required. Use is often made of standards and key figures obtained from precedents. For example:

The need is for a primary school to serve eight classes. The gross floor area is estimated at eight classrooms, each taking $56\,m^2 \times 1.7$ (to allow space for circulation area, sanitary provisions, technical services and constructional elements).

Once the floor area has been quantified, the required quality must be established in general terms, since this after all will largely determine the cost level. This means that something needs to be said about requirements relating to the site, any special requirements in respect of environmental control, security, accessibility, sustainability and the level of ambition as regards the materials to be applied and the expected visual quality. At the very least it must also provide a global view of any limiting conditions, internal and external.

b. Basic programme of requirements

The basic brief is a more detailed development of the global programme. It must be sufficiently detailed to provide a basis for a structural design and a provisional design. Precise technical details are not necessary at this stage. The main requirement is for a clear description of the organisation to be housed, e.g.:

- Mission statement
- Organisation structure (organisation chart)
- Number of employees (in total and per department)
- Relationships between departments or functions
- Work processes: activities and relationships between activities.

The level of detail required for a particular topic is determined by the extent to which that topic has spatial or architectural implications. Apart from the *functional programme*, the basic programme must also give some insight into the *spatial programme*, which means that the user requirements must be worked out in terms of functions and performance. The basic programme must also provide information about the symbolic function of the building (identity, presence, expected visual quality) and any internally and externally imposed requirements and conditions (time, money, quality, legislation and regulation) that will affect the development of floor plans and cross sections.

c. Detailed programme of requirements

A detailed brief also contains full technical information, allowing it to serve as a basis for the definitive design and the contract documentation (specification and contract drawings or specification of requirements) preparatory to execution. The detailed brief is generally only prepared while the definitive design is being developed or at the same time as the working drawings. Sometimes use is made of a *workbook* or *space book*, containing details of the use and the spatial and architectural requirements for each room or workplace.

Box 3.8 Possible arrangement of a workbook for a nursing home

Include for each room:

- Characteristics of the users or target group (number, type of user)
- Activities
- Equipment, permanent and temporary (table, chairs, beds, bedside cupboards, lifting equipment)
- Spatial requirements (accessibility, spatial orientation, privacy, view)
- Technical and physical requirements (temperature, humidity, ventilation, natural light, noise and acoustics, water, electricity, telephone, wiring, lighting, protection against the sun, oxygen, fire precautions)
- Finish for floors, walls and ceilings (decoration, resistance to wear and moisture, homely appearance, etc.)
- Dimensions of the room (as required by the programme and in accordance with standards)
- Useful floor area (square metres)
- Number of rooms of this type required
- Notes for clarification, as required.

Source: Waalwijk, 1995.

---

d. Strategic brief, project brief and fit-out brief

Like the five-phase division used by the Building Research Foundation and the more usual division into three parts – rough, basic and definitive – Blyth and Worthington (2001) too emphasise that briefing is a process of refinement leading from a general expression of need to a particular solution, making a distinction between a 'strategic brief' and a 'project brief'. During the pre-project stage the client defines the need for the project and sets it down in a *strategic brief*, written in business language, with clear statements of intent. The strategic brief should deal with 'ends' rather than 'means'. The nature of the business and its objectives are examined and different options tested. At the end of this stage the type of project is defined. Once appointed, the design team validates the strategic brief. This will give the design team an opportunity to clarify the client's objectives and the client has an opportunity to ensure that the team understands his priorities, particularly those relating to quality, time and cost. The design team then reformulates the strategic brief and produces a *project brief*, whose aim is to convert the organisational and business language of the strategic brief into building terms, fixing functional relationships, giving initial sizes, areas and volumes and establishing quality and image. A draft project brief allows the client to review the direction of the project. Value management and risk management techniques allow the brief to be tested against the priorities and objectives set out in the strategic brief. The draft project brief is refined to a greater level of detail and becomes the project brief, giving dimensions, finishes, colours and a cost plan. The project brief leads on to the production of the detailed constructional information required for building or extending the building. To allow for change, separate briefs may be developed for fit-out and operations. The *fit-out brief* aims to define the client's requirements for internal building spaces in building terms and gives detailed information on the dimensions of spaces and elements to be provided. The *operating brief* sets out the concept, guidelines and management databases for the project so that it can be used to inform continuing planning and design decisions. According to Blyth and Worthington (2001), the manager who will be responsible for the project after completion should be part of the team developing this brief. There can also be detailed briefs on related topics such as furniture, information and communication technology requirements, environmental issues and facilities management.

3.3.4 Presentation of the requirements

Many programmes of requirements consist of no more than text, tables and diagrams: e.g. a space table (presenting required m^2 per space) (Table 3.1) and a matrix or spatial relationship diagram showing the desired relationships between different activities or rooms (Figures 3.8 and 3.9). Sometimes small sketches are used. The increasing use of modern word-processing programs, drawing programs and multimedia techniques makes it easier to present requirements and wishes visually, e.g. in the form of alternative solutions, with comments, or by reference to precedents. This last factor is of particular importance when it comes to the expected visual effect. The danger with pictures, however, is that they can easily come to live a life of their own or be

Table 3.1 Example of a space table for an office building

Department	Sub deptartment	Room	Functions*		Area*	
Management		Director	Cat	N	m²	Total
			f	1	28	28
Human Resources	HRM	Manager	e	1	18	
		Staff	c	1	18	
	Office	Security	d	1	11	
		Receptionist	d	1	11	
		Manager	d	1	11	69
Finance		Controller	e	1	18	
		Supervisor	d	2	22	
		Staff	b	13	117	157
Business		Staff	b	3	27	27
Business unit 1		Manager	e	1	18	
		Team members	b	20	180	198
Business unit 2	Management	Manager	e	1	18	
		Team members	b	7	63	
	Other	Team leaders	b	2	18	
		Team members	b	9	81	180
Business unit 3		Manager	e	1	18	
		Team members	b	11	99	117
Subtotal				77		776

*The categories (a–f) and associated areas were derived from the Dutch standard NEN 1824, Ergonomic recommendations for office sizes.
Source: Programme of requirements for commercial premises (DHV/AIB, 1995).

wrongly interpreted, blurring the boundary between programming and design. This is why some designers prefer to seek inspiration in a metaphor. Another much used option is to go together to visit a number of buildings and to work out the kind of visual quality that is wanted by discussion with the client, the prospective users (or their representatives) and the designer.

The requirements must of course really have something to say. Obvious remarks like 'the building must not leak' should be avoided. The requirements should also be clearly expressed and wherever possible be verifiable. There is an important distinction between functional requirements and performance requirements.

Functional requirements or *user requirements* indicate what activities must be possible within the building. Such requirements are generally expressed in qualitative terms, e.g. 'the building must be integrally accessible'.

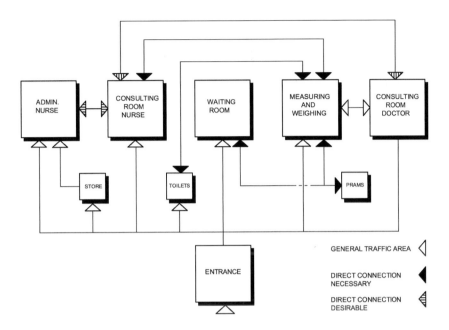

Figure 3.8 Visualisation of the spatial organisation of activities in a health centre. Source: Van Hoogdalem et al., 1985.

There is often a description of the activities to be housed, e.g. 'there must be space to hold 12,000 books available on public loan, for lending out and receiving returned books, for reading books and magazines and for consulting works of reference'.

Performance requirements indicate the conditions that the building must satisfy if it is to be possible to use it in the way intended. *Performance requirements* means quite literally the way the building is required to perform. Performance requirements should be expressed in as concrete terms as possible, in terms that are measurable but not based on any particular solution. Requirements that are measurable are objectively verifiable, so wherever possible the desired level of quality should be expressed in quantitative terms, for example 'a gross floor area of 12,500 square metres' or 'doors should provide unobstructed passage at least 850 mm wide'. In the library example: 'an 1800 m^2 lending area for 12,000 books, a 20 m^2 counter for lending and returns and a 90 m^2 reading room with seating for 30'. If requirements are expressed in a way that is not tied to any particular solution, the designer is left with sufficient freedom to select his own solution to satisfy the required performance specifications.

Care should be taken with descriptive requirements that contain their own solutions, e.g. 'the floor must be finished in white marble'. This kind of formulation leaves little scope for alternative solutions. On the other hand, there is no point in providing a detailed summary of performance specifications when the client has already said that there is only one solution that he is prepared to accept. However, in many cases the solution demanded expresses some underlying wish, e.g. 'easy to keep clean and giving an impression of luxury'. When such underlying wishes are included in the programme explicitly, there is still room for alternative solutions, equally capable of meeting the requirements.

3.4 Steps leading to a programme of requirements

The most important steps to be taken in preparation for a programme of requirements are as follows:

■ A careful analysis of the organisation of the activities to be housed, mainly prepared with the help of information and experience obtained from the client and the users.

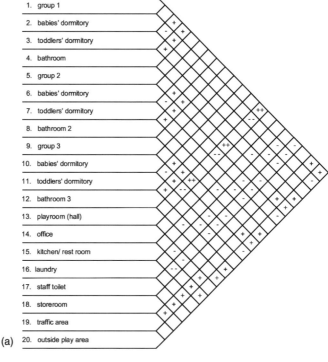

Figure 3.9 Spatial relationship diagrams for a children's day care centre with three groups. (a) A semi matrix with '+'=needing to be close or connected;'−'=not needing to be close or connected. (b) Plan of individual locations showing rooms to scale. The closeness of a relationship is indicated by the nearness of the relevant rooms to one another in the plan. Direct relationships are emphasised by connecting lines indicating a connecting door. Source: Van der Voordt et al., 1984.

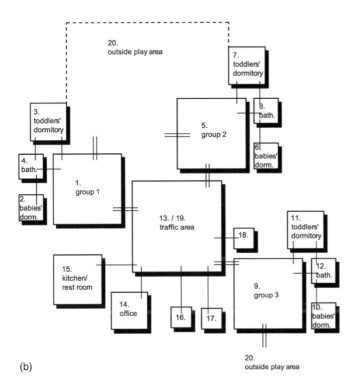

20.
outside play area

7.
toddlers'
dormitory

3.
toddlers'
dormitory

8.
bath.

5.
group 2

6.
babies'
dorm.

4.
bath.

2.
babies'
dorm.

1.
group 1

13. / 19.
traffic area

18.

11.
toddlers'
dormitory

15.
kitchen/
rest room

12.
bath.

9.
group 3

14.
office

16.

17.

10.
babies'
dorm.

(b)

20.
outside play area

Figure 3.9 Continued.

- A spatial translation into functional requirements and performance specifications, prepared with the help of the knowledge and experience of the client and those responsible for preparing the brief (architects or specialists), the literature and standards.
- Visits to comparable projects and the study of information relating to those projects.
- A comparative analysis and evaluation of precedents.

The first two steps are known collectively as *functional analysis* or *function analysis* (Figure 3.10). The task of translating a functional analysis into a functional design is referred to, appropriately, as functional designing. This systematic approach follows in the footsteps of the work study analyses carried out by Taylor in America. In the Netherlands in the 1960s and 1970s his approach was developed to cover architecture by Zweers and de Bruijn (1958), de Bruijn and Korfker (1969) and Polak (1973), all of whom taught in the Faculty of Architecture at Delft. Recent thinking on functional design can be found in van Duin et al. (1990), Sanoff (1992) and Blyth and Worthington (2001). We shall first discuss how a function analysis is done and then explain how precedents can be used in the preparation of a programme of requirements.

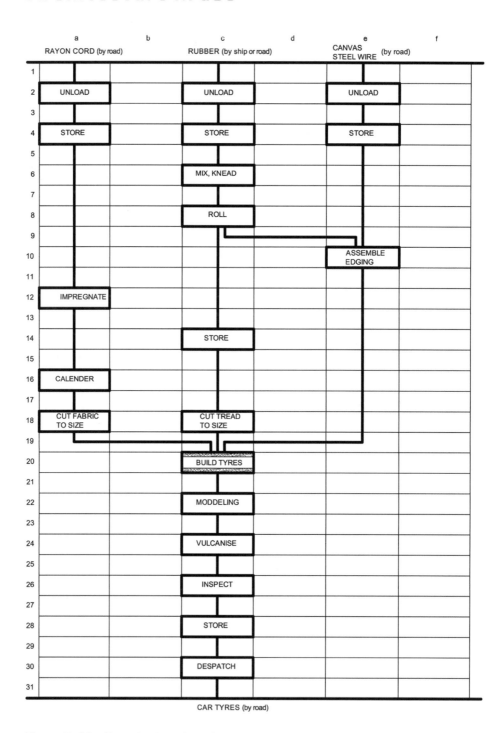

Figure 3.10 Organisation chart for a tyre factory. Source: De Bruijn and Korfker, 1969.

3.4.1 Function analysis: dimensioning, separating and connecting

Programming starts with an analysis of the organisation and activities that need to be housed. The analysis involves establishing the nature of the activities and the spatial conditions to be satisfied, such as the floor area needed, any minimum breadth or depth, physical conditions (temperature, lighting and noise) and requirements for a psychologically acceptable environment (view, privacy, social contact, territoriality, identity and recognisability). Proper consideration must be given to the question of which activities need a specific space of their own and which activities can be accommodated in shared space. Should the photocopier and the fax be in the room occupied by the secretaries, in a separate room or in some area, possibly a public area, in the middle of the building? Should every office be given its own conference area? Or should there be conference rooms for common use and informal seating areas? Once it has been established which activities require their own space and which activities can make do with shared space, it will be possible to determine the spatial conditions required for each room individually, so largely determining the requirement for space in terms of individual rooms and conditions to be satisfied. This is not to say that there is a specific spatial solution for each activity. From the point of view of flexibility and future value it is important to design rooms in such a way that they are not merely capable of accommodating the activities currently envisaged but other activities as well. A closely fitting, 'tailor-made' solution, where form corresponds perfectly to function, will not be easy to adjust to changing circumstances.

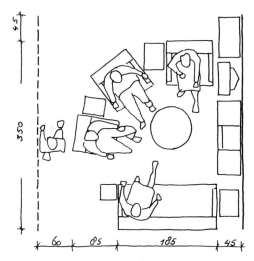

Figure 3.11 Dimensional data in the literature. Source: Haak and Leever van der Burgh (1992).

Dimensional data in the literature

It is preferable for closely related activities and spaces to be situated near to one another. Other considerations bearing on spatial proximity or the grouping of rooms (zoning) are common properties, i.e. public or private, hot or cold, quiet or noisy, outward looking or walled in, etc. In simple buildings, spatial relationships can easily be analysed by hand. For more complex buildings, it is desirable to use a computer.

Box 3.9 Example of a space requirement estimate

The floor area required for a works canteen is determined by the number of people who will be using the facility at the same time. The following guidelines for a works canteen can be found in the specialist literature:

1. Canteen section: number of seats $\times$ 1.4 m^2
2. Counter, kitchen and storage: number of seats $\times$ 0.7 m^2
3. Staff rest room and changing room, office etc.: 0.4 m^2 per seat

The programme consultant makes the following calculation:

- Number of staff: 400
- Maximum occupancy at any one time about 90% (10% absent sick, on holiday, etc.)
- People eat between 12.00 noon and 1.30 p.m., in two shifts
- Assume that 60% use the canteen
- Assume that all tables are occupied at peak periods, though not completely (e.g. three people at a table for four), so requiring an uplift factor of 1.15:

$$\text{Number of seats} = \frac{400 \times 0.90 \times 0.60 \times 1.15}{2} = 125$$

Space required:

- Public space   125 $\times$ 1.4 m^2 = 175 m^2
- Counter, kitchen   125 $\times$ 0.7 m^2 = 87.5 m^2
- Other rooms   125 $\times$ 0.4 m^2 = 50 m^2
- Total   313 m^2

Source: Internal report on basic technical principles for rented office buildings.

It is advisable to avoid wording the brief too tightly, as if the design must follow logically and unambiguously from the programme analysis. Apart from the target use, there will after all be many other considerations affecting the design, e.g. adjustment to fit in with the surroundings or indeed a desire for contrast, aesthetic and financial considerations and future value. This last factor requires a certain degree of flexibility. A building 'tailor-made' to suit a programme can easily mean uneconomically large differences between different rooms, or a building that is impossible to use for any other function.

3.4.2   Tools and references

Of course the client and the programme consultant working on the brief will take advantage of their experience with their own organisations and in the preparation of programmes of requirements. Programme consultants often make use of a programme prepared for a comparable task at some earlier date, going through it, perhaps together with the client, and making adjustments to suit the present task. To find out about the organisation, use is made of such techniques as interviews, workshops for users (or their representatives), occupancy measurements, scenario techniques and dimensional studies using a full-scale model. Not everything needs to be worked out afresh every time. Over the years countless publications appear which can help with function analysis and be useful in formulating internally and externally imposed conditions. The following list, which makes no claim to be complete, gives a number of important publications:

- Publications specifically concerned with the preparation of programmes of requirements, including *SBR 258, Programma van eisen* [Programme of requirements]; *Handleiding Ruimtelijke Programma's van eisen* [Spatial programmes of requirements manual] published by the Building Research Foundation (1998); *SBR 421, Bouwstenen voor het Programma van eisen* [Stepping stones leading to a programme of requirements] (Building Research Foundation, 1998); *Integrating Programming, Evaluation and Participation in Design* (Sanoff, 1992); *Professional practice in facility programming* (Preiser, 1993); *Architectural Programming* (Duerk, 1994); *Better construction briefing* (Barrett and Stanley, 1999); *Managing the brief for better design* (Blyth and Worthington, 2001).
- Dimensional studies which translate activities into spatial measures, e.g. *Human dimensions & interior space*, Panero and Zelnik (1979), *De menselijke maat* [The human dimension], Haak and Van der Burgh (1992) (Figure 3.11) and *Architect's Data* (2000), the English updated edition of Ernst Neufert's classic *Bauentwurfslehre* (1970).
- Studies of buildings for particular types of function, such as office buildings, school buildings, libraries, museums and hospitals.
- Studies of specific features such as integral accessibility, safety and security, flexibility, the sick building syndrome, comfort, low-energy and sustainable

Box 3.10 Examples of questions to establish user requirements for a brief

- What kind of organisation is it?
- Why is accommodation needed?
- What does the organisation structure look like?
- How big is the organisation?
- What are the organisation's commercial activities?
- What activities need to be accommodated?
- What is the present accommodation like (quantitatively and qualitatively)?
- Are there any particular trends in progress which may affect the accommodation?
- What is the organisation's policy for the medium and long term?
- Is it essential to have good parking facilities on the site?
- How important is accessibility by public transport?
- Will there need to be rooms to which only a limited number of people will be admitted?
- Which rooms must be simple to increase or decrease in size?

Source: Building Research Foundation, Rotterdam (1998): SBR 421.

Box 3.11 Sample description of the requirements for integral accessibility (design for all)

Regular users and visitors to the building must be able to access and use the functions (spaces, rooms and equipment) for the purposes of the activities in which they are involved in as independent and standard a way as possible. The facilities on the way to and at the places where the functions used by regular users are situated must therefore satisfy the basic accessibility requirements laid down in the Manual for Accessibility. Facilities also used by visitors must satisfy the additional requirements for visitors laid down in the Manual for Accessibility.

Source: Wijk, Drenth and Van Ditmarsch (2003).

Box 3.12 Interactive leitmotif

N.D. Huijgen's 'Interactive Leitmotif' is a new way of providing programme and design guidelines and could be thought of as an electronic variant of Ernst Neufert's well-known handbook 'Architect's Data'. The design principles are presented in both 2-D and 3-D visualisations, so allowing different requirements to be handled by a single illustration. The leitmotif has so far only been developed for setting up a public hall in the building of a local authority. The visualisations provide basic solutions for the layout and organisation of the hall, the application of materials, acoustic aids, use of light, window areas, etc. The illustrations are explained and supported by passages of text. The leitmotif has been placed on the Internet at www.bk. tudelft.nl/bt/toi/afstuderen and so can be easily accessed. The advantage of an Internet page is that it can be used as a kind of encyclopaedia that is easy to adapt and extend. Solutions can be presented in a way that allows a good deal of interaction. The user of the leitmotif can make his own changes, e.g. to the layout and the materials and colours used.

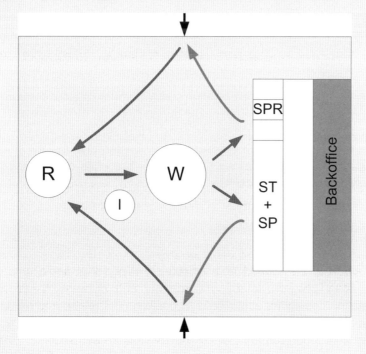

Figure 3.12 R = reception; W = waiting area; I = information; SPR = consulting room; ST = standard desk; SP = specialised desk.

(Continued)

Figure 3.13 3-D simulation of a reception area.

building, and investment and exploitation costs. Chapter 6 discusses a number of these subjects in more detail and makes suggestions for further reading.

- Standards and guidelines, such as the Dutch NEN standards, the German DIN standards, the American ANSI standards and the international CEN standards.
- Building standards and guidelines for particular branches of industry, such as schools, childcare centres, hospitals and libraries.
- Summaries of laws and regulations, e.g. SBR258a (1997).

3.4.3 Precedents

There is much to be learned from existing buildings that could help develop ideas for one's own project by observations and discussions on the spot. Documentation containing evaluations of buildings in the use and management phase can also be extremely valuable. This kind of evaluation is known as a *post-occupancy evaluation (POE)*. When the evaluation also extends to aspects other than use and experience – e.g. costs, technology and aesthetics – it is known as a *building performance evaluation (BPE)* or *total building performance evaluation*.

Evaluative studies are even more valuable when they compare character-istics of and experiences with a range of related buildings (Van der Voordt et al.,

1997). Comparative building analysis has an advantage over traditional research methods such as observation and interviews, because the information obtained relates to different spatial solutions. Each building is the result of a complicated decision-making process, in which basic aims and principles are translated into organisation structure and activities and then incorporated into a spatial design covering such matters as floor plans, cross-sections, materials and facilities. Ex post analysis makes it possible to rediscover the thoughts, ideas and basic assumptions that underlay different choices.

It goes without saying that this kind of process can suffer from problems of interpretation. After all, the design as realised is always affected by the designer's interpretation and limiting conditions, internal and external, such as the size of the budget and the characteristics of the site (zoning plan, dimensions and shape of the building site, neighbouring functions, etc.). It is therefore a good idea to supplement the analysis with research into how the building came into being, interviews with whoever was the client at the time and others involved in the building process, e.g. the architect and the consultants. Further details of how a building is evaluated in the use phase are given in Chapter 5.

Bibliography

Ang, K.I. (1995), *Werken met prestatiecontracten bij vastgoedontwikkeling* [Performance contracts in real estate development]. Department of Housing, Regional Development and the Environment/Government Buildings Agency and Coordination of Building Policy, The Hague.

Barrett, P., C. Stanley (1999), *Better construction briefing.* Blackwell Science, Oxford.

Blyth, A., J. Worthington (2001), *Managing the brief for better design.* Son Press, London.

Bruijn, W.N. de, D. Korfker (1969), *Voorbereiding en methodiek bij het ontwerpen van bedrijfsgebouwen* [Preparation and methodology for the design of commercial buildings]. Parts I and II. Bouwwereld, 29 August and 12 September 1969.

Building Research Foundation, Rotterdam (1995), *Het prestatiebeginsel: begrippen en contracten* [The performance principle: concepts and contracts]. SBR 348. W.J.P. Bakens, Rotterdam.

Building Research Foundation, Rotterdam (1996), *Programma van eisen. Instrument voor kwaliteitsbeheersing* [Programme of requirements. An instrument for quality control]. SBR 258, 3rd edn. E.A.M. ten Dam, F.J. Smits and D. Spekkink, Rotterdam.

Building Research Foundation, Rotterdam (1997), *Programma van eisen. Instrument voor kwaliteitsbeheersing. Externe eisen en voorwaarden* [Programme of requirements. An instrument for quality control. Externally imposed requirements and conditions]. SBR 258a. J.J. Rip, Rotterdam.

Building Research Foundation, Rotterdam (1998), *Bouwstenen voor het PVE* [Steps to a programme of requirements]. SBR 421. M. Wijk and D. Spekkink, Rotterdam.

Duerk, D.P. (1994), *Architectural Programming*. Information Management for Design. John Wiley & Sons, New York.

Duin, L. van, J. Zeinstra (eds) (1990), *Functioneel ontwerpen*. Ontwikkeling en toepassing van het doelmatigheidsbeginsel in de architectuur [Functional design. Development and application of the efficiency principle in architecture]. Architectural Publications Office, Delft.

Dutch Standards Institution (1993a), *NEN 2658, Programma's van eisen voor gebouwen en bijbehorende projectprocedure*. Algemene regels [Programmes of requirements for buildings and associated project procedure. General rules]. Delft.

Dutch Standards Institution (1993b), *NPR 3401, Programma's van eisen voor gebouwen en bijbehorende projectprocedure*. Algemene nalooplijst [Programmes of requirements for buildings and associated project procedure. General checklist]. Delft.

Dutch Standards Institution (1993c), *NPR 3405, Programma's van eisen voor gebouwen*. Indeling en aspecten van gebouwdelen en voorzieningen op het terrein [Programmes of requirements for buildings. Division and features of parts of the building and on-site facilities]. Delft.

Haak, L., D. Leever van der Burgh (1992), *De menselijike meat* [The human dimension]. Delft University.

Hoogdalem, H. van, D.J.M. van der Voordt, H.B.R. van Wegen (1985), *Bouwen aan gezondheidscentra. Functionele grondslagen voor programma en ontwerp* [Building for health centres. Functional foundations for programme and design]. Delft University Press.

Huijbrechts, R. (1997), *Case studies on build operate transfer*. Faculty of Architecture, Delft University of Technology.

Laarschot, J. van de (1998), *Functionele heroriëntatie van het architectenbureau* [Functional reorientation of the architectural practice]. Faculty of Architecture, Delft University of Technology.

Neufert, E., P. Neufert, B. Baiche, N. Walliman (2000), *Architect's data*. Blackwell Scientific Publications, London.

Panero, J., M. Zelnik (1979), *Human dimension & interior space*. A source book of design reference standards. Whitney Library of Design, New York.

Polak, B.M. (1973), *Functioneel ontwerpen* [Functional design]. Amsterdam/Brussels.

Preiser, W. (1993), *Professional practice in facility programming*. Van Nostrand Reinhold, New York.

Rijksgebouwendienst (1995), *Handleiding ruimtelijke programma's van eisen* [Programmes of spatial requirements manual]. Department of Housing, Regional Development and the Environment, The Hague.

Sanoff, H. (1992), *Integrating programming, evaluation and participation in design*. Avebury, England.

Voordt, D.J.M. van der, D. Vrielink, H.B.R. van Wegen (1984), *Kinderdagverblijven*. Richtlijnen voor de bouw [Children's day care centres. Building guidelines]. Delft University Press.

Voordt, D.J.M. van der, D. Vrielink, H.B.R. van Wegen (1997), *Comparative floorplan-analysis in programming and design*. Design Studies (18) No.1, 67–88.

Voordt, D.J.M. van der, D. Vrielink, H.B.R. van Wegen (1999), *Reader programmakunde* [Programming technique reader]. Module M1. Faculty of Architecture, Delft University of Technology.

Vrielink, D. (1991), *Kwaliteit maken , meten en vergelijken* [Quality creation, measurement and comparison]. *Bouw* 23, 17–19.

Waalwijk, W. (1995), *Betere gebouwen door gebruikersparticipatie bij het opstellen van het programma van eisen* [Better buildings by user participation in the preparation of the programme of requirements]. Dutch Association for Nursing Care, Utrecht.

Wijk, M., J. Drenth, M. van Ditmarsch (2003), *Handboek voor Toegankchijkheid* [Accessibility Manual] 5th edition. Elsevier Bedrijfsinformatie, Doetinchem.

Zweers, B.H.H., W.N. de Bruijn (1958), *Een analytische methode voor het ontwerpen van bedrijfsgebouwen* [An analytical method for designing commercial buildings]. Doelmatig Bedrijfsbeheer (10) No. 11. Also included in L. van Duin et al. (eds) (1989), *Functioneel ontwerpen* [Functional design]. Faculty of Architecture, Delft University of Technology.

CHAPTER 4

From brief to design

4.1 Introduction

A programme of requirements or brief may be expected to embody the most important requirements and desires of the client as they relate to intended user quality. As the previous chapter made clear, the traditional distinction between the programme phase and the design phase should not be taken too literally. In practice the programme continues to develop even in the design phase, partly under the influence of questions and ideas that come up during the design. Sometimes the programme of requirements hardly exists, or is at most very brief, so that it has to be developed (often by implication) during the design process. In such cases alternative routes need to be found to guarantee that the design will produce optimal user quality. Whether or not the designer starts the design phase with a properly developed programme, he still has personal responsibility for user quality. After all, the design largely determines the extent to which the building will provide the proper level of support for the activities to be accommodated. This chapter looks at the question of how to decide on a design and how and by whom it can be ensured that the design will yield a building that is as usable as it can be. Two types of research and discussion relating to this kind of question can be found in the professional literature:

- *Descriptive*, attempting to answer the question of how design processes work. Empirical research and analysis of logical structures are used in an attempt to understand the structure of the design process and design methods used in practice.

■ *Prescriptive*, attempting to answer the question of how to go about the design process so that it will work effectively and efficiently and achieve the best possible result.

The first approach starts from the facts and describes what the reality *is*. The second approach is normative and deals with what the reality *should* be. Both approaches give an insight into the way in which designers work and the problems they face. This chapter describes, with the help of references to the specialist literature, how the design process works, the different phases that can be distinguished within the process, what design methods can be used and the effect they have on the user quality of buildings. But the first thing to be discussed before getting down to design methodology and design methods is design itself.

4.2 What is design?

Webster's Dictionary defines design as 'the arrangement of elements that make up a work of art, a machine, or other man-made object'. *The Dutch Van Dale Dictionary* defines design as: 'devising and incorporating in a sketch, drawing a sketch of something', where 'sketch' is a synonym for 'plan' or 'design'. A design is defined as a description of the main features of something. A design is a plan – something that is devised rather than executed. A plan is a design that indicates how something should be arranged and executed. None of this gets us very far. Reference to the specialist literature is more successful. For example, Foqué's book *Ontwerpsystemen* [Design systems] (1975) gives an extensive list of definitions. Different definitions and descriptions can also be found elsewhere. The multiplicity of definitions shows that opinions differ about the essential nature of designing. To illustrate, this point Box 4.1 contains a number of definitions dating from different periods and derived from different disciplines.

The definitions of Mick Eekhout, professor in building technology at the Faculty of Architecture in Delft, present two significantly different views of design, one conceptual, the other integrated. According to the conceptual view, design is no more than preparing a draft design. Everything else is development, working out the detail. The integrated view is that design embraces the whole process, from initiation to production, from the first sketch to the definitive working drawings. Over the years the role played by the designer in the building process has undergone radical change. Today the traditional role of the designer as the client's chief representative – the master

Box 4.1. Definitions of design

The use of scientific principles, technical information and imagination in the definition of a structure, machine or system to perform prospected functions with the maximum economy and efficiency.

Fielden et al. (1963)

The formulation of a prescription or model for a finished work in advance of its embodiment, with the intention of embodiment as hardware, including the presence of a creative step.

Archer (1965)

The translation of information in the form of requirements, constraints and experience into potential solutions, which are considered by the designer to meet required performance characteristics.

Luckman (1967)

Designing is devising and setting down geometry, materials and manufacturing techniques for a new product. This is more than just drawing. It is a goal-oriented mental process in which problems are analysed, goals set and reset, proposed solutions developed and the properties of solutions assessed.

Roozenburg and Eekels (1991)

The translation of the analytical and still abstract data in the programme of requirements into a synthesis that is the building plan.

(Association of Dutch Architects)

An efficient process for taking decisions on an original, ingenious, practical, physical and spatial solution to a spatial problem, from initiation to execution.

Eekhout (1996)

The conceiving of an original, technical, physical and spatial solution to a new spatial problem.

Eekhout (1996)

builder, guiding and directing the entire process – is often taken over by a building manager, someone who generally has few artistic pretensions and is mainly concerned with ensuring that the building is completed on time and within budget (Eekhout, 1998). It also often happens that part of the designer's task is taken over by others. In some building processes the role of the architect is reduced to that of aesthetic designer, so significantly reducing the original significance of architectonic design.

Despite all this diversity, it will be noted that a number of elements recur with some regularity:

- the search for a *creative solution* to a *spatial problem*,
- that satisfies *requirements set in advance* (e.g. usability and technical feasibility),
- based on an analysis and an attempt to translate *information*.

The Working Party on Assessment Criteria for Design Disciplines and the Advisory Board for Technological Policy at the Delft University of Technology also listed criteria for determining whether a design is *scientifically* sound:

- Originality (the design must contain a demonstrable element of novelty).
- Utility (an effective solution to a concrete problem).
- Efficiency (ability to fulfil its function over an extended period of time, i.e. a long useful life).
- The usual criteria applicable to any scientific exercise: reliability, verifiability and a methodical approach (in this case to design), with an adequate level of objective validity or substantiated subjective validity.
- Applicability (capable of being executed and applied in other situations or contexts).

4.3 Design methodology

The 1960s and 1970s saw a boom in dissertations about design methodology, i.e. the theory or science of methods used in the design process that considered both how the design process works and the methods used in that process (see Sections 4.4 and 4.5). The characteristics of a methodical approach are that the various steps are formulated explicitly and are capable of being communicated, controlled and verified. This increasing interest in design methodology came about partly because of the increasing complexity of the design process (the size and novelty of the tasks, the range of available materials and techniques) and partly because of the need to make design more scientific (more systematic, less a matter of trial and error). It was hoped that the application of the computer would allow complex design tasks to be dealt with more effectively. Work on devising a clearly defined conceptual framework for the design process has been going on for more than 20 years. The start of the period was marked by the first British conference on design methods, held in London in 1962 (Jones and Thornley, 1963), and the end by the conference on design policy, also in London, in 1982 (Langdon et al., 1984). After this the debate on design methodology took something of a back seat. For years now, only limited attention has been paid to the subject in training and research carried out by Delft's Faculty of Architecture. Despite the many architectonic studies on ideas about architecture, design strategies and typology as a design method, there is no current handbook for design methodology. In recent years, however, interest in design methodology and design methods seems to have been on the increase. In 1998 the Faculty of Architecture organised a fresh conference on design methods. In the same period the project *De Architectonische Interventie* [The Architectonic Intervention] was set up to consider methods and techniques for design studies and study by design. The results of this 2-year project were presented at the international conference 'Research by Design' in Delft (Langenhuizen et al., 2001) and later on in a book on *Ways to study and research architectural, urban and technical design* (De Jong and Van der Voordt, 2002). According to Rosemann (2001) a spatial plan is no longer just a plan, but also a tool to explore the potential of the site and a means of communication and negotiation between the parties involved. Design is increasingly becoming a collective process undertaken by collaborating specialists, in which tasks are divided between design and construction and between architect, constructor, developer and other participants.

Interest in design methodology is also on the increase in other countries; witness the great interest in the reissue of the work of Donald Schön (1991) and Brian Lawson (1997). If we confine ourselves to the main points, it appears that four different generations of design methodology can be distinguished over the last 40 years.

The beginning of the 1960s

At the beginning of the period the emphasis was on design as a goal-oriented, problem-solving activity. Design methodologies attempted to find a systematic and efficient approach to design tasks. There was much confidence in the possibilities offered by the computer, and enthusiastic use was made of insights gained from problem-solving techniques, such as systems analysis and operational research, developed in the 1940s and 1950s. Important representatives of the period include Jones (1963), Alexander (1963, 1964) and Luckman (1967). Design tasks were broken down into the finest detail to produce small sub-problems. First these sub-problems were solved separately, then an attempt was made to synthesise the individual solutions into an integrated whole.

The second half of the 1960s to the mid 1970s

The second period was characterised by growing criticism of the failures of the technological approach. Attention was transferred to the solution of social problems. It was a time of participation by residents in the creation and management of the built environment. There was increasing interest in experimental types of housing and forms of communal housing (Cooper, 1971; Meyer-Ehlers, 1972). Herman Herzberger built his 'Diagoon' houses in Delft. The Belgian architect Lucien Kroll became known for his La Mémé in Leuven, a project realised with much input from residents. Further development took place in new disciplines such as environmental psychology and the sociology of building and housing. Well-known names in the field of scientific research include De Jonge (1960), Priemus (1969) and Burie (1972, 1978) in the Netherlands, and Sommer (1969), Proshansky et al. (1970), Altman (1975) and Canter and Craik (1981) outside the Netherlands.

Mid 1970s to 1980s

During this period it seemed likely that the 'design methods movement' would come to an untimely end. There was much criticism of a one-sided emphasis on rational thought. A pioneer like Christopher Alexander, whose *pattern language* (1977) is still much used to this day, fiercely resisted the labelling of every idea as a methodology (Alexander, 1971). Various authors pointed out that the design process does indeed correspond to some extent with the cycle analysis–synthesis–evaluation, but that every design process is unique and so cannot be described in a standard way. But the debate on design methodology never stopped completely. Broadbent (1978) referred to the coming of a third generation. In contrast to the quantitatively analytical approach of the 1960s and the attention to user participation in the 1970s, this third generation was mainly concerned with a search for solutions which would leave scope for the user to arrange the details of the interior to suit himself, and so necessitated further development of methods used by the first and second generations. Van Duin and Engel (1991) distinguished two types of design strategies current during this period, both of which can be seen as a reaction to the modernistic pretensions of earlier generations: the rationalistic approach and the postmodern approach. The central feature of the rationalistic view is the autonomy of architecture and the designer. Apart from its role as a support for function, form has an independent role in the design process. Van Duin took as example Carel Weeber's design for a prison in Rotterdam. The postmodern approach was interpreted by Van Duin as a protest as much against the social ambitions of modernism as against rationalistic no-nonsense architecture.

Box 4.2   Pattern language

In 1977, on the wave of a search for design methods, Christopher Alexander et al. published a new tool for building and planning: *A pattern language*. It is strongly connected to an earlier volume – *The timeless way of building* – that provides the theory and instructions for the use of the language. A pattern language includes 253 patterns ordered in three themes: towns, buildings and construction. Patterns are guiding principles in order to support designing with user needs in mind, based on facts. Each pattern refers to a number of other patterns, and is referred to by other patterns, to create coherence and consistency. As such, patterns form a pattern language. Each pattern has the same format, including a picture that shows an archetypical example, a brief (problem) statement, an exploration of the body of the problem, and a description of the core of the solution, without limiting the freedom of the architect to make his own choices. An example is pattern 183, Workspace enclosure. It states that 'People cannot work effectively if their workspace is too enclosed or too exposed. A good workspace strikes the balance'. This statement is elaborated in 13 variables which might influence a person's sense of enclosure, such as presence or absence of a wall immediately behind you or beside you, the amount of space in front of you, view to the outside, and so on. Then 13 hypotheses are formulated, e.g. 'You feel more comfortable in a workspace if there is a wall behind you', 'There should be no blank wall closer than 8 feet in front of you', or 'Workspaces where you spend most of the day should be at least 60 square feet in area'.

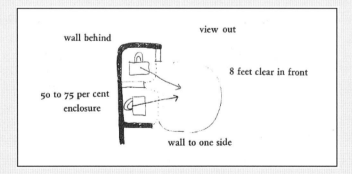

Figure 4.1   Pattern 183: workplace enclosure.

(*Continued*)

The theory behind a pattern language is clearly a product of the 1970s. Much attention is paid to the need for social contact and close relationships with nature. It shows a preference for traditional and labour-consuming building methods and traditional building materials. The empirical background of the patterns is often not completely clear. As a consequence, a lot of statements seem quite subjective. Nevertheless, the systematic approach with a standard format, the straight linear sequence and, at the same time, the structure of a network of patterns linked to other patterns is still very helpful in briefing and design processes.

The 1990s to the present day

In recent years there has been a noticeable increase in the attention paid to information processing systems and design decision support systems (Bax, 1995). According to Foqué (1982), design involves working with messages containing extremely complex information, so it is important to know how accurately, meaningfully and effectively information is conveyed and processed. Foqué believed that the traditional conflict between methodologies that he termed 'artistic' and 'scientific' could be resolved by the use of design and design-directed methods which combined both ways of working. The design process can certainly involve hypotheses and the testing of hypotheses, but expressed in terms not of cause and effect (causal connections) but rather of change and chaos. Foqué based this idea on Prigogine's chaos theory (1984). Research by Hamel (1990) into the way that designers think and work suggested that in practice design does in fact almost always involve a combination of intuition and an analytical and systematic approach. In the words of Eekhout (1996a): 'Design is an iterative process requiring brains to do the thinking and hands to do the visualising, both sides being stimulated by a mind to do the dreaming'.

An essential design tool nowadays is computer-aided design (CAD). The former head of the MIT Media Lab, Professor Nicholas Negroponte, wrote already about the possibilities of CAD in 1969 in his book *The architecture machine*. In this book he discussed the idea of a partnership and dialogue between the designer (architect) and an intelligent computer – an 'architecture machine' (Cotton and Oliver, 1994). A couple of years earlier, Marshall McLuhan had published his *Understanding media* (1964), stating that the computer would produce changes in the proportion, rhythm or schemes of human relations, and changes in the way we think, in which we articulate language, in which we live. The computer allows new experiences in the field of virtualisation. Architecture may become the spatialisation and concretisation for the development of thought (Puglisi, 1999). For a number of years now there has been increasing use of a new type of design, influenced by the use of computers and involving a search for abnormal, non-rectangular building geometries. This development has been stimulated by Frank Gehry's Guggenheim Museum. Dutch exponents of 'blob' architecture include Oosterhuis, Van Egeraat and Spuybroek (see also Chapter 2). Interesting in this context is the PhD thesis of Vollers (2001) on twisted facades. Its central feature was his computer-assisted search for spatially interesting facade shapes, the mathematical principles underlying them and the technical feasibility of curved outer surfaces.

An important point to note here is that design is less and less the individual activity of a single designer and more and more a process involving many individuals (Heintz, 1999). The complexity of the building task has meant that designs are influenced not only by architects but also by building techni- cians, contractors, future residents, etc. Van Loon, in his 1998 thesis, speaks of inter-organisational design, requiring an open, transparent design process and specific methods to take account of different aims and priorities and to achieve the best possible solution. One approach to limiting the range of possible solution is to express all the preconditions set by the different stakeholders as linear equations (Figure 4.2). Mathematical algorithms can then be used to give an idea of the range of solutions within which design variants would still be

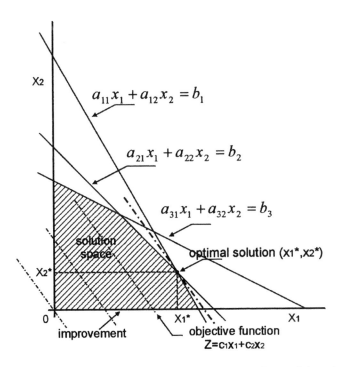

Figure 4.2 Defining the range of possible solutions by determining the precondi- tions and requirements specified by the different parties involved. Source: Van Gunsteren and Van Loon (2000).

able to satisfy each individual's minimum requirements (Van Gunsteren and Van Loon, 2000). If different opinions and levels of authority are also taken into account, it should be possible to discover the 'best' solution. What is 'best' is defined here according to the criterion of Pareto. A design is at optimum when it can no longer be improved to the benefit of one or more of those involved without diminishing the benefits enjoyed by one or more of the others that they would enjoy if one of the earlier versions of the plan were implemented.

4.4 Design processes

One of the best-known design methodologies from the early period is that of J.C. Jones. In 1963 he published the article *A method of systematic design.* He was also the author of a manual on design methods (1970), frequently reprinted (Jones, 1982). According to Jones, the design process starts with divergence (the production of a programme of requirements), moves on to transformation (structuring the problem, conceiving partial solutions, transformation) and then to convergence (combination of partial solutions, evaluation of different designs). Jones recognised the three main phases in this process:

- *Analysis:* describing the problem in its entirety and breaking it down into individual components, identifying each requirement the design has to satisfy and arranging the results to form a consistent set of performance requirements.
- *Synthesis:* developing solutions for parts of the problem and ways of satisfying special performance requirements and achieving the best possible integration of partial solutions into a complete design.
- *Evaluation:* determining the extent to which total or partial solutions satisfy the requirements set in advance.

This three-stage process, analysis–synthesis–evaluation, is frequently encountered in works in the Anglo-Saxon tradition (e.g. Archer, 1965; Luckman, 1967; Broadbent and Ward, 1969; Cross, 1984; Lawson, 1997) and in works by Dutch authors (e.g. Boekholt, 1984, 1987; Roozenburg and Eekels, 1991; De Ridder, 1998), although often in a slightly amended form.

Roozenburg and Eekels (1991), for example, add two more steps: 'simulation', as an extra step between synthesis and evaluation, and 'decision' following evaluation. By 'simulation' they mean applying reasoning or tests on models to reach a judgement about the behaviour and properties of the product under design before actual production commences.

Designing as a cyclic iterative process

According to Archer (1965) the division into the phases analysis, synthesis and evaluation not only applies to the design process as a whole but also can serve as a model for each phase of the process. After subjecting the design process to detailed analysis, Archer distinguished no less than 229 different activities, which he classified into the analytical phase (data collection, programme of requirements), the creative phase (analysis, synthesis, development of solutions) and the execution phase, with much communication and feedback. Hamel (1990) also stated that analysis, synthesis and evaluation take place not so much sequentially as rather in parallel, interactively. The central questions raised in his PhD thesis on how designers think were what components make up architectonic design and how these components are organised in the design process. He constructed a descriptive model based on a study of the literature and then tested it by asking 15 experienced architects to think aloud during the process of designing a youth club. His research led him to conclude that the design process often involves going through a cycle consisting of the following main steps:

- *Analysis:* analysing the task, collecting additional information and splitting the task into sub-problems (decomposition) on the basis of various dimensions such as user function, aesthetics, construction and urban design.
- *Synthesis*: solving sub-problems and then solving the total design problem by synthesising the solutions to the sub-problems. The aim of the synthesis is to integrate the solutions to the sub-problems for each dimension individually and then to integrate these solutions to provide a single overall solution.
- *Design*: giving shape to the solution so that the design is 'architecture', i.e. aesthetically justified, exciting and elegant (while remaining economical with resources).

Each of these steps involves three stages, orientation, execution and evaluation. The results of each step are evaluated on the basis of criteria specific to the task. The task of the designer consists to a large extent of transforming (from text to drawings, from activities to floor space requirements), switching (from draft to detail and back, from one sub-problem or dimension to other sub-problems or dimensions) and providing feedback (from solutions to aims).

Analogy with problem-solving

Roozenburg and Eekels (1991) pointed out that the basic design cycle has a good deal in common with the accepted problem-solving cycle used for dealing with complex problems of technical and socio-economic development. Following Hall (1968), they distinguished five phases: (1) defining the problem; (2) formulating goals; (3) devising solutions; (4) selecting the best solution; and (5) executing the plans. Boekholt (1987) used a similar division, but limited himself to four phases which merge gradually into one another (Figures 4.3 and 4.4):

1. Developing a statement of problem and goals.

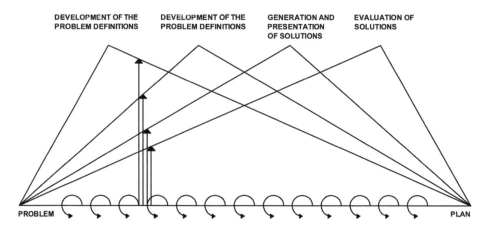

Figure 4.3 From problem statement to design in four phases. Source: Boekholt, 1987.

2. Formulating basic physical and spatial principles.
3. Generating significantly different and original variants.
4. Assessing and selecting variants with the help of explicitly formulated criteria.

Steps 3 and 4 bear some relationship to the well-known TOTE model (Test–Operate–Test–Exit) used in systems analysis. Information obtained by the senses is examined for congruence between the existing situation and the desired situation, using predetermined criteria (Test). If there is any lack of congruence, an attempt is made to use physical or psychological methods to restore it (Operate). In principle this attempt continues until congruence is achieved, at which point design is stopped. According to Boekholt, the sequence is not fixed. The process may often run from the formulation of goals to the generation and evaluation of solutions, sometimes prematurely. But it can equally well happen that a solution generates new goals, or that an evaluation prompts fresh analysis before devising new solutions, total or partial.

Design conjectures and primary generators

In spite of the similarities between the basic design cycle and the widely used problem-solving cycle, there are dissimilarities, too. In the early 1970s, Bryan Lawson examined the problem-solving process in two different groups: students of architecture and students of science (Lawson, 1980, cited in Downing, 1994). An experimental design-like problem was used to test whether differences existed. The problem-solving process that worked for students in science was found to be ineffective for design students. The results indicated that the science students used a problem-focused process while design students favoured a

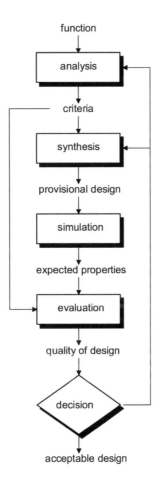

function

→ analysis

criteria

synthesis

provisional design

simulation

expected properties

evaluation

quality of design

decision

acceptable design

Figure 4.4 Basic design cycle. Source: Roozenburg and Eekels, 1991.

solution-focused process. Problem-focusing was time-consuming in that it involved learning as much as possible about the structure of the problem before attempting a solution. Solution-focusing involved the immediate identification of a solution based upon some match made in the designer's mind between the problem statement and an exemplar stored in his or her own experience. Evaluation of the solution was accomplished by the examination of the exemplar against the background of programmatic criteria and other forces that had an impact on the design problem. In this context, Hillier et al. (1972) developed a conjecture–analysis model that accounts for a designer's tendency to use subjective knowledge, with a more objective accountability for behaviour research, programme information and evaluation. In this model 'conjecture' is an 'if' statement that is based on knowledge of problem/solution relationships. Analysis is the 'then' response, referring to the manipulation and adjustment of principles found in the conjectured solution to test for fit to the design problem. In the conjecture–analysis model, design becomes a series of if–then speculations (Schön, 1983). Conjectures are a form of stating hypotheses with a more tentative and action-oriented nature than most scientific hypotheses. Memory of prototypes and precedents can be very useful in this process (Downing, 1994). According to Jane Darke (1978), architects' value systems play an important role in initial design decisions. In her research concerning public housing designs, she noticed that architects had not only used conjectures of a solution-oriented nature in formulating their responses to design projects but also that they relied on a hidden agenda she called the primary generator. This is a set of values held by the designer or client that generates the initial conjectures concerning what a future place might be like. In Darke's research, the generator was the high value placed on the site. In addition to her research outcomes, Darke adapted the conjecture–analysis model into a generator–conjecture–analysis model.

Foqué's three stages

Another interesting way of dividing the process into different elements was proposed by Foqué (1975). He distinguished a structuring stage, a creative stage and an informational stage. The *structuring* stage is the preparatory phase of problem analysis, using both descriptive and prescriptive models. The thought process here mainly involves reconciling objectively observed facts with subjective value judgements. The stage also involves synthesis, in which the designer acts on the structure as analysed by replacing or regrouping individual elements, so radically changing the way they cohere. The *creative* stage is the stage in which people come up with new ideas that can potentially lead to new solutions. Research into creative processes shows that these processes involve interplay between subconscious intuition and rational, conscious thought and action. The *informational* stage is the phase in which abstract knowledge, not yet materialised, is coded and converted into messages and signals. Information from the real world is transformed into a mental model that is then converted into a formal model. Three questions are important to this processing of information:

- *Syntax*: how accurately can the signs be transmitted to convey design information within an information processing system?
- *Semantics*: how accurately do the signs transmitted interpret the meaning intended and desired by the sender?
- *Praxis*: how effectively do the signs influence the receiver of the information?

These three stages merge gradually into one another and alternate constantly with one another. The process is not linear, with a fixed sequence of steps, but cyclic, with continuous feedback.

From function to form or vice versa?

Roozenburg and Eekels (1991) saw design as a thought process in which the same cycle of activities is repeated over and over again: observation, supposition, expectation, checking and evaluation. They referred back to the empirical cycle proposed by De Groot (1969), who distinguished between observation, induction, deduction, testing and evaluation, and believed that in essence the design process reasons from function to form. Design is a means (M) to achieve an end (E), which is to provide the function envisaged. The end is what matters. Determining the spatial and architectural means best capable of achieving that end is the next step. Expressed as a formula, $M = f(E)$.

De Jong (1993) took the opposite approach, arguing that design should be based on research; designers should look for possible solutions that would then be examined to establish their desirability. In urban design, for example, designers should devise and record new forms capable of serving social goals. Various means would be suggested and then examined one by one to see what they could achieve. Comparison with goals is therefore just as relevant here, but by definition the goals are not formulated in advance and are less stringent. It might be said that the goals are derived from the means: expressed as a formula, $E = f(M)$. Goal-directed design starts from a programme of requirements: means-directed design starts from an inventory of the features available and the way they interconnect (topography, the nature of the location and its morphological typology). The next step is to establish the functions for which the location is suitable. Form by itself gives no indication of probable function, only of possible function, e.g. natural or recreational. What De Jong was trying to do was to find a set of tools to generate hypotheses and design new possibilities, to add to the range of tools used in the empirical sciences, which are primarily concerned with determining probabilities.

One process with many faces?

One might well ask whether there are really only two choices possible – design from end to means or from means to end. From the extensive literature on design methodology one could conclude that designers are constantly switching between general and detail, problem and solution, function and form and aims and means. As a consequence, any suggestion of tribal conflict is unnecessary, being based on an incorrect understanding of one another's methods. In essence the difference between the two approaches is one of degree rather than kind. Even the more analytical, goal-directed designers are happy to work from a provisional general solution. It is true that the means-directed approach may skip the first analytical phase, but the provisional design solution will be subject to cyclic feedback between analyses and evaluations to achieve an increasingly suitable result.

It should also be realised that despite the differences in opinion amongst theorists and architects about the 'correct' sequence for analysis, synthesis and evaluation, these three steps can be found in every design process. Design always involves analysis, synthesis and evaluation, in the creative stage or in the structuring stage, when generating solutions or evaluating solutions. In the words of Donald Schön (1991) 'Designers are reflective practitioners': Thinking and acting, generating ideas and making choices, constantly alternate with one another.

4.5   Design methods

A method is a fixed, properly thought out way of acting to achieve a particular goal. Eekhout (1998) speaks of a specific, rational, general, observable method of working, in this case in the process of design. The word 'methodology' is also used instead of 'method', although a methodology is in fact a collection of methods and techniques. The word 'strategy' is also used, it is defined by Roozenburg and Eekels (1991) as a broad outline of the way in which people aim to achieve a particular goal, without laying down the method of working in any detail. Goals and strategy combine to form part of policy. According to Foqué, design methods contribute to increasing the capacity of the designer to structure, think creatively and process information. Foqué believed that design methods should have the effect of deepening one's understanding (process analysis and problem analysis), stimulating participation (information and communication) and have a definite effect on the design environment (design and building).

As Eekhout saw it, intuitive working is not methodical. After all, 'intuitive' implies uncontrollable and inexplicable, and therefore dependent on good luck. It therefore fails to satisfy the elementary requirement for a methodical approach, that the various steps must be formulated explicitly. Besides the intuitive approach and the methodical approach, Eekhout also distinguished the routine approach, an approach lying somewhere between the two extremes. On the other hand, many authors have treated the intuitive approach as a fully accept-able method, part of the total package of methods available to the designer. From this it follows that design methods may be divided roughly into analytical and creative.

4.5.1   Analytical methods

Analytical design methods are primarily concerned with analysis and systematic definition of the problem. As already stated, the early 1960s saw the beginning of a strong movement in favour of a more analytical and systematic approach to design. Features common to the methods of the time were a broad detailed exploration and analysis of the problem, division of the task into sub-tasks, charting relevant factors and their possible interrelationships, and the synthesis of partial solutions into a whole. Almost all these methods combined systematic logical analysis with intuition and creativity.

The three-step method

In *A method of systematic design*, based on the three phases analysis, synthesis and evaluation, Jones (1963) presented a method involving the following steps:

1. With the help of consultants and others involved, draw up a list of factors that might possibly be relevant, initially without limitation of any sort. Make a separate list of requirements with which the design must satisfy, and a list of suggestions and ideas for solutions. Look for sources of information. Classify the factors, check priorities, analyse interrelationships and develop the most complete sets possible of mutually consistent performance specifications. Ensure sufficient support.
2. Look for as many total or partial solutions as possible to all performance specifications. Take into account any preconditions or restrictions. Combine partial solutions into a total design that satisfies as many of the requirements as possible.
3. Before choosing the final design solution, judge each solution variant on the extent to which it satisfies the requirements, making use of earlier experiences with comparable solutions, simulations, logical forecasts of what is likely to happen to the design product during its lifetime and the testing of prototypes.

Hierarchical decomposition

In the same period Christopher Alexander presented his 'hierarchical decomposition' method, based on a design for a village in India (Alexander, 1963). The method is described at length in his book *Notes on the synthesis of form* (1964). Briefly, the method involves dissecting the design task into as many components as possible. First a list is prepared of all possible requirements to be satisfied by the design. These requirements are then analysed in sets of two at a time to determine mutual dependencies. A dependency is defined here as the extent to which the satisfaction of one requirement makes it easier or harder to satisfy another requirement. Once these dependencies have been determined, a computer and graph theory are used to formulate subsets of independent requirements. The task of the designer is to develop draft solutions satisfying these subsets and then to produce a total design based on the partial solutions.

Function analysis

Function analysis is the analysis, development and description of a functional structure. A functional structure is an abstract model of the product to be designed, ignoring physical characteristics such as dimensions, shape, colour and material usage. In a function analysis the product is viewed primarily as a technical and physical system. The first step in such an analysis is to describe the product's primary function. The second step is to develop a simple functional structure, including the most important technical processes, as a consistent set of sub-functions. The third step involves devising variants on the functional structure, e.g. by separating or combining sub-functions or changing their order. This method is in frequent use, particularly in mechanical engineering applications. In architecture, people more often speak of functional analysis. The methodical approach starts with a thorough analysis of activities and relationships between activities. The Delft lecturers De Bruijn and Korfker (1969) and Polak (1981) were important founders of this approach, later adopted by Van Duin et al. (1989). For further details the reader is referred to Chapter 3 on programming and programmes of requirements.

Analysis of interconnected decision areas (AIDA)

This method, developed by Luckman (1967), starts by identifying 'decision areas', factors about which decisions must be made during the design process. In an architectural design problem these factors might include the height of the building, the direction of the span and the selection of building components, e.g. windows, doors and door handles. Next, a chart is prepared showing the range within which partial solutions to sub-problems could be varied while still satisfying the requirements laid down (the extent to which it is possible to choose between different solutions) and the extent to which decisions relating to individual parts of the picture are mutually consistent. Finally, decision areas, options and relationships between options are represented in an 'option diagram', making it possible to make decisions in parallel rather than sequentially and giving a general overview of possible solutions, partial and total. This method has some affinity with the *morphological method*, a method which is mainly concerned with generating solutions. Here the first step is to search for all theoretically conceivable solutions to the problem. The next step is to determine which elements are 'significant' to the solutions found. Finally, an inventory is prepared of the ways it is theoretically possible to realise each element. This kind of analytical method often makes use of *decision trees*, a method of structuring a number of possibilities by determining what choices are possible at each level.

4.5.2 Creative methods

Examples of creative methods include 'associative methods' and 'creative confrontation methods' (Roozenburg and Eekels, 1991). *Associative methods* involve the encouragement of spontaneous reactions to or associations with particular statements or ideas. The thought process used is one in which connections are made between individual ideas, sometimes obvious (snow → white), sometimes surprisingly innovative. The assumption is that the number of creative ideas increases with the total number of associations produced. Brainstorming is one of the best known of such methods. *Creative confrontation methods*, like associative methods, are characterised by the linking of ideas which were originally unrelated, but in this case connections are 'forced' by regulation. This method is capable of revealing totally new and unexpected combinations of viewpoints, which bring the participants nearer to solving the problem. One example of this method is *synectics*, developed by Gordon and Prince as long ago as 1955. Synectics uses thinking based on analogies and metaphors. Sometimes an attempt is made to find a problem analogous to the original problem but coming from a different situation or field of application, e.g. the legs of a grasshopper as a model for an aircraft landing system. Another

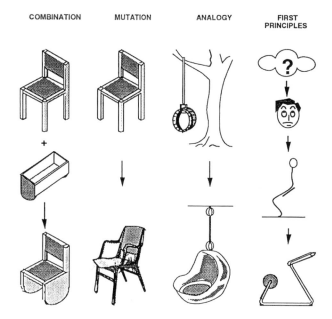

Figure 4.5 Examples of free association. Source: Rosenmann and Gero, 1993. New ideas about how to design a chair can be developed by combining or changing existing forms, making use of analogies and applying ergonomic principles.

application is the fantasy analogy, in which an attempt is made to devise the ideal solution to a problem as a child might dream it up. Rosenman and Gero (1993) give four related and to some extent overlapping design methods which provide scope for creative design (Figure 4.5):

- Combination: combining existing concepts into an entirely new configuration.
- Mutation: changing the form of all or part of an existing design.
- Analogy: applying analogous forms.
- Determining the most significant features of the desired product ('first principles').

An example of the use of analogies in architecture is the design process followed by Le Corbusier for l'Unité d'Habitation. In a reconstruction, Tzonis (1993) showed how Le Corbusier developed the spatial concept for this building,

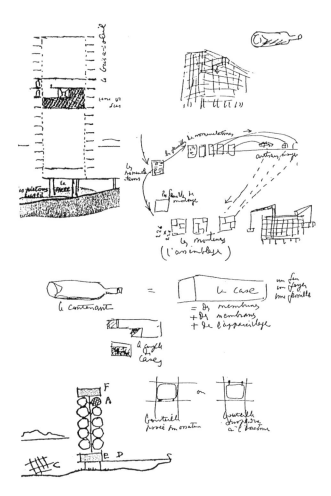

Figure 4.6 A hut, a seagoing vessel and a bottle rack as sources of inspiration for a designer.

and what precedents played a role in the development (Figure 4.6). Le Corbusier searched his memory for artefacts, constantly bearing in mind three criteria to be applied to the final solution: it must not disturb the natural continuity of the countryside; it must be responsive to the requirement for public spaces with a view; and it must involve a load-bearing structure with modular units capable of accommodating individual apartments. The combination and amalgamation of elements from precedents with identical or similar requirements led to his achievement of an entirely new composition. The three main precedents used by Le Corbusier were the hut, which satisfied the requirement for natural continuity; the seagoing vessel, with its decks and view; and the bottle rack, evoking associations with a modular load-bearing structure.

4.5.3   Typology as a design method

Typology is the study of types, i.e. their classification and description, and the study of a type, i.e. its investigation and interpretation. A type is an abstract schematic representation of a series of persons or objects (in this case buildings) with similar characteristics, a concise method of representing reality by including only its essential characteristics. It is a conceptual construct that distinguishes similar from dissimilar. Types may refer to particular, concrete buildings or places, but also to abstract images of places and ideas about places. Whereas an architectural precedent is a building or part of a building that exists or has existed physically, a type can be studied without reference to actually existing physical objects. The characteristics which determine the type of a building can include its function, i.e. what people do in the building or what it is for (houses, shops, schools, hospitals, etc.); its form, i.e. what buildings look like (e.g. high rise or low rise, postmodern or neo-classic a cottage or a single family row house); or its technology and materials used (e.g. a steel frame versus load-bearing concrete walls, brick or high tech). Formal typology is concerned with questions such as what basic forms can be recognised, or which formal characteristics have remained constant over a significant period. Functional typology represents the functions of a building and analyses these functions without making aesthetic judgements. Naming is a way of classification, too. A canteen, a restaurant, a mess, a pub, and a cafeteria are all eating places, but the names represent places with very different connotations.

Typology and design

Typology structures our environments by classifying an almost infinite variety of functions and forms into a limited number of categories, classes or types. Types and acts of typing organise thinking, understanding, communicating and acting in all domains of life. Typology and typological analyses on a material, imaginary or conceptual level are important means in description, explanation and prescription

(Franck and Schneekloth, 1994). Types summarise and hold together a whole range of already interpreted information about the detailed implications of possible actions. As such, types can be interpreted as a corpus of shared knowledge. Typology can help to uncover general lessons and principles. Types offer a 'shortcut' that can be economically sensible for producing a form, educationally satisfactory for explaining ideas to clients, and personally reassuring to professionals if they fear the risk associated with innovation (Symes, 1994, referring to Schön, 1988). Existing types that fit with design requirements can become a model for the programming of other projects and can provide a starting point with general validity even while they are being adapted to site conditions, budgets and local patterns of needs. Economy of effort and a sense that the acceptance of the built result can be predicted are obvious benefits. But typologies can also become outdated and redundant, with a risk of being a prison instead of a promise. Changes in society's expectations and views, another political or socio-economic context, new technologies, new opportunities or constraints, etc., may have radical effects on our thinking about types. As a consequence, typological thinking can become a drag on problem-solving instead of a stimulus to it (Symes, 1994). For that reason, the idea of type should be treated as a point of departure or a temporary destination rather than as an end point (Robinson, 1994). It is through imagination rather than simple mental imagery that the designer should apply and test ideas (Downing, 1994).

In his study of the typology of residential blocks, van Leusen (1994) endorses the importance of typology in design training, research and practice. A typological system can make a valuable contribution to knowledge and understanding of architecture. It makes it easier to access the huge number of precedents from which the designer can choose when working on a particular commission. Van Leusen referred to the 19th century architecture theorist Quatremère de Quincy (1755–1849) who had the following to say about the term type:

> ... to understand the reasons, is to discover their origin and primitive cause. This is what must be called 'type' in architecture. The original reason of the thing is founded in the use that one makes of it and the natural habits for which one intends it. . . .

Like his contemporary Auguste Durand (1760–1834), De Quincy was one of the founders of the application of the typological approach to architectural design. The chief aim of Durand's typological research into historical buildings was to develop a method of design to be used in training and practice. To do this Durand prepared an extensive vocabulary of building components, with detailed descriptions and examples. According to Leupen (1997), Durand's typology can be seen as a catalogue of empty forms, which may well refer to a particular programme but are capable of accepting any type of content. In design practice forms can be copied quite literally, whereas a precedent is rarely copied exactly (Fang, 1993).

All the newly designed building has in common with its precedent is a particular combination of characteristics. This makes design a matter of assembling components. Here Leupen pointed out a significant difference between the thinking of Quatremère and Durand. Quatremère argued that a typology should only be viewed in the context of the relevant historical and cultural conditions, whereas Durand claimed that a typology can be applied without reference to the original context.

Criticism and resurrection

Not everyone subscribes to the value of typology in architectural design. In a design school like the Bauhaus, the dominant view is that design problems can be solved by rational means, with no need to fall back on tradition, precedents or preconceptions. Typology was also resisted as a design method by the modern movement, which believed that it too often led to the rigid application of design principles. After the movement away from modernism and disappointing experiences with user participation in the 1970s, a kind of vacuum developed, giving an opportunity for new ideas, and all kinds of different ideas began to appear. Besides historicism, postmodernism and deconstructivism, fresh attention began to be paid to the idea of typology. According to Colquhoun (1969) it is impossible – or nearly impossible – to solve complex design problems by analytical methods. Designers seeking solutions to contemporary problems will therefore often fall back on artefacts developed at some previous time. In a much quoted article on architectural typology, Argan (1963) points out that architectural design can not only be understood as an individual invention. Designers wanting to avoid having to go back to first principles are constantly on the look out for correspondence with something experienced earlier in the history of architecture. Architects refer to types in design to structure their memories and experiences, to negotiate with clients and to respond to changes in society. They use types to understand the built landscape and to generate new kinds of places. In the book *Ordering space* (1994), edited by Karen Franck and Lynda Schneekloth, 19 architects, landscape designers, historians, planners and an artist offer diverse views on the past, present and future uses of type. The authors illustrate how the language of building types may help to create and preserve social and spatial order. This more or less universal awareness has led to much typological research into architectural forms and the application of typology in design practice right up to the present day.

Function and form

The fact that there are two kinds of typology, functional and formal, means that typological research is often applied to design in two different ways:

- As an instrument for *functional* analysis and the generation of spatial and functional ideas, using graphical representations and schematic floor plans.

■ As an instrument for *morphological* analysis and the generation of forms, involving a designer drawing on a vast stock of precedents in the search for a formal typology.

The functional approach is illustrated in *Bauentwurfslehre,* the standard work by the German architect Ernst Neufert (translated into English as *Architect's data*). The examples and design details it presents have been stripped of their spatial and formal characteristics and reduced to functional organisation diagrams (Neufert et al., 2000). Representatives of the morphological movement were often directly opposed to the functionalistic approach, more or less ignoring functional typology as a basis for function or programme. They believed that the important question is how morphological research into typologies can be used in the understanding and processing of forms (Aymonino and Rossi, 1965). Aldo Rossi viewed formal architecture as architecture that lacks any reference to its possible use. A design will of course support a number of possibilities, but it is up to the user to mobilise services and functions (Rossi, 1982).

Use of precedents in education

An example of the use of research into precedents in education occurs in the second year CAD practical organised by the Faculty of Architecture of Delft University of Technology (Koutamanis, 1994). The task set is to design a school building from a programme of requirements and a few precedents from which trainee designers can find out how various principles, rules, types and norms have been implemented. Existing solutions that seem to be appropriate to all or part of the current task can encourage the inclusion of similar solutions in the design. Thus, the use of precedents as an aid to design means making use of elements and concepts found in precedents to help the designer find a solution to his own design task. In practice, students go about this in two different ways. Some use precedents, singly or in combination, as prototypes for the spatial organisation of their own designs, taking an existing spatial organisation and adjusting it to suit the new programme of requirements by adding, changing or removing spaces. Other students take components of precedents as prototypes for the solution of specific sub-problems in the new design. Neither of these approaches involves the indiscriminate adoption of elements derived from precedents. Some transformation is always required to adjust the old solution to fit the new task and to integrate existing solutions into a homogeneous design.

4.6 Quality control

It would seem plausible to assume that combining a systematic analytical approach to the design process with working from function to form will ensure the greatest likelihood of producing buildings with a high utility value, from which it follows that functional requirements will have a major influence on controlling the way the plan develops. Alternative solutions are explicitly checked against these requirements. But a single-minded concentration on functionality can easily lead to a building that is undoubtedly functional but otherwise very unexciting. Moreover, functions are highly subject to change, so that too close a correspondence between function and form will leave little scope for new developments (see also Chapter 2). The converse is true when a more intuitive approach is combined with designing from form to function, so that the designer first looks for beautiful, interesting and meaningful forms and only then checks whether they satisfy the functional requirements. There will be a greater chance of producing a building with architectonic merit and experientially attractive, but also a risk that the building will be functionally unsatisfactory. This risk can be substantially reduced by regularly checking the developing plan for user quality. In fact a combination of the two styles of approach, applying design methods which are both analytical and creative, turns out to be the best way of guaranteeing a result in which functional, aesthetic, technical and economic requirements are kept properly in balance.

Comparing one's own design process with findings in design methodology literature makes the process easier to discuss and more transparent, provides opportunities for better management practice and encourages further efforts to make the design process more scientific. As we have seen, design is not a linear process with a completely explicit final goal and methods that are defined unambiguously. It is much more often a cyclic, iterative search for the best possible design solution. And the process involves not merely the designer or designers but also countless other participants. There must be scope for thinking logically and analytically, for using analogies and associative thinking, reason and feeling, head and heart, commercial arguments and creative inventions. The final solution must satisfy a wide range of different, partly conflicting, demands and desires. Managing this process is by no means simple. The management of a creative process requires a readiness to deal flexibly with rules, to make mistakes, to listen to ideas which are not yet fully formed and to live with chaos, if only temporarily. It calls for a proper balance between the inputs from generalists and specialists and between art and expertise. This explains the constant search for new forms of management, partly under the influence of the changing roles of the parties involved. The rise of *architectural design management* (ADM) is particularly interesting in this context (see for instance the *Journal of Architectural Management Practice and Research*; Cooper, 1995; Augenbroe and Prins, 2000; Emmitt and Yeomans, 2001; Gray and Hughes, 1994, 2001; Tunstall, 2001; Van Doorn, 2004). ADM involves the full range of activities undertaken by the architect, firm of architects or project team to ensure that the design process goes well and to achieve the best possible design. This does not, by definition, mean the introduction of a new discipline. After an extensive study of the literature, interviews with architects and project managers and a number of case studies, Van Doorn (2004) argues that design management needs to be the collective responsibility of everyone involved. The firm of architects or project manager will often play the leading role. In practice, it will often happen that the architect concentrates mainly on the design and the architectural concept, leaving the control of the process to others. An interesting example is the design process for the Arnhem and Nijmegen Polytechnic. For this and various other projects use was made of the services of MVDRV architects and the Bureau Bouwkunde partnership. The design task was handled collectively. There was a single contract with the client. MVRDV was mainly concerned with the overall concept and working out the architectural details. Bureau Bouwkunde was mainly responsible for managing the design process, technical details and cost control. Arcadis handled the management of the project as a whole (Pos, 2000).

Design management requires the various parties involved to take measures at strategic, tactical and operational levels (Van Doorn, 2004). Guiding a successful design process requires:

- A properly balanced correspondence between the design task and the means available.
- Adjustment of the form of project organisation to suit the design task.
- Matching the choice of architect to the client's level of ambition, e.g. whether the client is looking primarily for original ideas and architecture that will attract attention or is more concerned with functionality and durability. Although these requirements are not mutually exclusive, individual firms of architects often present themselves rather more emphatically as specialised in one or the other.
- Proper consideration of the selection of consultants, on the basis not only of cost but also of professionalism, willingness to work in a team and communicative skills.
- Clear agreements on tasks and authority. A proper understanding of contracts with other parties, ensuring that their interpretation is unambiguous and making interim adjustments where necessary on the basis of newly gained insights are all important if the anticipated quality is to be achieved and the project is to be completed satisfactorily, on time and within budget.
- Clarity and openness about the various parties' demands, desires and interests. Joint workshops and round-table discussions, particularly in the start phase, can help potential conflicts to come to light faster and a better estimate to be made of the chance of reaching agreement. Too much conflict increases the risk of failure. Too little conflict means insufficient challenge to do one's utmost.
- Phased development of the programme of requirements. The programme must be timely and clear about performance requirements and visual expectations;

but must at the same time leave sufficient room for new ideas during the development from general to detail.

■ Continuous control to ensure that the flow of information is timely, accurate, complete and reliable, both as regards the sender and receiver of the information and the media by means of which the information is transmitted, e.g. drawings, documents and information in digital form.

■ Application of tools for the proper management of the process and considerations to be borne in mind when making choices.

Bibliography

Alexander, C. (1963), The determination of components for an indian village. In: J.C. Jones and D. Thornley (eds), *Conference on design methods*. Pergamon, Oxford.

Alexander, C. (1964), *Notes on the synthesis of form*. Harvard University Press, Cambridge, Mass.

Alexander, C. (1971), The state of the art in design methods. *DMG Newsletter* 5(3), 3–7.

Alexander, A., S. Ishikawa, M. Silverstein (1977), *A pattern language*. Oxford University Press, New York.

Altman, I. (1975), T*he environment and social behavior: privacy, personal space, territoriality and crowding*. Brooks-Cole, Monterey, California.

Archer, L.B. (1965), *Systematic method for designers*. The Design Council, London.

Argan, C.G. (1963), On the typology of architecture. *Architectural Design* 33(12), 564–565.

Augenbroe, G., M. Prins (eds) (2000), *Design management in the architectural and engineering office*. Proceedings of CIB W96 Commission on Architectural Management, Atlanta 2000. CIB, Rotterdam.

Aymonino, C., A. Rossi (1965), *La formazione del cencetto di tipologia edilizia*. Instituto universitario di arcitettura, Venice.

Bax, M.F.T. (1995), From ideology to methodology. In: R.M. Oxman, M.F.T. Bax and H.H. Achten (eds), *Design research in the Netherlands*. Eindhoven University of Technology, Eindhoven.

Boekholt, J.T. (1984), *Bouwkundig ontwerpen* [Architectural design]. PhD Thesis, Faculty of Architecture, Eindhoven University of Technology.

Boekholt, J.T. (1987), *Ontwerpmethodieken. 1. Methodisch ontwerpen* [Design methodologies. 1. Methodical design]. In: Vademecum voor Architecten [Architects' vademecum].

Boekholt, J.T. (2000), *Ontwerpend leren, leren ontwerpen* [Learning by design, learn to design]. Bouwstenen No. 57. Faculty of Architecture, Eindhoven University of Technology.

Broadbent, G. (1978), *Design in architecture*. John Wiley and Sons, Chichester.

Broadbent, G., A. Ward (eds) (1969), *Design methods in architecture*. Lund Humphries, London.

Bruijn, W.N. de, D. Korfker (1969), *Voorbereiding en methodiek bij het ontwerpen van bedrijfsgebouwen* [Preparation and methodology for the design of industrial buildings] . Vols I and II. Bouwwereld 29.8.69 and 12.09.69.

Burie, J.B. (1972), *Wonen en woongedrag. Verkenningen in de sociologie van bouwen en wonen* [Housing and lifestyle. Explorations in the sociology of building and housing]. Boom, Meppel.

Burie, J.B. (ed) (1978), *Handboek bouwen en wonen* [Manual of building and housing]. Van Loghum Slaterus, Deventer.

Canter, D., K.H. Craik (1981), Environmental psychology. *Journal of Environmental Psychology*, 1–11

Colquhoun, A. (1969), Typology and design method. In: C. Jencks and G. Baird (eds), *Meaning in architecture*. Barrie & Rockcliff: The Cresset Press, 267–277.

Cooper, D. (1971), *The death of the family*. Fletcher & Son, Norwich, UK.

Cooper, R. (1995), *The design agenda: a guide to successful design management*. Wiley, London.

Cotton, B., R. Oliver (1994), *The cyberspace lexicon; an illustrated dictionary of terms from multimedia to virtual reality*. Phaidon, London.

Cross, N. (ed.) (1984), *Developments in design methodology*. John Wiley and Sons, New York.

Cross, N. (1997), Descriptive models of creative design: application to an example. *Design Studies* 18, 427–455.

Darke, J. (1978), *The primary generator and the design process*. Proceedings EDRA 9, University of Arizona, Tucson.

Doorn, A. van (2004), *Ontwerp/proces. Ontwerpmanageent in theory en praktijk.* [Design/process. Architectural Design Management – Theory and Practice]. SUN, Nijmegen.

Downing, F. (1994), Memory and the making of places. In: K.A. Franck, L.H. Schneekloth (eds), *Ordering space. Types in architecture and design.* Van Nostrand Reinhold, New York.

Duin, L. van, J. Zeinstra (eds). (1989), *Functioneel ontwerpen. Ontwikkeling en toepassing van het doelmatigheidsbeginsel in de architectuur* [Functional design. Development and application of the efficiency principle in architecture]. Faculty of Architecture, Delft University of Technology.

Duin, L. van, H. Engel (1991), *Architectuurfragmenten: typologie, stijl en ontwerpmethoden* [Architectural fragments: typology, style and design methods]. Faculty of Architecture, Delft University of Technology.

Eekhout, M. (1996a), *Inleiding over ontwerpen, ontwikkelen en onderzoeken* [Introduction to design, development and research]. Course on design methodology, 15 October, 1996.

Eekhout, M. (1996b), *POPO, ProcesOrganisatie voor ProduktOntwikkeling* [Process organisation for product development]. Faculty of Architecture, Delft University of Technology.

Eekhout, M. (1998), *Ontwerpmethodologie* [Design methodology]. Faculty of Architecture, Delft University of Technology.

Emmitt, S., D.T. Yeomans (2001), *Specifying buildings: a design management perspective*. Butterworth-Heinemann, Boston.

Evans, B., J.A. Powell, R.J. Talbot (1982), *Changing design.* John Wiley and Sons, New York.

Fang, N. (1993), *Architectural precedent analysis.* Publications Office, Faculty of Architecture, Delft University of Technology.

Fielden, G.B.R. (ed) (1963), *Engineering design.* HMSO, London.

Foqué, R. (1975), *Ontwerpsystemen* [Design systems]. Het Spectrum, Utrecht/ Amsterdam.

Foqué, R. (1982), Beyond design methods. Arguments for a practical design theory. In: B. Evans, J.A. Powell, R. Talbot (eds), *Changing design.* John Wiley and Sons, New York.

Franck, K.A., L.H. Schneekloth (eds) (1994), *Ordering space. Types in architecture and design.* Van Nostrand Reinhold, New York.

Gray, C., W. Hughes (1994), *The successful management of design.* University of Reading, Whiteknights, CB VBD 194.

Gray, C., W. Hughes (2001), *Building design management.* Butterworth-Heinemann, Oxford.

Gunsteren, L.A. van, P.P. van Loon (2000), *Open design. A* collaborative approach to architecture. Eburon, Delft.

Hall, A.D. (1968), *A methodology for systems engineering.* Van Nostrand, Princeton, New Jersey.

Hamel, R. (1990), *Over het denken van de architect* [How an architect thinks]. AHA Books, Amsterdam.

Heintz, J.L. (1999), *Coordinating collaborative building design.* PhD thesis, Delft University of Technology.

Hillier, B., J. Musgrove, P. O'Sullivan (1972), Knowledge and design. In: W.J. Mitchell (ed.), *Environmental design: research and practice.* University of California, Berkeley.

Jones, J.C. (1963), A method of systematic design. In: J.C. Jones and D. Thornley (eds), *Conference on design methods.* Pergamon, Oxford.

Jones, J.C. (1982), *Design methods: seeds of human futures,* 9th edn. John Wiley and Sons, Chichester.

Jones, J.C., D. Thornley (eds) (1963), *Conference on design methods.* Pergamon, Oxford.

Jonge, D. de (1960), *Moderne woonidealen en woonwensen in Nederland* [Modern housing ideals and housing desires in the Netherlands]. Vuga, Arnhem.

Jong, T.M. de (1992), *Kleine methodologie voor ontwerpend onderzoek* [A small methodology for design research]. Boom, Meppel.

Jong, T.M. de (1993), *Onderzoekthema's gericht op ontwerp en beleid* [Research topics relating to design and policy]. Faculty of Architecture, Delft University of Technology.

Jong, T.M. de, D.J.M. van der Voordt (eds) (2002), *Ways to study and research architectural, urban and technical design.* Delft University Press, Delft.

Koutamanis, A. (1994), *Ontwerprepresentaties en ontwerpprocessen 1994–1995* [Design representations and processes 1994–1995]. Faculty of Architecture, Delft University of Technology.

Langdon, R. (ed) (1984), *Design policy.* The Design Council, London.

Langenhuizen, A., M. van Ouwerkerk, J. Rosemann (eds) (2001), *Research by design.* Proceedings of the International Conference on Research by Design, Faculty of

Architecture, Delft University of Technology, in cooperation with the European Association for Architectural Education. Delft University Press.

Lawrence, B.R. (1992), Characteristics of architectural design tools. *Architecture & Behaviour* 8(3), 229–240.

Lawson, B.R. (1994), *Design in mind.* Butterworth Architecture, Oxford.

Lawson, B.R. (1997) [1980], *How designers think. The design process demystified*, 3rd edn. Architectural Press, London.

Leupen, B., C. Grafe, N. Körning, M. Lampe, P. de Zeeuw (1997), *Design and analysis.* 010 Publishers, Rotterdam.

Leusen, M. van (1994), *A system of types in the domain of residential buildings.* Publications Office, Faculty of Architecture, Delft University of Technology.

Loon, P.P. van (1998), *Interorganisational design.* Faculty of Architecture, Delft University of Technology.

Luckman, J. (1967), An approach to the management of design. *Operational Research Quarterly* 18(4), 345–358.

Meyer-Ehlers, G. (1972), *Wohnung und familie.* Verlags-Anstalt, Stuttgart.

Neufert, E., P. Neufert, B. Baiche, N. Walliman (2000), The handbook of building types – Neufert's architect's data, 3rd edn. Blackwell Science, Oxford.

Polak, B.M. (1981), *Functioneel ontwerpen* [Functional design]. Faculty of Civil Engineering, Delft University of Technology.

Pos, M. (2000), *Inquiry into the management of innovative architectural design.* Graduate thesis, Faculty of Architecture, Delft University of Technology.

Priemus, H. (1969), *Wonen, kreativiteit en aanpassing.* [Housing, creativity and adaptation]. Mouton, The Hague.

Prigogine, I., I. Stengers (1984), *Order out of chaos. Man's new dialogue with nature.* Bantam Books, Toronto.

Proshansky, H.M., W.H. Ittelson, L.G. Rivlin (1970), *Environmental psychology. Man and his physical setting.* Holt, Rinehart and Winston, New York.

Puglisi, L.P. (1999), *Hyper architecture. Spaces in the electronic age.* Birkhäuser, Basel.

Ridder, H.A.J. de (1998), Ontwerpmethodologie in de civiele techniek [Design methodology in civil engineering]. In: M. Eekhout (ed.), *Ontwerpmethodologie* [Design methodology]. Symposium, Faculty of Architecture, Delft University of Technology.

Robinson, J.W. (1994), The question of type. In: K.A. Franck and L.H. Schneekloth (eds), *Ordering space. Types in architecture and design.* Van Nostrand Reinhold, New York, 179–192.

Roozenburg, N.F.M., J. Eekels (1991), *Produktontwerpen, structuur en methoden* [Product design, structure and methods]. Lemma B.V., Utrecht.

Rosemann, J. (2001), *The construction of research by design in practice.* In: Proceedings Part A, Research by Design. International Conference. Faculty of Architecture and EAAE/AEEA. Delft University Press.

Rosenman, M.A., and J.S. Gero (1993), Creativity in designing using a design prototype approach. In: J.S. Gero and M.L. Maher (eds), *Modelling creativity and knowledge based creative design.* Lawrence Erlbaum, New Jersey.

Rossi, A. (1982) [1967], *The architecture of the city.* MIT Press, Cambridge, Mass.

Schön, D.A. (1988), Designing: rules, types and worlds. *Design Studies* 9(3), 181–190.

Schön, D.A. [1983] (1991), *The reflective practitioner. How professionals think in action.* Aldershot, Avebury.

Sommer, R. (1969), *Personal space: the behavioral basis of design.* Englewood Cliffs, NJ: Prentice-Hall.

Symes, M. (1994), Typological thinking in architectural practice. In: K.A. Franck and L.H. Schneekloth (eds), *Ordering space. Types in architecture and design.* Van Nostrand Reinhold, New York, 165–178.

Tunstall, G. (2001), *Managing the building design process.* Butterworth-Heinemann, Oxford.

Turpijn, W., H. Venema (1979), *Bewonersparticipatie* [Resident participation]. Van Loghum Slaterus, Deventer.

Tzonis, A. (1993), Huts, ships and bottleracks. Design by analogy for architects and/or machines. In: N. Cross, K. Dorst, N. Roozenburg (eds), *Research in design thinking.* Delft University Press, 139–164.

Vidler, A. (1977), The idea of type: the transformation of the academic ideal, 1750–1830. *Oppositions* 8, 95–115.

Vollers, K.J. (2001), *Twist and build: creating non-orthogonal architecture.* 010 Publishers, Rotterdam.

CHAPTER 5

Evaluating buildings

5.1. Introduction

Taken literally, evaluation means determining a value or establishing what some-thing is worth. Originally the term came from the financial world, where evaluation means calculating a rate of exchange or determining the value of money. In the world of architecture, evaluation is mainly concerned with establishing the value of all or part of the built environment (*product evaluation*) or the process of construction and management (*process evaluation*). Apart from their subjects, evaluations can be performed for different reasons and be intended for different target audiences: they can differ in breadth and depth, method of evaluation, time of evaluation and the people involved in the evaluation such as clients, research workers, daily users and so on (Kernohan et al., 1992). All these points need to be considered when preparing an evaluation. There must be as clear a picture as possible of what is to be evaluated, why, how, when, for whom and by whom. In this chapter these decision points are used to form the basis for a number of aids to setting up and carrying out an evaluation. The main subject is the evaluation of buildings in use. This chapter provides a summary of the factors relevant to such an assessment and the methods and techniques used to measure those factors.

5.2. Product and process, ex ante and ex post

In the world of architecture, product-related evaluations can deal with matters such as a programme of requirements, a plan or design, a specification or a building as realised. An evaluation may, for example, check a programme of requirements to see that it corresponds with the desires and requirements of future users, with legislation and regulations, with results produced by research and with the budget. These factors are just as relevant when a plan is being evaluated. From an architectonic point of view, another primary evaluation criterion is visual quality or, in more general terms, architectonic quality, here understood as a synthesis of form, function and technology. Evaluation of a programme of requirements or design is referred to as *evaluation ex ante* or evaluation before the event, i.e. before the building is realised. It could be thought of as an evaluation of a 'model' of the building, whether on paper, in the form of a scale model or, in the case of building components, a full-size model. The term used in the American literature is 'pre-design research' or sometimes 'impact assessment'. A well-known example is the environmental effect report, in which a plan is examined for its possible effect on the environment, often in comparison with the null option, i.e. doing nothing, and other variants of the plan. 'Evaluation after the event', when the building has been completed and is in use, is referred to as *ex post evaluation* or *post-occupancy evaluation* (POE).

The distinction between ex ante and ex post can also be drawn for process-related evaluations (Table 5.1). A process-related evaluation can be concerned with the building process as a whole, from initiation all the way through to use and management, or to elements in that process, e.g. the design process.

5.3. Why evaluate?

Evaluation allows lessons to be learnt which could lead to an improvement in the project under investigation and more generally improve the quality of programming, designing, building and management of the built environment. The reasons for the exercise can be both ideological and economic, e.g. the promotion of health and welfare or a reduction in the amount of property standing empty in an expanding market. Besides such practical goals, there can also be scientific goals, such as contributing to the formation of new theories or developing new tools, and there may be subsidiary goals derived from these main goals (Box 5.1).

Table 5.1 Sample questions for the evaluation of buildings

	Ex ante	Ex post
Product	■ Does the brief give a clear and complete account of the required or desired user quality, visual quality and technical quality? ■ Do the requirements correspond to the wishes of the future users? ■ Can the design be expected to lead to a usable building? ■ Does the design have sufficient visual quality? ■ Is the design affordable? ■ Does the design conform with the building regulations?	■ Is the building being used in the way anticipated by the client and the architect? ■ Are the users satisfied? ■ How does the actual energy usage compare with the usage estimated in advance? ■ What do experts and laymen think about the building's architectonic quality? ■ Does the building conform with accepted quality standards?
Process	■ How best can the building process be organised? ■ Who should be involved in the process? ■ What are the tasks and powers of the various participants? ■ What input is required from future users? ■ How much time will be needed for the programming phase, design, contracting out and execution? ■ What information is needed, by whom and when? ■ What tools are available to ensure that the process runs efficiently and effectively? ■ What factors might affect the success or failure of the process?	■ How was the decision-making organised? Who took what decisions, when and on the basis of what information? ■ How long did the process take, in total and by phase? ■ What tools were used to prepare the brief, to develop and test plan variants, to coordinate different activities and to monitor cost and quality? ■ What was done well and what went wrong? ■ What lessons can be drawn?

Box 5.1. Objectives of evaluation

Project-related

- Determining whether expectations were fulfilled
- Determining whether goals were reached
- Drawing attention to unintended and unforeseen effects
- Increasing understanding of the decision-making processes
- Letting off steam
- Providing material on which to base improvements

Not project-related

- Theoretical development
- Development of tools
- Design guidelines
- Policy recommendations
- Database of reference projects

a. Testing aims and expectations

People involved in the planning process often have all kinds of wishes and expectations relating to 'their' building. The user wants a building that is usable and performs the functions for which it was intended but also one that is good to look at and pleasant to be in or to visit. The client has similar wishes and expectations, but will often be unwilling to pay more than was budgeted in advance. He may possibly also want the building to contribute to a corporate identity, or to serve as an example in the field of sustainable building. A designer will often set himself the goal of erecting a building that is not only functional and attractive but also sufficiently original to attract attention in architectural discussion. Thus, everyone participating in the building process has his own, often implicit, aims and expectations. Ex ante evaluation enables an estimate to be made of the likelihood that these aims will be achieved — aims which may perhaps conflict with one another – and what programme or design concept has the greatest chance of success. Ex post evaluation establishes whether expectations were fulfilled and aims actually achieved. When the work being carried out involves an existing building, evaluation both before and after the event can give a better idea of the effectiveness of the measures taken (Shepley, 1997; Fraley et al., 2002).

b.   Drawing attention to unintended and unforeseen effects

Besides checking against explicitly formulated aims and expectations, evaluation can also bring to light unintended and unforeseen phenomena, positive and negative. This applies as much to a product as to a process, ex post and ex ante. A critical evaluation can give an insight into the strengths and weaknesses of the design, opportunities and threats (a SWOT analysis) and the factors most relevant to its success or failure.

c.   Understanding the decision-making processes

Decisions are often based on a wide variety of different considerations. The role played by emotions, intuition, judgements and prejudices, social ideals and norms and values is at least as important as that played by rational argument. Evaluation of a building or a design process can lead to a better understanding of the motives, expected or actual, underlying the decisions and roles of the various participants (Preiser, 1988; Vischer, 1989). Such understanding is also important to the interpretation of the result of a product evaluation and the design guidelines and policy recommendations derived from it (Zimring, 1988). Points requiring attention include the significance of research in decision-making, the use of tools, the influence of limiting preconditions and the resolution of conflicting interests.

d.   Letting off steam

There is also a psychological reason for evaluating a building or the process that led to its creation. Renovation or constructing new buildings is exciting, but can also involve a good deal of stress. Everyone involved will have spent a good deal of time and energy searching for optimal solutions consistent with the budget, reaching compromises, moving and rearranging, etc. Scheduling an opportunity for evaluation will allow people to let off steam and express their enthusiasm or dissatisfaction.

e.   Material on which to base improvement

The results of an evaluation can be applied in various ways. One application of project-related evaluation is to use the results to improve the product or process. Ex ante evaluation of a programme or design can allow bottlenecks to be identified in good time. Changes are often easier and less expensive in the programme or design phase than improvements after the event. The same applies to the organisation of the building process. Once a building is complete, the results of an ex post evaluation can be used to solve teething troubles, to suggest minor adjustments or radical improvements possibly extending as far as renovation or replacement by a new building (Kernohan et al., 1992; Teikari, 1995). Depending on the problems identified, possible solutions might be functional (splitting or combining rooms, adding lifts), technical (better maintenance, different technical services, insulating the elevations), social (changing the target group, moving personnel internally) or involve adjusting the price/performance ratio (e.g. by reducing the rent). If there is a major mismatch between supply and demand (or wish and reality), replacement by a new building or moving to better premises may be an option. Careful evaluation will increase the likelihood of successful decisions and a positive return on investment.

f.   Theoretical development

Apart from allowing optimisation of the building under evaluation, there are other higher-level arguments in favour of evaluation, above and beyond the individual project. Evaluation makes it possible for others to learn from one's own experiences during the construction process and in the use and management phase. Individual evaluations and comparisons with other buildings and planning processes can make a significant contribution to theoretical development and the testing of existing theories, e.g. the relationship between the arrangement of the built environment and human behaviour or between design decisions and cost, environmental effect and visual quality (Shepley, 1997).

g.   Tools, design guidelines and policy recommendations

Nothing is as practical as a good theory. Knowledge and understanding are essential preconditions for well-considered decisions. Consequently, the results of research into evaluation need to be 'translated' into a form which will be quickly and easily accessible to clients, designers, people responsible for policy and for checking plans and indeed everyone involved in the building process. Results are often presented in forms such as checklists, seals of approval and manuals. Examples which contain information in a form that is compact, well structured and explicit include the *Delftse checklist sociaal veilig ontwerpen* [Delft checklist – designing for public safety] (Van der Voordt and Van Wegen, 1990a and b, 1993; Figure 5.1 and Box 5.2), *Keurmerk veilig wonen* [Safe housing seal of approval] given by the Social Housing Experiments Steering Committee (Reijnhoudt and Scherpenisse, 1998; Hooftman et al., 1999) and the *Handboek voor toegankelijkheid* [Accessibility manual] (Wijk et al., 2000). A summary is given in Chapter 6. Tools of this kind turn out to be highly suitable for developing and checking building plans, avoiding disasters, guiding policy and developing legislation and regulations.

Box 5.2. Sample design guidelines – multistorey car parks

Multistorey car parks have the advantage of cars being less visible from the street and often allow the same piece of ground to be used for two different purposes. As against this, multistorey car parks have the disadvantage that many people feel that they are unsafe. Measures which can be taken to increase safety and reduce the chance of vandalism, theft from or of cars and physical violence include:

- Integrating the car park in the residential environment.
- Putting the entrance somewhere where there are generally people around.
- Siting entrance doors on the building line; avoiding dark nooks and crannies.
- Avoiding obstacles that reduce visibility. Columns should preferably be round and slim: massive columns and load-bearing walls should be avoided.
- Compartmentalising the car park into small manageable units.
- Giving walls, floors and ceilings an attractive finish (light colours, artwork).
- Providing good illumination that conforms to the level specified in guidelines and standards such as the Dutch NPR 2442.
- Providing openings in the roof or elevations (or both) to admit daylight.
- Adjusting the acoustics to avoid 'hollow' sounds.
- Providing good ventilation.
- Denying admission to unauthorised visitors. Emergency exits should be self-closing and only openable from inside .
- Ensuring that the route to be followed is obvious and clearly signed.
- Making clear agreements about management.
- Providing regular maintenance and laying down clear procedures for dealing with complaints, etc.
- Arranging for supervision by the police or a private security organisation, either permanently or at special times.

Source: Van der Voordt and Van Wegen, 1990b.

Figure 5.1 Checklist – designing for public safety.

h. Database of reference projects

Systematic documentation of the findings of evaluation investigations can lead to the creation of a database of interesting projects, containing a number of key items of information about the project and the findings of the evaluation. In principle, developments in the field of information and communication technology allow the results of research to be stored on a computer and linked with drawing and analysis software. It seems likely that in due course it will be relatively simple to check building plans for user and experiential quality during the design phase.

Of course it is not suggested that evaluation research and design guidelines based on such research should be used to create a blueprint for the ideal building or building process; any such blueprint would lead in no time to standardisation and uniformity. All kinds of things need to be considered, quite apart from standard items like a straightforward layout, space for anticipated activities, a pleasant interior climate and an affordable price, each in turn affected by such things as location, the characteristics of the organisation, the personal preferences of the client, users and designer, and changes in limiting conditions. Moreover, every design has to strike a balance between partially conflicting desires and requirements. The result of this balancing process is highly variable, which means that there is no such thing as the 'ideal' building. But evaluation research teaches that complex decision-making process should take careful account of experience and lessons from earlier projects. Thus, evaluation research is important to everyone involved in the building process, whether in the process of producing buildings (clients, designers, consultants, project developers, process managers and the authorities) or in using and managing buildings (daily users, facility managers, plant managers, etc.).

5.4. Quality assessment

As has already been said, evaluation means determining the value of something. This is closely related to the determination of quality: the extent to which a product satisfies the requirements specified. Strictly speaking this definition of quality would allow us to call a building 'good' when it fulfils the programme of requirements. After all, the programme of requirements specifies the client's requirements. But it is not sufficient merely to check a design or building against the programme of requirements. In most cases there are a number of wishes and requirements which are never stated explicitly, either because the client was not consciously aware of them or has ignored them, or because some requirements are thought to be self-evident. Moreover, the client is often not aware of all the different possibilities, nor are the requirements and wishes of everyone else involved generally laid down completely and explicitly in the programme of requirements. Take for example the wishes of users and visitors and the private regulations imposed by various pressure groups. Thus, any assessment must take account of other criteria, not just the programme of requirements. We shall therefore follow Burt (1978) (in Giddings and Holness, 1996) and use a wider definition of quality:

> Quality is the totality of attributes that enables to satisfy needs, including the way in which individual attributes are related, balanced and integrated in the whole building and its surroundings.

Four steps need to be taken to determine the quality of a building (Van der Voordt and Vrielink, 1987):

1. Determine which factors are to be taken into account by the assessment.
2. Measure the relevant variables.
3. Evaluate the outcome of those measurements.
4. Assign weights according to the importance of each different factor.

When all this has been done, an assessment can be made of the quality of individual aspects of the building and the building as a whole, i.e. the weighted sum of the values assigned to each separate aspect.

5.4.1. Factors to be assessed

Before starting any product evaluation, it is important to decide what precisely is to be evaluated. Since the 1970s there has been noticeable increase in

POE (see, for instance, Friedman et al., 1978; Keys and Wener, 1980; Zimring and Reitzenstein, 1980; Zimring, 1987; Preiser et al., 1988; Wener, 1989; Preiser, 1989, 1994; Teikari, 1995; Preiser and Vischer, 2004). Literally, POE means evaluation of a building after it has been taken into use. POEs deal mainly with functional aspects, the most important being utility value and experiential value, i.e. the experiences and requirements of the people who use and visit the building day by day (Figure 5.2). The evaluation will assign values to such items as the basic layout and the layout of individual rooms, the way the general form is perceived, the interior climate and behavioural factors (use of space, privacy, social contact, spatial orientation, etc.). Design is generally either treated as an 'independent variable' or evaluated autonomously. Technical aspects (load-bearing structure, technical services, etc.) are only taken into account to the extent that they affect use and the well-being of the users. Sometimes the focus is on overall architectural quality (Marans and Spreckelmeyer, 1982).

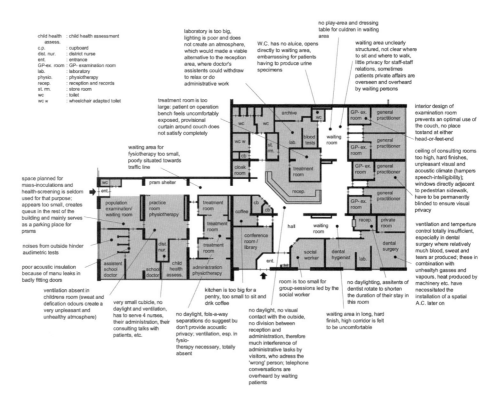

Figure 5.2 Result of a post-occupancy evaluation. Annotated floor plan of a health centre: a summary of complaints and bottlenecks as established by an evaluative investigation of users and visitors. Source: Van Hoogdalem et al., (1981).

Architects and architecture critics look at buildings mainly from the point of view of a designer. Dutch periodicals such as *De Architect* and *Archis* and foreign journals like *The Architectural Review, The Architects' Journal, Architektur Aktuell* and *l'Architettura* concentrate on such matters as design concepts and methods, spatial effects, size ratios, colours and materials, the coherence or lack of coherence between building components, and the considerations that underlie them. The design and approach of the designer involved is often compared with other designs by the same individual and reference projects (precedents) by other designers. This is also the central theme of many studies and plan analyses in the course on architectonic design given by the Faculty of Architecture at Delft University of Technology (see for instance Risselada, 1988). Most plan analyses include a documentation, description and architectonic analysis of the design in question, and often also a comparison with other designs of the same designer, in the same field and/or of the same or of a different period. But quite often a sound analysis of the functional quality and utility, supported by empirical data, is lacking.

In recent years there has been a visible widening in the scope of evaluations in the direction of *building performance evaluation* or *total building performance evaluation,* (BPE) (Preiser and Schramm, 1998). BPEs attempt to integrate user and aesthetic factors with technical and economic factors. Various summaries are to be found in the literature on evaluation (Preiser, 1988; Benes and Vrijling, 1990; Baird et al., 1996; Stichting REN, 1992, 1993, 1994). Although each source mentions different subjects and organises them differently, they have many points in common. Box 5.3 attempts to present the highest common denominator. Although the subjects are mainly concerned with evaluating buildings, many of them apply just as much to evaluating a programme of requirements or design and to judging the suitability of a building location.

For the sake of simplicity, the factors to be assessed are divided into four categories:

a. Functional (utility value, future value).
b. Aesthetic (experiential value).
c. Technical.
d. Economic and legal.

This division is very much in line with Vitruvius' traditional three-way division into utilitas, venustas and firmitas, and the trio of function, form and technology much quoted by architects, but with added cost, legislation and regulation. Literature on environmental psychology often includes a separate section on behavioural factors, including such items as territoriality, privacy and social contact. Our own summary (Box 5.3) includes these items in the section on functional aspects. Box 5.4 shows a breakdown of building-related costs in investment costs and exploitational costs.

Box 5.3.   Items to be included in an evaluation of buildings

a. Functional

- Reachability and parking facilities
- Accessibility
- Efficiency
- Flexibility
- Safety (ergonomic, public)
- Spatial orientation
- Territoriality, privacy and social contact
- Physical well-being (lighting, noise, heating, draughts, humidity)

b. Aesthetic

- Visual quality
- Order and complexity
- Representational quality
- Symbolic and semiotic value
- Value as cultural history

c. Technical

- Fire safety
- Constructional safety
- Building physics
- Environmental friendliness
- Sustainability

d. Economic and legal

- Investment costs
- Exploitation costs
- Time investment
- Public and private regulations

This summary can be seen as an expanded version of another much used method of subdividing evaluation criteria into *quality, costs and time.* Costs and time are included in the section on economic factors. What did the building cost? Did savings have to be made to keep within budget? How do the investment costs and exploitation charges compare with those for similar buildings? How much time was required for the programming phase, for design and execution? Quality embraces the other three aspects and refers as much to the objectively measurable characteristics of the building as to the value, often subjective, put on those characteristics. Factors that can be determined objectively include the dimensions of the building, the materials used for the elevations and the roof and the colours applied to the walls and doors. The determination of whether these factors are functional, aesthetically justifiable and environmentally friendly can be left until later.

Box 5.4. Breakdown of building-related costs by the Dutch Standard Institution

Investment costs as laid down in NEN 2631:

- Land
- Building
- Incidental
- Management
- Inventory
- Other (reserves, interest during building, start-up costs)

Exploitation costs as laid down in NEN 2632:

- Fixed (interest and capital repayment, rent, service costs)
- Energy
- Maintenance
- Administration
- Specific business expenses arising from real estate activities
- Cleaning

Characteristics of the location and the building

Three levels of scale are significant when assessing the quality of a location and a building: the building in its setting, the building as a unit; and individual rooms. Boxes 5.5 and 5.6 summarise the relevant characteristics of the location and the building. The lists can be used as checklists to ensure that the description of the building to be evaluated is as accurate as possible.

Box 5.5. Site characteristics

- Geographical situation
- Location relative to the city centre
- Access:

  - Traffic infrastructure (motorways, routes for slow traffic, capacity, traffic density)

(Continued)

- Public transport stops and service frequency (aircraft, train, tram, tube, bus, taxi)
- Parking facilities (number of parking places, size, location)

- Size and dimensions of the building site
- Built/unbuilt ratio
- Building density
- Functions and intended purposes (capacity in m^2, assortment, target group):

  - Housing
  - Shops
  - Schools
  - Recreational facilities (sports and games, cinema, hotel and catering facilities)
  - Cultural facilities (theatre, museum, library)
  - Accommodation facilities (hotel, guest house)
  - Trade and industry
  - Services (health care, banks, post offices, and so on)
  - Police, fire brigade, private security services
  - Water and green space (canals, parks, public gardens, deer park, children's animal park)

- Demographic characteristics (inhabitants, number employed, visitors):

  - Age distribution
  - Composition of household
  - Country of origin

- Socio-economic characteristics:

  - Income
  - Disposable income
  - Turnover
  - Employment/unemployment
  - Criminality
  - Unoccupied buildings
  - Level of maintenance

- Environment (sun, wind, smell, noise)
- Mains services (gas, water, electricity)
- Legislation and regulation (zoning plan, parking standards, etc.)
- Pattern of ownership (owned, rented, leasehold)

Box 5.6. Building characteristics

■ Shell (elevation, roof, floor)
■ Load-bearing structure
■ Plant and main services:

  – Electrical
  – Mechanical
  – Other (climate control, sanitation)

■ Spatial division:

  – Floor area (gross, net, useful, rentable)
  – Net/gross, rentable/gross ratios (for definitions, see e.g. NEN 2630)
  – Compactness (elevation area/floor area ratio)
  – Basic layout of the building (mass, number of floors)
  – Access (number and location of entrances, halls, corridors, stairs, lifts)
  – Relationships between rooms, zoning

■ Special rooms:

  – Function (intended purpose, activities, number of users)
  – Shape and dimensions
  – Floor area (gross, net)
  – Nature of enclosure (open or closed, load-bearing or not, fixed or flexible)
  – Location relative to other rooms (distance, barriers)
  – Relationship with the outside (view, daylight, sunlight, distance from the entrance)
  – Interior climate (lighting, heating, ventilation)
  – Finish of walls, floors and ceilings (material, colour)
  – Permanent fixtures
  – Temporary fixtures

Match between supply and demand

In fact, an evaluation compares supply and demand. The demand consists of the wishes, preferences, expectations and goals of those directly involved: part is laid down in the programme of requirements, legislation and regulations; part is stored in people's heads and hearts; and part is hidden in the subconscious. The supply is the building as realised. The comparison checks the extent to which the site and building corresponds to the qualities required. Suppose we want to establish the functionality of a hospital building. This will mean finding out the physical characteristics of the supply, e.g. location in the city, gross floor area, how the building is arranged, the size of the grid and the dimensions of the rooms. The requirements – the demand – will need to be determined by looking at things like reachability, accessibility and usability by staff, patients and visitors. The question of whether the site and building are suitable, given the various requirements and desires, can be answered by comparing the two types of information. This will mean analysing walking distances, the frequency with which a particular route is travelled, the space required to accommodate and use things like beds, bedside tables, etc., and then comparing this information with what was required or desired. The process is represented schematically in Table 5.2.

Table 5.2 Comparison of supply and demand

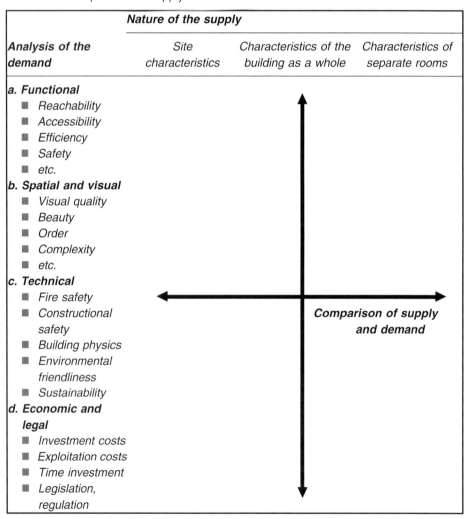

	Nature of the supply		
Analysis of the demand	*Site characteristics*	*Characteristics of the building as a whole*	*Characteristics of separate rooms*
a. Functional ▪ *Reachability* ▪ *Accessibility* ▪ *Efficiency* ▪ *Safety* ▪ *etc.*			
b. Spatial and visual ▪ *Visual quality* ▪ *Beauty* ▪ *Order* ▪ *Complexity* ▪ *etc.*			
c. Technical ▪ *Fire safety* ▪ *Constructional safety* ▪ *Building physics* ▪ *Environmental friendliness* ▪ *Sustainability*			
d. Economic and legal ▪ *Investment costs* ▪ *Exploitation costs* ▪ *Time investment* ▪ *Legislation, regulation*			

Comparison of supply and demand

It is vitally important to link quality aspects with the physical characteristics of the site and building if the results of the evaluation are to be correctly interpreted and translated into design guidelines, norms or dos and don'ts. It makes little sense to establish that there are problems with, e.g. spatial orientation or public safety, if no suggestions can be derived for improving planning, programming, designing, building or managing buildings. Unfortunately, evaluation studies often fail to include careful descriptions and illustrations (photos, floor plans, cross-sections) of the object evaluated, so it is difficult to see which design characteristics are responsible for which effects, positive or negative.

Selection of factors to be assessed

Only in exceptional cases will an attempt be made to produce a fully comprehensive evaluation. The choice of factors to be assessed depends largely on the purpose of the evaluation. There is often some practical reason for a project-related evaluation, e.g. a concern that the building might remain unoccupied, a mismatch between the organisation and the office concept or an excessively large energy bill. In such a case the obvious course is to concentrate on making a clear diagnosis of the problem and working out the way to go to find solutions to improve the situation. When innovative solutions have been applied, the evaluation will generally concentrate on the innovations. One example is the present boom in the evaluation of innovative office buildings (Vos and Dewulf, 1999; Vos and Van der Voordt, 2002). The well-known PROBE studies (post-occupancy review of buildings and their engineering) carried out in the UK in the 1990s were particularly interested in climate control, technical services and energy utilisation (Bordas and Leaman, 2001). When the aim is to establish guidelines for buildings with a specific function, it makes sense for the evaluation to concentrate on determining the spatial conditions that will best serve that function. Examples include the study of children's environments by Sanoff and Sanoff (1981), the study of health care centres by Van Hoogdalem et al. (1985a), and the study of design modifications in a general hospital (Becker and Poe, 1980). Recent examples, close to home, include the evaluations carried out by Delft University of Technology of buildings designed to provide assisted living for the elderly (Houben and Van der Voordt, 1993; Van der Voordt, 1997, 1998).

5.4.2. Measurement

When it is clear which factors are to be assessed, it needs to be established *how* these factors are to be measured. Sometimes this is simple: e.g. when all that is needed is to establish unambiguous characteristics such as date of construction, gross floor area or the colour of an elevation. Other quality criteria can be rather more complex to determine. How for example does one measure flexibility or user quality? A clear description of the concept is insufficient. Abstract concepts of this kind need to be made more concrete by translating them into variables that can be measured, a process known in the jargon as 'operationalising'. If, for example, we want to measure the flexibility of a building, we could define the concept of flexibility as 'the extent to which the building allows changes in the organisation to be dealt with without having to break down walls'. The next step is to establish which variables are relevant to flexibility as defined in this way. One might think for example of the nature of the load-bearing structure and the grid size (important to working out how easy it would be to rearrange the building), how easy it would be to replace an elevation (relevant to the possibility of extension), whether the plant could be changed or the dimensions of individual rooms could be adjusted (to allow space to be used multifunctionally). Finally, it must be possible to justify the way in which concrete variables are measured. If there is no obvious way to carry out a quantitative measurement, the only alternative is to resort to qualitative description. Box 5.7 shows some indicators for measuring user quality.

Box 5.7 Indicators for measuring user quality

- The use actually made of rooms and facilities (frequency of use, nature of use: for what activities, individual or communal, for one function or many)
- Valuation given by daily users, absolute and relative to alternative solutions
- Valuation given by the designer and others involved: the client, owner, manager and consultants
- Changes made to the building since delivery
- Rentability (figures on unoccupied periods, changes in occupancy, waiting lists, rent)
- Tendency to move
- Figures on maintenance, vandalism and burglary

Every method of measurement – interviews, questionnaires, observation, experiments and the use of measuring equipment – has its advantages and disadvantages. It is therefore sensible to use several methods in parallel. The choice of method depends in part on the desired breadth and depth of the evaluation and limiting factors such as time, money and expertise. The demands imposed by a rapid general diagnosis are different from those imposed by a searching scientific investigation. The accepted requirements for scientific research are objectivity, verifiability, validity and reliability. For detailed criteria for scientific exercises and different methods of measurement the reader is referred to the literature on research methodology. Apart from general introductions to research methodology, literature is available which is specifically geared to architecture (Zeisel, 1981; Bechtel et al., 1987; Baird et al., 1996). Scales have been developed to measure specific quality criteria, such as the 'real estate norm' for office buildings (Stichting REN, 1992, 1993, 1994). A summary of important quality criteria and measuring methods will be found in Chapter 6.

5.4.3. Valuation

When the results of the measurements are known, they have to be used to reach a value judgement. For example, a temperature of 30°C only becomes meaningful in relation to a wish or norm (e.g. no lower than 16°C, average 22°C and not higher than 30°C on more than 10 days a year). Use is often made of quality classes, e.g. a 3-point scale (poor, satisfactory, good) or a 5-point scale (unsatisfactory, poor, satisfactory, good, excellent). One example is the method used by consumer organisations to assess consumer products. Such organisations often test products against a number of different criteria and assess them on a 5-point scale, e.g. ++ + +\– – – –. The basis of the scale values must be indicated for each criterion, e.g. current norms, the judgement of a user panel or the judgement of an expert. Assessment criteria are not static but develop over time, as the result of critical reflection by experts and the development of new insights. Box 5.8 shows a number of references that can be used in a value judgement.

Box 5.8. Matters to be considered when assessing quality

- Programme of requirements
- Requirements, wishes and preferences of the client, users and visitors
- Experience of the building's management
- Judgements by professional specialists (designers, consultants, architecture critics)
- Guidelines and recommendations in the professional literature
- Results of an evaluative investigation (comparison with reference projects)
- Norms and seals of approval
- Legislation and regulation (relating to building, health and safety and private)

5.4.4. Weighting

In most cases, the person doing the evaluation perceives not all factors as equally important: some factors weigh more heavily than others. It can therefore be useful to assign weights to different factors, making it possible to reach a weighted conclusion based on a number of qualities each of which is given the importance it deserves. This method is referred to in the literature as the multicriteria method, and is used for such tasks as choosing between a number of potential building locations or design solutions (Table 5.3).

Table 5.3 Example allocation of weighting factors

	Main criteria	%	Sub-criteria
1. Physical environment	1.1 Public functions	5.8%	Through traffic Local traffic Accommodation Storage space
	1.2 Semi-public functions	3.1%	Shopping facilities Cultural facilities Hotel and catering facilities Social facilities
	1.3 Private functions	3.1%	Housing facilities Offices Businesses
	1.4 Separation of functions	2.9%	Between types of public transport Traffic↔accommodation Public↔semi-public functions Public↔private functions
	1.5 Reachability	5.5%	Public accommodation Public storage space (car parks) Semi-public functions Private functions
	1.6 Safety	5.2%	Traffic safety Manageability Environmental factors

(*Continued*)

Table 5.3 Continued

	Main criteria	%	Sub-criteria
2. Social environment	2.1 Expected level of activity	5.3%	Concentration of activities
	2.2 Public safety	6.2%	Feasibility of social control
3. Image	3.1 Individual identity of the plan	5.3%	Relationship with other areas Originality Orientation points Recognisability
	3.2 Cultural identity	2.4%	Use of historic features Autonomous style-related solutions
	3.3 Building structure	0.7%	Scale – large or small Variety ↔ unity
	3.4 Visual spatial image	5.7%	Arrangement of public space Urban intimacy View Relationships between different buildings
	3.5 Perceived form, colour and materials	3.6%	Coherence of the total composition Liveliness
	3.6 Design of green space	3.6%	Seasonal effects Liveliness
	3.7 Special features	3.9%	Suitability to total composition Design balance
4. Realisation factors	4.1 Costs	8.3%	
	4.2 Period required for realisation	5.6%	
	4.3 Possibility of phased approach	8.8%	
	4.4 Potential yield	6.7%	
Total		100%	

Source: Stichting Architecten Research (1991), *Kwaliteit van de openbare ruimte* [Quality of public space]. Design competition for Tilburg's railway district.

Box 5.9. Example of evaluative research not related to a single product

Health centres are cooperative arrangements in which one or more doctor, a district nursing service and social workers are accommodated under one roof. Larger health centres also often include physiotherapists and other health practitioners (dentists, pharmacists, psychologists). In the mid 1980s a wide-ranging investigation was carried out to develop guidelines for programming and design for such centres (Van Hoogdalem et al., 1985b). The investigation involved the following steps:

- trial investigation of the Merenwijk Health Centre, Leiden
- visits to 50 purpose-built health centres plus one or two interviews
- comparative analysis of the floor plans of these 50 buildings
- development of a spatial typology for the function
- establishment of criteria for the selection of four representative centres for further study
- extensive evaluation of the four selected centres (interviews, questionnaires, observation)
- general evaluation of the other centres (a brief survey of staff and visitors).

The comparative floor plan analysis was carried out iteratively and interactively with a study of the literature and evaluative research.

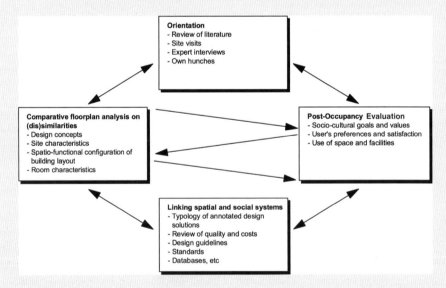

Figure 5.3. Interaction between Comparative Floorplan analysis and Post-Occupancy Evaluation.

The first step was to draw attention to similarities and differences (Figure 5.4). Next, hypotheses were set up for the underlying arguments, advantages and disadvantages, in use and as perceived. The hypotheses were presented to the people interviewed in the centres visited. As understanding increased, hypotheses were adjusted and typological solution variants were recorded, with comments. The notes were then used to develop guidelines for programming, designing and evaluating health centres. The same method was later applied to day nurseries, facilities for the mentally handicapped, assisted housing facilities for the elderly, etc.

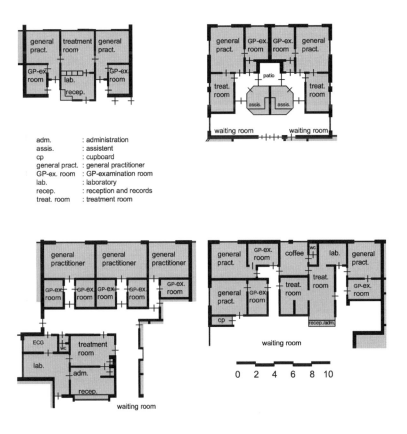

Figure 5.4 Ways of arranging the doctors' area in a health centre. A series of floor plans of buildings with the same function were systematically compared to produce a typology of solution variants. A number of different representative types of buildings were evaluated in use to identify actual and perceived advantages and disadvantages. The resulting 'annotated' typology may be used to assist in making more rapid decisions. Source: Van Hoogdalem et al., 1985a.

5.5. An integrated approach

This chapter has dealt at length with the evaluation of buildings, ex ante and ex post. Besides providing a summary of possible goals and items to be evaluated, it has also considered how evaluations should be carried out. It will have become apparent that there are a number of aids available to forming an objective assessment of the quality of a design or building. Although thorough evaluations are still the exception, it can be concluded that the methodological side of building performance evaluation and post-occupancy evaluation has by now outgrown the stage of being a new professional field. Both students and lecturers in faculties of architecture can benefit from these techniques, e.g. in design studios, in studying for a degree or guiding such study. In practice, too, a sound performance evaluation in different phases of the planning process may help to improve the quality of the built environment (Figure 5.5).

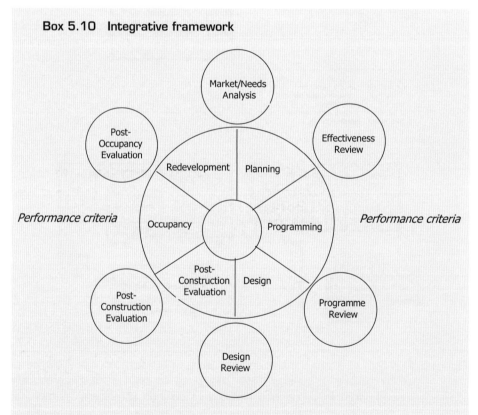

Box 5.10   Integrative framework

Figure 5.5   An integrative framework for building performance evaluation. Source: adapted from Preiser and Schramm, 1998.

(*Continued*)

The cycle includes six phases, each with internal reviews and feedback loops:

- *Planning*: starting with a strategic plan which establishes present and long-term needs of society through market/needs analyses. Loop 1 includes an effectiveness review of the outcomes of strategic planning in relation to quality, initial capital cost and operating cost.
- *Programming*: processing of information setting out design directions that will accommodate the needs of the users and other stakeholders and limiting conditions. Loop 2 refers to a programme review involving clients and other stakeholders.
- *Design*: from the first sketch ideas to construction documents. Loop 3 refers to design review, i.e. an ex ante assessment of the effects of design decisions from various perspectives.
- *Construction*: this phase includes administration and quality control to assure contractual compliance. Loop 4 includes post-construction evaluation, which results in punch lists of items that need to be completed prior to commissioning and acceptance by the clients.
- *Occupancy*: during this phase, move-in and start-up of the facilities occur, as well as fine-tuning by adjusting the facilities and its occupants to achieve optimal functioning. Loop 5 includes post-occupancy evaluation, providing feedback on what 'works' and what doesn't. POE may be used to test hypotheses and expectations, to identify problems in the performance of the built environment and ways to solve them.
- *Redevelopment*: e.g. recycling of buildings to similar or different uses, redesign of public areas, adding new functions or demolishing buildings. Loop 6 again includes market/needs analysis.

It will also have been noted that the emphasis in this chapter has been on functional quality. This to some extent follows from the subject of the present book. Another reason is that functional quality has received considerably more attention, scientifically speaking, than the assessment of aesthetic or technical quality. Although the assessment of aesthetic quality is and will always be strongly subjective, a more scientific exploration of the relevant criteria, definitions, operationalisations and methods of measurements would, we believe, also make this aspect easier to deal with, or at least easier to discuss. One example is the use of polar scales, e.g. beautiful/ugly, exciting/dull, original/traditional, monotonous/complex. It could be interesting to use such scales in the assessment of a number of recently completed buildings – and some rather older buildings – by users, architects, architecture critics and others involved in the building process. Comparing the results of the assessments with the character-istics of the various buildings might make it possible to devise a more scientific method of assessing form.

Bibliography

Baird, G., J. Gray, N. Isaacs, D. Kernohan, G. McIndoe (1996), *Building evaluation techniques*. McGraw-Hill, New York.

Bechtel, R., R. Marans, E. Michelson (1987), *Methods in environmental and behavioral research*. Van Nostrand Reinhold, New York.

Becker, E.D., D.B. Poe (1980), The effects of user-generated design modifications in a general hospital. *Journal of Nonverbal Behavior*, 4, 195–218.

Benes, J, J.K. Vrijling (1990), *Voldoet dit gebouw? Het bepalen van functionele kwaliteit* [Is this building satisfactory? The determination of functional quality]. SBR Report 222. Stichting Bouwresearch, Rotterdam.

Bordas, B., A. Leaman (eds) (2001), Assessing building performance in use. *Building Research & Information* 29, 2.

Burt, M.E. (1978), *A survey of quality and value in buildings*. Building Research Establishment, Walford, UK.

Fraley, I., J. Carmann, J. Anderzhon (2002), *Post-occupancy evaluations*. Making the most of design.

Friedman, A., C. Zimring, E. Zube (1978), *Environmental design evaluation*. Plenum Press, New York.

Giddings, B., A. Holness (1996), Quality assessment of architectural design and the use of design award schemes. *Environment by Design* 1(1), 53–68.

Haaksma, S.H.H. (1999), *Plannenmap voor de basis. Huis – Complex – Gebouw en Proces* [Portfolio of plans. House – Complex – Building and Process]. Faculty of Architecture, Delft University of Technology.

Hooftman, M., C. van Zwam, P. Reijnhoudt, R. Scherpenisse (1999), *Politiekeurmerk Veilig Wonen. Bestaande bouw.* [Safe housing seal of approval. Housing stock]. Nationaal Centrum voor Preventie, Utrecht.

Hoogdalem, H. van, D.J.M. van der Voordt, H.B.R. van Wegen (1981), *Ruimtelijk-functionele analyse van gezondheidscentra* [Spatial functional analysis of health centres]. Part 1: Procedure for research and experiment. Faculty of Architecture, Delft University of Technology.

Hoogdalem, H. van, D.J.M. van der Voordt, H.B.R. van Wegen (1985a), *Bouwen aan gezondheidscentra. Functionele grondslagen voor programma en ontwerp* [Building for health centres. Basic functional principles for programming and design]. Delft University Press.

Hoogdalem, H. van, D.J.M. van der Voordt, H.B.R. van Wegen (1985b), Comparative floorplan-analysis as a means to develop design guidelines. *Journal of Environmental Psychology* 5, 153–179.

Houben, P.P.J., D.J.M. van der Voordt (1993), New combinations of housing and care for the elderly in the Netherlands. *Netherlands Journal of Housing and Environmental Research* 8(3), 301–325.

Kernohan, D., J. Gray, J. Daish with D. Joiner (1992), *User participation in building design and management*. Butterworth Architecture, Oxford.

Keys, C., R. Wener (1980), Organizational Intervention Issues. A four-phase approach to post-occupancy evaluation. *Environment and Behaviour* 12(4), 533–540.

Marans, R., K. Spreckelmeyer (1982), Measuring overall architectural quality: a component of building evaluation. *Environment and Behaviour* 14(6), 652–670.

Preiser, W.F.E. (1988), Advances in post-occupancy evaluation: knowledge, methods and applications. In: H. van Hoogdalem, N.L. Prak, D.J.M. Van der Voordt, H.B.R. Van Wegen (eds), *Looking back to the future*. Proceedings of IAPS 10. Delft University of Technology, 207–212.

Preiser, W. (ed.) (1989), *Building evaluation*. Plenum Press, New York.

Preiser, W. (1994), Built environment evaluation: conceptual basis, benefits and uses. *Journal of Architectural and Planning Research* 11(2), 91–107.

Preiser, W.F.E., H.Z. Rabinowitz, E.T. White (1988), *Post-occupancy evaluation*. Van Nostrand Reinhold, New York.

Preiser, W.F.E., U. Schramm (1998). Building performance evaluation. In: D. Watson et al. (eds), *Time-saver standards*, 7th edn. McGraw Hill, New York, 233–238.

Preiser, W., J. Vischer (eds) (2004), *Assessing building performance: methods and case studies*. Elsevier, Oxford, UK.

Reijnhoudt, P., R. Scherpenisse (1998), *Politiekeurrmerk Veilig Wonen. Nieuwbouw*. [Safe housing seal of approval. New houses]. Zijp, Zoetermeer.

Risselada, M. (1988), *Raumplan versus Plan Libre. Adolf Loos and Le Corbusier 1919–1930*. Delft University Press, Delft.

Sanoff, H., J. Sanoff (1981), *Learning environments for children*. Edwards Bros., Humanics Limited, Atlanta.

Shepley, M. (1997), Design evaluation. In: S. Marberry (ed.), *Healthcare design*. John Wiley and Sons, New York.

Stichting Architecten Research (1991), *Kwaliteit van de openbare ruimte. Resultaten ontwerpprijsvraag Spoorzone Tilburg* [Quality of public space. Results of the design competition for Tilburg's railway district]. Eindhoven.

Stichting REN (1992), *Real estate norm. Methode voor de advisering en beoordeling van kantoorlocaties en kantoorgebouwen* [Method for advising on and assessing office locations and office buildings], 2nd edn. Nieuwegein.

Stichting REN (1993), *Real estate norm bedrijfsgebouwen* [Industrial buildings], 1st edn. Nieuwegein.

Stichting REN (1994), *Real estate norm quick scan kantoorgebouwen* [Office buildings], 1st edn. Nieuwegein.

Teikari, M. (1995), *Hospital facilities as work environments*. Faculty of Architecture, University of Technology, Helsinki.

Vischer, J.C. (1989), *Environmental quality in offices*. Van Nostrand Reinhold, New York.

Voordt, D.J.M. van der (1997), Housing and care variants for older people with dementia. Current trends in the Netherlands. *American Journal of Alzheimer's Disease* 12(2), 84–92.

Voordt, D.J.M. van der (1998), Spatial implications of policy trends and changing concepts of housing and care for the elderly. In: J. Teklenburg, J. van Andel, J. Smeets and A. Seidel (eds), *Shifting balances, changing roles in policy, research and design*. Proceedings of IAPS 15. European Institute of Retailing and Services Studies, Eindhoven.

Voordt, D.J.M. van der, H.B.R. van Wegen (1990a), *Sociaal veilig ontwerpen* [Designing for safety]. Check list for developing and testing the built environment. Publications Office, Faculty of Architecture, Delft University of Technology.

Voordt, D.J.M. van der, H.B.R. van Wegen (1990b), Testing building plans for public safety: usefulness of the Delft checklist. *Netherlands Journal of Housing and Environmental Research* 5(2), 129–154.

Voordt, D.J.M. van der, H.B.R. van Wegen (1993), The Delft checklist on safe neighborhoods. *Journal of Architectural and Planning Research* 10(4), 341–356.

Voordt, D.J.M. van der, D. Vrielink (1987), *Kosten-kwaliteit wijkwelzijnsaccommodaties* [Cost v. quality in district welfare accommodation]. Delft University Press.

Voordt, D.J.M. van der, D. Vrielink, H.B.R. van Wegen (1998), Comparative floorplan-analysis in programming and architectural design. *Design studies* 18, 67–88.

Vos, P.G.J.C., G.P.R.M. Dewulf (1999), *Searching for data.* A method to evaluate the effects of working in an innovative office. Delft University Press.

Vos, P., T. van der Voordt (2002), Tomorrow's offices through today's eyes. Effects of innovation in the working environment. *Journal of Corporate Real Estate* 4(1), 48–65.

Wener, R. (1989), Advances in evaluation of the built environment. In: E. Zube and G. Moore (eds), *Advances in environment, behavior, and design*, Vol. 2. Plenum Press, New York.

Wijk, M., J.J. Drenth, M. van Ditmarsch (2003), *Handboek voor toegankelijkheid* [Accessibility manual], 5th edn. Elsevier Bedrijfsinformatie, Doetinchem.

Zeisel, J. 1981), *Inquiry by design. Tools for environment-behavior research.* Brooks/Cole Publishing Company, Monterey, California.

Zimring, C. (1987), Evaluation of designed environments: methods for post-occupancy evaluation. In: R. Bechtel and W. Michelson (eds), *Methods in environmental and behavioural research.* Van Nostrand Reinhold, New York.

Zimring, C. (1988), Post-occupancy evaluation and implicit theories of organizational decision-making. In: H. van Hoogdalem et al., (eds), *Looking back to the future.* Proceedings of IAPS 10. Delft University Press, 240–248.

Zimring, C., J. Reitzenstein (1980), Post-occupancy evaluation: an overview. *Environment and Behaviour* 12(4), 429–450.

CHAPTER **6**

Quality assessment: methods of measurement

6.1 Criteria for functional quality

People involved in programming, designing and evaluating buildings are in general concerned to achieve the best possible quality in the circumstances, subject to limiting conditions such as time, money, legislation and regulations. It is therefore essential to be clear what quality means, what level of quality is wanted and how this level can be translated into spatial performance requirements and design solutions. This chapter presents a number of criteria for *developing* and *testing* plans (programme of requirements, structural design, provisional design and definitive design) and realised buildings, with the emphasis on functional quality.

A functional building is a building that is suitable for the activities for which it was intended. The people inside the building must be able to function efficiently, comfortably, healthily and safely. This means that people must be able to reach and get into the building easily and move round the building comfortably. The building must be sufficiently in harmony with human perceptions – in the way it looks, sounds, smells and feels. People must also feel physically comfortable, which means that the building must not be too hot or too cold nor must it be dirty, dark or noisy. People must be able to see how the parts of the building fit together and able to find their way round. All kinds of psychological needs must be taken care of, e.g. the need for privacy, social contact, freedom of choice and autonomy. The building must also be capable of being adjusted to suit changing circumstances, new activities and different users.

With this as a basis, the concept of functional quality can be divided into nine aspects:

a. Reachability and parking facilities
b. Accessibility
c. Efficiency
d. Flexibility
e. Safety
f. Spatial orientation
g. Privacy, territoriality and social contact
h. Health and physical well-being
i. Sustainability.

Aspects a–d relate mainly to the user value of the building (Is it easy to use?), f and g to psychological well-being, h to physical well-being and i to environmental quality. Safety embraces several aspects: utilitarian, psychological and physical. The nine aspects are to some extent interconnected. For example, accessibility and safety are preconditions for efficiency, and reachability and spatial orientation are preconditions for psychological accessibility.

Details of these nine aspects are presented below in a standard format:

- A description or definition of the concept.
- Thoughts about how to achieve a spatial translation of this aspect of quality and what design techniques can be used to achieve the anticipated user value.
- Sources for further reading, e.g. about tools for measuring particular aspects of quality, interesting research findings and 'exemplary' applications.

A. Reachability and parking facilities

Reachability is the ease with which people can get to the building as a whole and to its separate entrances. Internal reachability (of individual rooms and services) is a component of accessibility. The distinction between regular users and occasional visitors (e.g. clients) will often be relevant. A further distinction can be made between reachability by public transport (plane, ship, train, tram, metro or taxi) and by private transport (car, cycle or on foot, perhaps with some aid to mobility – a wheelchair, walking frame or pushchair).

Criteria for reachability are presented in detail in such publications as the *Real Estate Norm* (REN) for industrial buildings and the *Real Estate Norm Quick Scan* for office buildings. The REN distinguishes four criteria:

1. Reachability by goods vehicles and private cars
2. Reachability by public transport
3. Distribution channels (airport, seaport, inland port or railway)
4. Reachability in case of disaster (fire brigade, ambulance)

Each criterion is operationalised by two or more indicators. Indicators of reachability by public transport include nearness to a railway station, type of railway station and nearness of bus, tram or metro stops serving lines that connect to a railway station (Box 6.1).

Box 6.1   REN reachability criteria

1. Reachability by goods vehicles and private cars:

- Distance to the nearest motorway
- Distance to the nearest motorway intersection
- Traffic flow and presence of obstacles (traffic jams, traffic lights, bridges, level crossings)
- Nature of the route connecting the site to the motorway

2. Reachability by public transport:

- Distance to the nearest railway station
- Number and nature of connections (local train, Intercity, international)
- Walking distance to the nearest bus, tram or metro stop serving a line which connects to a railway station

3. Distribution channels:

- Distance to an airport for goods transport
- Distance to a seaport for goods transport
- Distance to an inland port for goods transport
- Distance to a rail trans-shipment point

4. Disaster:

- Fire brigade response time
- Ambulance response time

Each indicator is assessed on a five-point scale, ranging from 1 (unfavourable) to 5 (highly favourable). The following scale might be used for the nearness of a bus, tram or metro stop or the walking distance to the nearest stop serving a line which connects to a railway station:

1. $1 = 500$ m or more
2. $2 = 300–500$ m
3. $3 = 200–300$ m
4. $4 = 100–200$ m
5. $5 =$ less than 100 m

The REN does not go into the frequency of service provided by public transport nor the times at which the service begins and ends. Nor does it go into measurement criteria for reachability by people with mobility aids. For more details on this last point the reader is referred to the *Handboek voor Toegankelijkheid* [Accessibility manual] and *NEN 1814, Toegankelijkheid van gebouwen en buitenruimten* [Accessibility of buildings and outside areas].

Parking facilities

Once the user or visitor has reached the building he or she will often want to be able to park. At site level the REN checks both for public parking (number of public parking places for private cars and goods vehicles within a radius of 200 m) and for parking facilities on the building's own grounds (nature of the facilities, capacity and dimensions). A five-point scale is used for parking capacity for office buildings for private cars, expressed in terms such as the number of parking places on the building's own grounds per m^2 of gross floor area:

1. $1 = 1:200$ or less
2. $2 = 1:150$ to $1:200$
3. $3 = 1:100$ to $1:150$
4. $4 = 1:50$ to $1:100$
5. $5 =$ more than $1:50$

The zoning plan often includes a parking norm, related to the type of location (A, B or C) and expressed as 'one parking place per so many m^2 GFA', 'one place per so many FTE' or 'one place per so many employees'. In an attempt to reduce environmental pollution, local authorities sometimes attempt to reduce mobility and therefore specify the maximum capacity rather than the minimum. Parking norms will differ according to the particular local authority or private client involved.

B. Accessibility

The accessibility of a building can be described as good if regular users and anticipated visitors have no difficulty in getting to their destinations, are able to participate in the anticipated activities and can use the facilities required for the purpose. Accessibility breaks down into two components: physical accessibility and psychological accessibility.

a.   Physical accessibility

It is usual to distinguish three components of physical accessibility:

- Reachability: the ease with which users and visitors can get to the front of the building.
- Accessibility in the narrow sense: the ease with which people and goods can get into the building (Figures 6.2 and 6.3).
- Usability: the ease with which people are able to move through the building and make use of the rooms and services intended for them.

It is important to take the variability of human characteristics into account when dimensioning and designing passageways and bridging different levels. People have different builds, strengths and stamina. Some people use aids to mobility; others walk behind a pushchair or carry heavy shopping or other luggage. In this context, concepts are used such as 'design for all' or 'universal design': the built environment must be accessible and usable by everyone, regardless of physical and mental capacity or limitations (Preiser and Ostroff, 2001). In principle, every-one must be able to make equal and independent use of the built environment. Related expressions are 'access for all' and 'thinking inclusively', both of which require designs to be user friendly and ergonomically sound at all levels. Service features must be usable by all those for whom they were intended; slippery and uneven floors must be avoided (to prevent falls), counters must be neither too high nor too low, signing must be legible and understandable, etc.

In the Netherlands the criteria that an environment must satisfy to be usable by everyone are set out in detail in the *Handboek voor Toegankelijkheid* (Accessibility Manual) (Wijk et al., 2000) (Figure 6.1) and the standard *NEN 1814, Toegankelijkheid van gebouwen en buitenruimten* (Dutch Standards Institution, 2000). Most countries have similar guidelines. See for instance the ANSI Standard 117.1 of the American National Standards Institute (1992), and the Americans with Disabilities Act Accessibility Guidelines (ADAAG). Most stan-dards contain dimensional criteria, performance requirements and performance specifications relating to:

- Minimum clear passage required for doors and corridors.
- Manoeuvring space required for turning round and changing direction, also by people with luggage or wheeled equipment (shopping trolley, pushchair, tea trolley, wheelchair or walking frame).
- Bridging over differences in levels (riser/tread ratio for stairs, passenger lift, chair lift, lifting platform, ramp).

173

Operating height

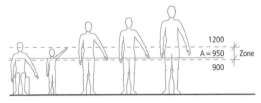

A = correct height for installing items such as door knobs, light switches, operating features for a public telephone or lift

Zone = range of heights within which items should be installed when they cannot be fitted at exactly the correct operating height (A)

Maximum reach   **Clearance**

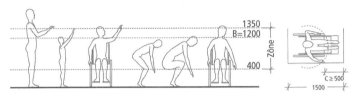

B = correct height for installing clothes hooks, bookshelves, etc.

Zone = range of heights within items should be installed when they cannot be fitted at exactly the correct height (B)

C = clearance required for any operating features fitted in a corner

Height, cross-section and operating clearance for handrails

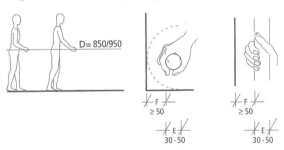

D = correct height for installing handrails

E = suitable diameter for handrails

F = clearance between a handrail or handle and its surroudings

Figure 6.1 Selected dimensional standards from the *Manual for accessibility*.

■ Optimum height of work surfaces, coat hooks, wall cupboards.
■ Facilities for people with a visual or auditory handicap.

Besides reachability, accessibility and usability, it is important for people to be able to escape quickly or to take an alternative route in the event of danger.

Figure 6.2 A building with good accessibility. In 1999 the Social Affairs and Employment Department of the city of Rotterdam published the report *Over de drempel* [Over the threshold]. This investigation into Rotterdammers' experiences with accessibility in their city showed that the city library scored high for accessibility. The wide revolving doors provide good accessibility for everyone, including wheelchair users and people with pushchairs. Within the building, good accessibility is ensured by lifts and escalators.

The term sometimes used in this connection is 'egressability'. It must be possible to close off routes to people and goods in the event of disaster.

b. Psychological accessibility

Psychological accessibility is the extent to which a building 'invites' a potential user or visitor to come inside and makes the building and its individual rooms and

(a)

Figure 6.3 (a and b) A building with poor accessibility. Neither the cultural centre (a) nor the new NEN building (b), both in Delft, honour the principle 'building for everyone'. It is true that someone had the idea of putting special parking places right by the entrance and that wheelchair users can get to the main entrance of the NEN building by means of a lifting platform, but it would have been preferable to provide simple access for everyone, without the need for additional arrangements for special categories.

equipment simple to use. Emotional aspects play a part – Do people feel welcome? Is the building a pleasant place to be in or do people find particular spots repellent? – as do cognitive aspects – Can people find their way round easily? Is the layout simple to understand? Relevant features include a recognisable entrance, possibilities for 'previewing' and obvious breaks between public and private areas. It is often intended that some or all of a building should *not* be accessible – physically or psychologically – to everyone. This can be achieved by technical devices (e.g. burglar-proof hinges and locks, alarm systems) or by legal devices (e.g. forbidding entrance to unauthorised visitors). Sometimes, inaccessibility can be an unintended side effect. For example, consider the inaccessibility of an imposing staircase, designed to give the impression of power or grandeur. When the accessibility of a building is being evaluated, attention should also be paid to any possible unintentional inaccessibility.

Figure 6.3 Continued.

As far as we know, the criterion of psychological accessibility has never been completely worked out anywhere in measurable units, although there are checklists and lists of attention points which deal with certain aspects of the criterion. This applies particularly to the cognitive aspect of legibility of the building in relation to spatial orientation and all those aspects that bear on physical and psychological well-being (safety, distinction between public and private, perception of the interior climate). Each of these aspects is treated separately below.

C. Efficiency

A building, or a design for building, is efficient if it serves the purpose, i.e. its intended use. People also talk about functional efficiency as against constructional or economic efficiency. Functional efficiency requires not only an efficient programme, i.e. a suitable supply of activities and favourable legal and economic conditions, but also that the building is spatially and architecturally efficient, i.e. that the anticipated activities are effectively and efficiently supported. 'Effective' here means 'doing the right things'. As applied to buildings, this means making design choices that will provide optimum support for the desired activities, maximising the extent to which the aims of the organisation are realised. 'Efficient' means 'doing things well'. It has to do with achieving one's goal without using more resources than necessary. As applied to organisations, 'efficient' means achieving the optimum ratio between a company's output and the input in terms of labour, energy and other resources.

The main criteria for the efficiency of a building are:

- A location that is favourable to the purpose of the building. A favourable location provides suitable routes for people and goods arriving and departing, adequate parking facilities and synergy effects produced by the proximity of interesting functions and facilities. Figure 6.4 shows an example of efficiency in a nursing home ward.
- Adequate access arrangements in the building as a whole (logical location of the entrance or entrances, adequate facilities for moving between floors, clear traffic routes, sufficient capacity in corridors, stairs and lifts) and for individual rooms (doors which open in a convenient direction, no traffic routes through occupied areas, etc.).
- An efficient layout, e.g. short walking distances because related functions are grouped near one another, locating functions requiring natural light against an outside wall, maintaining a clear hierarchy between public and private space, providing separate zones for different levels of activity and different temperatures.
- Sufficient floor area to allow all the desired activities to be carried out. This applies both to the building as a whole and to the separate rooms, traffic space, space for technical services and constructional space. An important attention point is the space required to stand and use furniture, whether fixed or mobile.
- Sufficient vertical dimensions: ceiling height, clear headroom for doors, height of worktops, working surfaces and kitchen cupboards.
- Functional use of colours and materials to support spatial orientation, recognisability and identity, cleaning and maintenance and technical maintenance.
- Adequate equipment and arrangement of water and electricity, sanitary facilities, sun blinds, blackout facilities where necessary.
- Sufficient plant and services and careful materialisation and detailing of separations between spaces (partition walls, outside skin) to achieve the desired physical conditions (temperature, humidity, clean air, light, noise).

Like 'functionality', 'efficiency' is a term that covers a multitude of different aspects. Reachability, accessibility, safety and flexibility are all essential preconditions for an efficient building. Because of their importance, these aspects are treated separately below.

D. Flexibility

We live in a dynamic society. Organisations are constantly subject to change, caused for example by expansion or contraction. Functions become outdated and are discarded. New functions are added. As time goes by, existing activities

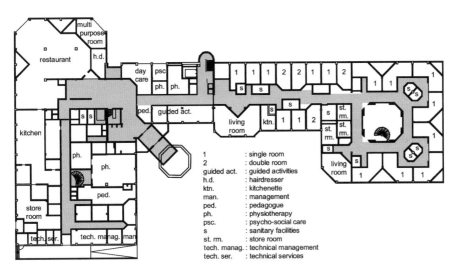

Figure 6.4 Example of an efficiently laid out floor plan. The ground floor of the St. Elisabeth Nursing Home, Amersfoort. The clear zoning of common facilities (left) and a nursing department (right) means short walking distances between activities that belong together and simplifies spatial orientation. The positioning of the sanitary facilities in the nursing department means short walking distances between bedrooms and bathrooms. A degree of separation can be seen on the right of the picture between the semi-public pedestrian area and the space used for more private traffic (the 'pyjama passage') between single rooms and bathrooms.

are often organised differently. Quality requirements change under the influence of new legislation and regulations, economic or technological developments, changes in use, etc. Buildings, on the other hand, are relatively static. According to Brand (1994), a building can be considered as composed of six components that vary dramatically in their longevity: site (permanent); structure (30–300 years); skin (20 years); services (7–15 years); space plan (3–30 years); and the building's content. To deal with dynamism, buildings must be flexible, both *internally* (within the building) and *externally* (capable of expansion and contraction), preferably without having to do much in the way of breaking down walls and without incurring high costs. This will increase the future value of the building. Not surprisingly, many programmes of requirements give high priority to the requirement for flexibility. Arguments are sometimes advanced in favour of function-neutral buildings, suitable for a large number of very different functions, but because function and form are always interrelated this seems to be going rather too far.

A number of other terms are related to flexibility in one way or another, some more or less synonymous, others distinguished by the extent to which the assistance of a builder is required to adjust the building to meet new require-ments (Tables 6.1 and 6.2, and Figure 6.5). The terms most frequently used are listed below:

- *Flexible*: easily adjusted to suit changing circumstances.
- *Adjustable*: the same, whether or not concentrating on a particular target group. In house building, adjustable or 'adaptable building' is often defined as 'not spe-cially adapted in advance or intended for people with disabilities, but designed in such a way that later adaptation can be done easily and relatively cheaply as and when the occupier becomes handicapped'.
- *Changeable*: made so that it can be changed if so desired.
- *Variable*: allowing changes to be made to dimensions, form, location, etc.; the opposite of fixed. Also defined as 'capable of being adjusted without exorbitantly high costs by the movement, removal or addition, by a builder, of non-load-bearing architectural elements.
- *Multifunctional*: suitable or able to be made suitable for different functions without requiring changes to the structure or built-in features.
- *Polyvalent*: capable of being adjusted to changes or differences in user prefer-ences or needs by changing the relationships between different spaces without the assistance of a builder (e.g. by the use of sliding doors or folding partitions).
- *Neutral*: capable of being adjusted to changes without changing the location of the various functions and without the architectural elements required by those functions needing to be moved, removed or augmented. Examples include:

Table 6.1 Conceptual framework for flexibility of buildings in the use phase

Flexibility of:	Change requires:		
	No building operations	Moderate building operations not requiring the use of a builder	Building operations requiring the use of a builder
Arrangement of rooms	Arrangement neutrality Multifunctionality	Arrangement flexibility	Arrangement variability
Room boundaries	Polyvalent room boundaries	Flexible room boundaries	Variable room boundaries
Division of the building	Division neutrality Shell neutrality Function neutrality	Division flexibility Spatial flexibility Constructional flexibility	Division variability Variability of the shell

Source: Boerman et al. (1992).

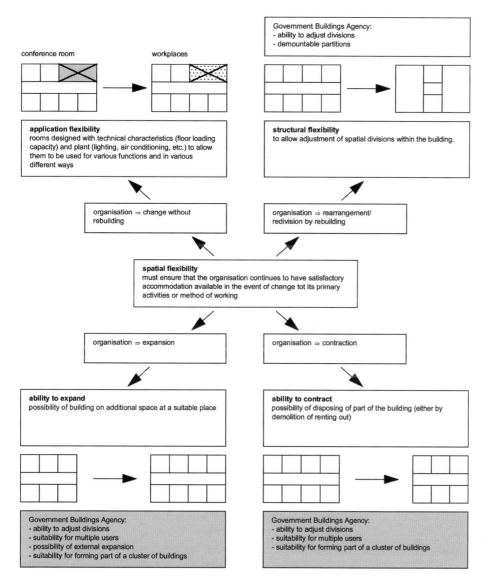

Figure 6.5 Examples of flexible solutions. Source: Lotze (1997, based on Nicolai and Dekker, 1991).

- *Layout neutrality*: the possibility of laying out rooms in different ways.
- *Division neutrality*: the possibility of dividing up a building in different ways.
- *Functional neutrality*: the possibility of giving a building a different function.
- *Shell neutrality*: the possibility of incorporating different floor plans in the same shell or achieving different arrangements within the same shell.

Table 6.2 Examples of design techniques for incorporating flexibility

Technique	Description
Arrangement neutrality	Extra floor area Generous length/breadth ratio Sufficient wall length to allow for furnishing units Extra ceiling height Extra electrical outlets Movable fittings
Arrangement flexibility	Demountable fittings
Arrangement variability	Provisions for future wiring
Polyvalent room boundaries	Sliding doors, sliding partitions, folding partitions
Flexible room boundaries	Movable or demountable partitions
Variable room boundaries	Removable partitions
Division neutrality	Division neutral spaces Neutral parapet height Wall finish to suit several functions Sound installation to suit several functions Extra wiring and services Zoning
Division flexibility	Separation of load-bearers from inbuilt features Demountable walls, elevation, roof Generous grid size for the shell Over-dimensioning of load-bearing structure
Division variability	Removable walls, elevation, roof Demountable wiring, placed accessibly Alternative methods of attaching walls/elevation Avoidance of differences in floor levels Neutral, flexible or variable shell Space or facilities for later addition of a lift

Sources: Boerman et al. (1992) and Geraedts and Cuperus (1999).

The cost of any measures taken to achieve flexibility must of course be carefully weighed against the benefit, i.e. savings on later adjustments.

E. Safety

The following types of safety can be distinguished:

- User or ergonomic safety: the least possible chance of falls, being trapped, or injured.

- Public safety: subjective (a feeling of safety) and objective (little risk of any criminal offence).
- Fire safety: the least possible chance of fire (prevention) and, if fire does break out, little likelihood of it spreading rapidly; a rapid response from the fire brigade, adequate fire fighting equipment and ways to escape quickly and safely.
- Constructional safety: a load-bearing structure with sufficient strength, rigidity and stability.
- Traffic safety: the safest possible transportation of people and goods, horizontally and vertically. Traffic safety *in* buildings falls under user safety.
- Chemical safety: the least possible chance of explosion or escape of dangerous materials (e.g. in laboratories or factories); protection against air, water and ground pollution.

Fire safety criteria include such things as the presence of smoke detectors, use of fire-resistant materials, compartmentalisation of the building, easily recognisable escape routes and the availability of a fire safety plan. Criteria for constructional safety are mainly concerned with the load-bearing properties and durability of the structure. Chemical safety imposes requirements such as safe storage of dangerous materials and shielding of hazardous spaces. For the purposes of this book, we consider these aspects to be too technical for further attention here, and instead concentrate on user safety and public safety.

User safety

Apart from factors personal to the individual, such as reduced mobility, limited vision or a tendency to giddiness, user safety is also affected by environmental factors, e.g. slippery floors, lack of support on stairs and in traffic areas (banisters, handrails), steep steps, obstacles such as high thresholds or dangerous projections, insufficient lighting and inadequate management of space. The significant contribution made to user safety by good accessibility means that publications dealing with accessibility are also relevant to safety checks. In summary, the main points are:

- Safely accessible rooms (no obstacles, e.g. high thresholds).
- Safe passageways (sufficient clear space, no risk of getting trapped).
- Avoidance of sharp edges and corners.
- Safe stairways (favourable riser/tread ratio, banisters, non-slip treads).
- Handrails and banisters where appropriate.
- Level, non-slip floor finishes.
- Unsafe places screened off.
- Sufficient illumination.
- Avoidance of loose leads.
- No glass (or use of safety glass instead of ordinary glass) at vulnerable points.

■ Function-specific measures, e.g. in hospitals and nursing homes, thermostatic taps to avoid scalding, safe bedside tables, foldaway seats in showers and lifts, measures to prevent demented patients wandering off, easily operated system to call a nurse.

Public safety

A building is safe for the public when people can use it without being or feeling threatened. People in buildings can suffer (or be afraid of suffering) violence, indecent assault, robbery, vandalism, theft or burglary. Detailed public safety criteria are given in the *Checklist – Sociaal veilig ontwerpen* [Checklist – Designing for public safety] (Van der Voordt and Van Wegen, 1990), published by Delft University of Technology. The basic principle underlying this checklist is that the chance of (or fear of) criminality is greater when there are one or more potential offenders present, the victim is attractive or vulnerable and the environment provides insufficient barriers between offender and victim. The checklist divides measures that can be taken at the design stage or by management once the building is in use into five groups (Figure 6.6):

■ presence of protective eyes ('social control')
■ visibility
■ attractiveness of the environment
■ involvement of users in 'their' environment
■ accessibility and escape routes.

'Social control' means the actual or probable presence of people who are expected to get involved if the need arises. Taken together with 'visibility', the requirement can be expressed as 'sight and supervision' or 'see and be seen'. People feel safer and more in control of the situation when they have a clear view of their surroundings and can themselves be seen by others, because this allows them to anticipate possible dangers, take an alternative route, take flight or call for help. Being seen gives one the confidence or at least the hope that in the event of threat some third party will get involved, either directly (e.g. by stopping potential offenders behaving aggressively) or indirectly (by calling for help or warning the police). Seeing and being seen increases the chance that offenders will be caught, which reduces both the feeling of insecurity and the level of criminal behaviour.

Attractiveness and involvement are important factors in designing a psychological threshold for potential offenders. Accessibility and escape routes relate to physical thresholds, and affect safety in two ways. It is important both to restrict physical access by undesirables and to ensure that potential victims are able to escape from a threatening situation. This demands a careful balance between accessibility and enclosure.

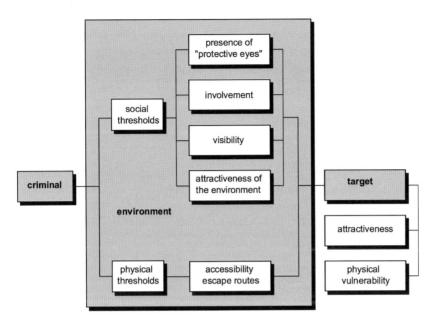

Figure 6.6 The built environment as intermediary between potential offender and victim. A well-designed and carefully managed built environment encourages positive behaviour and can contribute to the creation of physical and psychological barriers between potential offenders and their victims.

The Delft *Checklist – Sociaal veilig ontwerpen* distinguishes two types of measure:

- Techno-prevention (i.e. prevention by technical means): reinforcement, burglar-proof locks and hinges, security lighting.
- Socio-prevention (i.e. prevention by social means): the actual or probable presence of people who are expected to get involved if the need arises. Possible ways of achieving this include functions that will attract the public, surveillance and proper management (e.g. the prompt removal of graffiti and repair of damage).

Many measures use methods which are both technical and social, e.g. an alarm button with an intercom connection or a surveillance camera.

F. Spatial orientation

In general, people feel happier when the layout of a building is understandable. An understandable layout makes it easier for people to know where they are and how to get where they want to be. In a complex building it is harder to work out one's position and the right way to go. A well-designed building, on the other hand, can make a significant contribution to one's spatial orientation.

In his classic work *The image of the city,* the urban designer Kevin Lynch (1960) developed clear criteria for the legibility of towns and districts. He recommended the application of identity, structure and meaning. *Identity* is a quality in itself, referring to the recognisability of an object as a separate unit, distinguishable from other objects. Identity plays an important role in supporting spatial orientation and can contribute to emotional and cultural values. For example, the Eiffel Tower defines the image of Paris: this distinctive feature makes the city uniquely recognisable anywhere in the world. *Structure* refers to the way objects relate to one another and the position occupied by individual objects in an interrelated whole. Simple structures are easier to recognise, comprehend and remember than complicated structures, and so are simpler to find one's way round. *Meaning* refers to the relationship, practical and psychological, between an object and its user. Here one might think of affective values (attractive or unattractive, beautiful or ugly), emotional significance (e.g. the pleasant or painful memories associated with a particular place), symbolic value (e.g. the association of a tall building with commerce or the power of big business) and cultural or historic significance. Lynch believes that spaces are particularly legible when all three ingredients are present to a sufficient extent.

Lynch used these concepts as a basis for a number of urban design principles, which can equally well be used for buildings. For instance, whereas cities have an urban structure, buildings have also a spatial structure, with corridors analogous to streets, rooms analogous to small buildings, and atria or meeting places analogous to squares. Here, too, paths create the layout, the sequence of spaces and events and the skeleton of the building. With the layout, a structure is given to the sequence of experiences, to the relationship within the building and to the relationship between building and context.

Combining Lynch's principles with the insights of Paul and Passini (1992) and Van der Voordt (2001) results in the following list of attention points and criteria for developing and checking plans:

- Clear overall shapes and easily understandable access routes.
- Recognisable functional units.
- Individual identities for rooms as regards function, design and layout (fittings, lighting, choice of colours and materials), avoiding the repetition of identical departments and rooms.
- Clear distinction between public, semi-public and private spaces.
- Differentiation by colours and materials used for floors, walls and ceilings.
- Sufficient points of recognition: signposts and 'natural' elements such as conspicuous functions, street furniture or works of art.

Box 6.2   Gestalt laws

a. Figure/background principle: an element is more easily visualised when it is recognisable as a separate figure against a wider background.

b. Law of proximity: the smaller the space or time interval between two or more elements, the stronger the tendency to group those elements and see them as a single object.

c. Law of similarity: two or more similar objects are perceived and recalled as belonging together. The objects can be similar in form, colour or material usage for example, but also in their non-physical properties such as function.

d. Law of continuation: elements situated in a continuous line can readily be perceived as a unit.

e. Law of simplicity of shape: when perceiving or recalling, people tend to reduce complicated perceptual stimuli to simple geometrical shapes. For example, a square with a minor indentation will be remembered as a simple square, an almost complete circle will be remembered as complete. Shapes that are already simple will therefore be easy to remember.

■ Application of Gestalt principles (Box 6.2), e.g.:

- Singularity: unique properties which give an element an identity of its own.
- Continuity: characteristics produced by continuation, where separate elements are perceived and visualised as a coherent whole.
- Dominance: the way one element predominates because of its size or importance.

■ Kinaesthetic qualities: formal properties which create a feeling of movement, e.g. a sharp turn or a right angle.

■ Directional clarity: spatial characteristics which show the direction in which one is going, e.g. a difference in design between the two sides of a corridor, or the use of ornamental paving to indicate direction.

■ Extending 'visual scope' by viewing holes and visible connections.

■ Extra support at important decision points (where a choice has to be made between turning right or left or going to a different floor), e.g. by hanging up a stylised floor plan with a 'you are here' mark and the most important functions shown in different colours.

■ Proper signing, with good colour contrast between symbols or letters and background, clearly specified names, combinations of simple recognisable symbols and texts, and repetition of information (Figure 6.7).

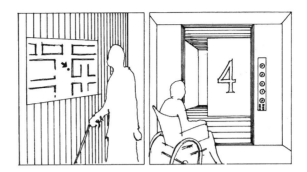

Figure 6.7 Signposting in a hospital: simplified map and floor indications.

- Consistent information, e.g. consistent use of colours and pictograms to indicate similar places, both in the rooms themselves and in information about the underground space (brochures, information panels).
- Organisational measures, e.g. a reception desk or information point.

G. Privacy, territoriality and social contact

The built environment plays an important role in maintaining or avoiding social contact. An environment can stimulate contact by providing favourable physical and social conditions. The converse also occurs: an environment which generates too much contact may be perceived as too crowded; where there is too little contact, people may find themselves socially isolated. Osmond (1966) spoke of spaces as 'sociopetal' (encouraging contact) or 'sociofugal' (encouraging contact-avoiding behaviour) (Figure 6.8).

A good deal has been written, particularly in the 1960s and 1970s, about the relationship between space and social contact. In *The hidden dimension*, by the American anthropologist Edward Hall, published in 1966, a relationship is established between the way people behave towards one another and the spatial environment. Hall introduced the term 'proxemics', an umbrella term for the spatial environment as a device for regulating social interaction. He distinguished three components:

- Privacy: control of access by others to one's own person.
- Personal space: the invisible area ('space bubble') round one's body into which others are not routinely admitted.
- Territoriality: making an area one's own personal property and protecting it against or shielding it from others.

Privacy

Privacy can be seen as the personal control and selective management of access to oneself or one's own group (Altman, 1975). Definitions of privacy

Figure 6.8 Example of a sociofugal space. In this Paris metro station the space between the seats literally distances people from one another. Users create extra space by occupying alternate seats, a form of behaviour which illustrates an underlying need for privacy and territoriality. Conversely, the probability of contact decreases.

often emphasise the elements of separation and control. In essence, however, privacy is about self-determination and freedom of choice in accepting or avoiding contact with other people. In the ideal situation an optimal balance is maintained between being inward-looking and being outward-looking. In the best case there is congruence between the degree of privacy available and the degree of privacy desired (Altman, 1975). Too much privacy or too little contact leads to loneliness and social isolation. Too little privacy, on the other hand, leads to irritation, feelings of discomfort, stimulus overload and crowding (Figure 6.9). Westin (1970) pointed out the importance of privacy to the opportunity for emotional outlet (crying, laughing, screaming) and self-evaluation. Privacy gives the individual the opportunity to process his experiences and think about his future behaviour. Thus, privacy also satisfies the need to process and interpret information gained from contact with others and so determine the relationship between oneself and those others.

Three forms of privacy can be distinguished (see also Figure 6.10):

- Visual privacy: freedom of choice about whether to see others or be seen by others.

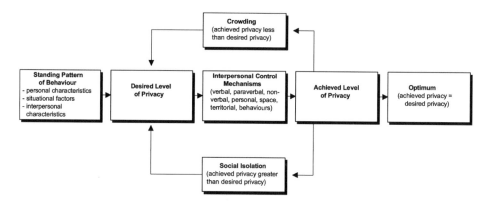

Figure 6.9 Irwin Altman's privacy model.

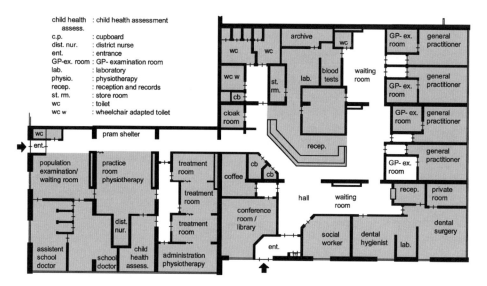

Figure 6.10 Privacy (and lack of privacy) in a health centre. The spatial conditions in the health centre in the illustration are not favourable to privacy. a. Auditory: insufficient sound insulation means that conversations can be followed almost word for word between different workspaces; the reception desk is so near to the waiting room that people waiting can overhear confidential conversations being held at the desk. b. Visual: the route between the examination rooms and the communal treatment room and consultation rooms runs through the waiting room, which means that waiting patients are regularly confronted by people carrying bottles of urine or blood samples. c. Territorial: when someone who has just been given bad news leaves the consulting room in tears, there is no alternative to leaving the centre through the waiting room. No more separate traffic space is available.

- Auditory privacy: not being disturbed by noise made by others or being unwillingly overheard by others.
- Social or territorial privacy: the ability to exercise personal control on social contacts by spatial connection or separation.

The desired level of privacy is achieved by psychological and spatial control mechanisms (Box 6.3). If someone feels that he is being looked at he can ask the other to look away or he can close the curtains. If someone is annoyed by loud

---

Box 6.3 Privacy in healthcare buildings

In the field of healthcare, things are often done which normally only take place in private, e.g. physical contact with patients, undressing before a stranger and carrying on confidential discussions. The stress that this creates calls for extremely discreet behaviour on the part of the professionals involved and the assurance of a sufficient level of privacy and respect to the boundary between 'I' and 'others'. Behaviour that crosses this boundary is subject to all kinds of limitations, mainly behavioural and culturally determined. There are for example all sorts of unwritten rules about what can and what cannot be asked or said, and about the circumstances in which a person may or may not touch another. The design and arrangement of the spatial environment plays an important role here. Different functions do of course call for their own furnishings and equipment. For example, a consultation room which is also used for confidential discussions demands a certain warmth in its furnishing and decoration. Surroundings of this kind are a less readily associated with a situation in which people get undressed to be examined. A more clinically equipped examination room, on the other hand, is more suggestive of the medical world, in which undressing is accepted as normal and necessary. For this reason many doctors prefer a clear separation between consultation rooms and examination rooms.

Apart from a discreet approach on the part of the professional involved and a proper arrangement of the room used, privacy can also be assured by a well laid out floor plan. For example, doors that are correctly placed relative to an examination table and that open the right way, can be very important to visual privacy. An important principle developed by Ruth Cammock (1977), an English doctor and architect, involves division into three zones:

1. Public zone: the area visited by patients and where patients spend some time, e.g. entrance hall, traffic spaces, waiting rooms and toilets.

(Continued)

191

2. Staff zone: the area used exclusively by professional staff and where confidential information is stored, e.g. the administrative department, private rooms, meeting rooms and the coffee room – places where people talk with one another, often in confidence, *about* the patient.
3. Interaction zone or meeting area: the area where contact take place between staff and patients. This is the area in which 'the public' become individual patients and 'the staff' become individual doctors and nurses, and where confidential discussions take place *with* the patient.

According to Cammock, assuring maximum privacy involves striving to achieve:

- a clear distinction between public, staff and interaction zones
- separate entrances to the public zone and the staff zone
- separate routes from the staff zone to the interaction zone and from the public zone to the interaction zone
- no direct connection between the public zone and the staff zone.

Source: Van Hoogdalem et al. (1985).

music on the radio coming in from outside, he can go and sit somewhere else (distance himself, literally), close the window (a spatial regulation mechanism) or politely ask the other to turn down the radio a bit (a social regulation mechanism). Examples of the regulation of territorial privacy include applying codes of conduct (hanging up a 'Do not Disturb' sign), defining one's own space and marking space as personal by making personal additions. In this way, one's surroundings are, as it were, 'appropriated' and so made more private.

Personal space and territorial behaviour

Altman (1975) described territorial behaviour as the regulation of the boundaries between one's own space and space belonging to others. Personalisation (making something one's own) indicates that a space belongs to a particular individual or group. In biology, the term 'territoriality' generally means territorial behaviour by animals. Animals appropriate a particular space and then defend it against intruders, often aggressively. Although generalising from animal behaviour to human activities is often unjustifiable, the terms and methods used in biology can equally well be used in the study of human behaviour and spatial relationships. For human beings territoriality means the need for a place of one's own, under one's own control, temporary or not, and to different degrees (Box 6.4).

Examples, in increasing order of privacy and permanence, are a reserved table in a restaurant, one's own workplace in the office, one's own room in a nursing home and one's own home.

Territoriality and personal space are closely related. Both terms deal with the distance between one individual and another. Territory is visible, reasonably static and tied to a particular location. Personal space on the other hand is invisible, mobile, tied to a particular individual and 'portable'. In his book *Personal Space*, Sommer (1969) developed the concept of personal space in more detail, showing how the mechanism can be recognised in the way people use the built environment. Hall, referred to earlier, distinguished four different types of distance used by people in their interactions with others, differing in the degree of intimacy and the amount and type of information exchanged:

- Intimate (0–15 cm)
  Characteristics: actual or potential bodily contact, perception of bodily odours, soft speech. This distance is observed for example between mother and child or between lovers. In public it is generally considered undesirable, but when it does occur, as for example in a metro, train or lift, defence mechanisms come into operation (turning one's head away, avoiding eye contact and standing perfectly still).
- Personal (45–75 cm, increasing to as much as 125 cm)
  At this distance (arm's length) it is still possible to touch somebody. There is no visual distortion. Details can be clearly perceived. Speech volume is moderate. Bodily heat is not perceptible. Personal conversations can take place.
- Social (125–200 cm)
  This distance is used for more impersonal conversations, for example at a reception.
- Public (3.5–7.5 m or more)
  At this distance the choice of spoken words and sentences is more careful. Voices are relatively loud. Details of skin, hair and eyes are no longer clearly visible. This distance is observed for example at a lecture or class. At still greater distances a microphone is necessary.

Box 6.4 Psychological effects of non-territorial offices

A typical feature of flexible workplace solutions is the combination of desk-sharing and desk-rotating. Personnel work here and there, irrespective of time and place. This provides some with a positive feeling of freedom while others find the constant need to switch a burden. Desk-sharing is at odds with the need for personalisation

(Continued)

and an individual territory. Users often try to claim a familiar place by arriving at work earlier or by leaving items behind during their absence. The same (flexible) workplace for everyone provides fewer opportunities to express one's status. Some employees are fairly laconic, whereas others make an issue of it. The principle of 'clean desk' makes personalisation (personalising the desk) difficult or outright impossible. Although personnel are able to deal with this properly in the long run, this is a negative point. The effect of flexible working on social interaction is a mixed one. The ability to choose one's desk is generally appreciated. Besides dynamics, it also provides people with the opportunity to establish new contacts. As a result, they can become better acquainted with less familiar colleagues and acquire new knowledge and experience: a significant point that is scored both from an individual perspective as well as for 'learning' organisations. At the same time, close contact between colleagues who sit close to each other and work well together may be unintentionally disrupted. Evaluation of the Interpolis office in Tilburg reveals that autonomy at work and informal contacts have increased while cooperation has improved. On the other hand, opportunities for formal contact have hardly changed. The same applies to opportunities for concentrated work and participation in decision-making. The 'person–office fit' (the extent to which the workplace is tailored to the personal needs and wishes of employees) is experienced in a far more positive manner than during the old situation. In spite of this, no improvement in general well-being could be measured. (Source: Van der Voordt, 2003.)

Design principles

The conceptual framework outlined above can be used to assist in the development and checking of plans to ensure they will achieve an optimum level of privacy and contact. Criteria for favourable spatial conditions include:

- recognisable distinction between areas which are public, semi-public and private
- places available to which people can go to be private, by themselves or with one or two others
- private areas with sufficient visual, auditory and territorial screening
- facilities for locking private rooms and storage spaces (cupboards, safes)
- meeting places for communal activities
- places whose location, design and arrangement encourage accidental, spontaneous meetings.

H.   Health and physical well-being

According to the World Health Organisation, health is not merely the absence of disease and infirmity but a state of optimal physical, mental and social well-being. Building characteristics may affect health and well-being in a positive or negative way by such things as light, noise, indoor air quality, colours and materials. The well-known studies of Ulrich (1984, 1991, 2000) show that views from a window may influence recovery of hospital patients. Later studies have been carried out into the positive effects of nice environments, leading to the so-called *healing environments* (Malkin, 1992; Hasking and Haggard, 2001; College Bouw Ziekenhuisvoorzieningen, 2002). For a summary of the effects see Table 6.3.

A special approach is designing according the principles of feng shui (Lip, 1997). This approach comes from China. The underlying hypothesis is that a right position of buildings, entrances and interior objects and the right use of colours and materials may support health and welfare. Right here: means the right use of energy: e.g. a mirror will reflect energy, a toilet stall absorbs all energy. A so-called ba-gua is used to understand how energy flows. Time also matters, according to the astrological calendar. On some days it is better not to start piling, because that will bring unhappiness.

A stream of studies has considered the negative effects of poorly designed environments and the *sick building syndrome (SBS)* (Hedge et al., 1986; Burge et al., 1987; Molhave, 1987; Valjborn, 1989; Norback et al., 1990; De Boo, 1990; Ryan and Morrow, 1992). In 1982 the World Health Organisation officially recognised SBS as a medical condition where people in a building suffer from symptoms or illness or feel unwell for no apparent reason. The symptoms tend to increase in severity with the time people spend in the building and improve over time or even disappear when people are away from the building. SBS results in substantial disruption of people's work performance and personal relationships and considerable loss of productivity (Clements-Croome, 2000). Below, a brief summary is given of a number of regulations and guidelines in the Netherlands with respect to health and prevention of illness.

Light

Environmental variables relating to lighting include the quality of the light (daylight, artificial light, sunlight), the quantity of light (to allow things to be seen properly and to avoid dazzle and excessive contrast between light and dark), the direction of the light and the colour of the light. Besides these stimulus-related characteristics, the properties of the surroundings also affect the way light is perceived: the way light is reflected (depending on colour and the material used) and the extent to which the users can influence the lighting themselves.

Table 6.3 Environmental effects on health and well-being

	Environmental factor	Proved favourable effect on health and welfare	Patients	Staff	Visitors	Neigh-bours
Light and view						
1	Good natural lighting	Faster recovery of biorhythm after an aesthesia; better physical condition	×			
		Better management of vitamins and minerals; 2–3% increase in productivity		×		
2	View of natural light	Better sense of time, weather and location	×	×	×	
3	Proper artificial lighting	Reinforcement of identity; improvement in atmosphere; increased security in and around buildings	×	×	×	×
		Increase in productivity		×		
4	Functional and ergonomic use of colour	Reduction in restless-ness; increase in character; recognition and sense of direction	×	×	×	
		Increase in productivity	×			
5	Quality of light	Improvement in atmosphere; support of function; relaxation	×	×	×	×
Atmosphere and identity						
6	Single patient's room	More privacy; less infection; faster recovery	×			
		Less movement of patients; reduced demand for support	×	×	×	

(*Continued*)

Table 6.3 Continued

	Environmental factor	Proved favourable effect on health and welfare	Patients	Staff	Visitors	Neighbours
7	Special-purpose room	Meeting; distraction; relaxation; regeneration; active recreation; cultural expression; reduced stress	×	×	×	
		Private conversations; privacy; mental relief	×	×	×	
		Reflection and prayer; mental relief; spiritual strength; consolation				
	Cellular offices (<4 persons)	Less disturbance; more concentration; 2–4% higher labour productivity		×		
8	Design suited to desired level of social interaction	Encouragement of meetings; distraction; relaxation or simply privacy; individuality	×	×	×	×
9	Integration of art	Relaxation; contemplation; appreciation of the organisation	×	×	×	
Sound and vibrations						
10	Peace and quiet, less noise pollution	Less sleep disturbance; fewer irritations; fewer stress and heart rhythm problems; faster recovery	×			
		Better concentration; less tiredness		×	×	
		Increase in productivity		×		
11	Individual choice of music	Distraction; relaxation; less need for painkillers	×			
Being self-handy						
12	Ring main for hearing aids	Increase of being self-handy; good information; relaxation	×	×	×	

(*Continued*)

Table 6.3 Continued

	Environmental factor	Proved favourable effect on health and welfare	Patients	Staff	Visitors	Neighb-ours
13	Personal control of sun blinds, heating, etc.	Increase in perceived control and being self-handy	×	×		
Air						
14	Locating sensitive facilities in less critical places	Less risk of transfer of infection; fewer problems with biological, physical and chemical contamination	×	×	×	
15	Separation of sources of contamination	Less risk of transfer of infection; fewer problems with biological, physical and chemical contamination	×	×	×	
16	Fewer sources of air pollution	Less irritation to airways; less infection; fewer smell problems	×			
		Lower risk of disease development in the long term	×	×		
		3–8% increase in prod-uctivity; considerable reduction in sick leave		×		
17	Flow from clean to foul	3–8% increase in prod-uctivity; considerable reduction in sick leave	×	×	×	
18	Pleasant smell	Positive impression of space; positive memory of stay	×	×	×	
Climate						
19	Internal environment uniformly good	Comfort; well-being; 10–15% gain in prod-uctivity; reduction in sick leave	×	×	×	

(*Continued*)

Table 6.3 Continued

	Environmental factor	Proved favourable effect on health and welfare	Patients	Staff	Visitors	Neighb-ours
Accessibility						
20	Good signing	Ability to find one's way round; increase in being self-handy	×		×	
21	Flat and non-slippery floors	Better sense of balance; safer movement; fewer accidental falls	×	×	×	
22	Entrance sheltered from wind and rain	Physical security; increased being self-handy	×	×	×	
Ergonomics						
23	Extra space for proper movement and use of aids for heavy work	Proper movement; fewer injuries and accidents; less sick leave; more work satisfaction	×	×		
24	Ergonomic sizing of workplaces	Correct posture; relaxation; fewer physical com-plaints; higher productivity	×	×		
25	Ergonomic sizing of routes	Unobstructed movement; fewer accidents; increase of physical and social privacy	×	×	×	
Green space						
26	Good access to parkland	Relaxation; recrea-tion; improvement in physical condition	×	×	×	
27	View of greenery + natural objects	Relaxation; regen-eration; appreciat-ion; faster physical recovery	×	×	×	

Sources: Adapted from Versteege and Van Heel (2004); see also Devlin and Arneill (2003).

Criteria to be used when developing or checking plans are laid down in various standards and guidelines, including the Dutch NEN standards and the Dutch Working Conditions Act [*Arbeidsomstandighedenwet* or Arbo]. For example, the Arbo states that rooms in which people spend a significant amount of time must satisfy the following requirements:

- total area of windows or openings admitting light, e.g. in an atrium or greenhouse, >1/20 of floor area
- total width of windows >1/10 of the room's perimeter; if total width <1/10 of the perimeter, the shortfall must be made good by extra window area.

These requirements for the admission of daylight do not apply to workspaces for staff members with many contacts (reception), enclosed spaces (conservatories) and rooms where the admission of daylight must be avoided (e.g. a photographic dark room). Rooms that are used less than 2 hours a day and rooms with a glass wall that borders on rooms that satisfy the stated requirements are also excluded. Sunblinds must be fitted to avoid discomfort from direct sunlight. Outside awnings are the most effective, because they protect against heat as well as sunlight. Further details can be found in the Dutch standard *NEN 3087, Visuele ergonomie in relatie tot verlichting* [Visual ergonomics in relation to lighting], which also provides guidelines for orientation lighting, the level of illumination required for workplaces and lighting requirements for people working with display screens (see also *ISO 9241, Ergonomische eisen voor kantoorarbeid met beeldschermen* [Ergonomic requirements for office work involving the use of display screens]).

Noise

Too much noise is distracting and reduces user value. Some rooms require special attention to be paid to ensuring that speech is intelligible. The level of background noise may not be too high, not more than something in the order of 30 dB for listening to speech or music, or 35 dB for telephone conversations or confidential discussions. The signal-to-noise ratio, i.e. the ratio of the strength of the signal (e.g. the speaker) and any interference or noise (e.g. background noise) is also important. A 1 dB improvement in the signal-to-noise ratio produces an immediate 15% improvement in intelligibility. Most people are able to follow a conversation without difficulty with a signal-to-noise ratio of -3 dB. It is also important to have a short reverberation time, i.e. the time taken for the level of sound some distance from the source to drop 60 dB after that source has been switched off abruptly. Reverberation time can be reduced by avoiding parallel walls and smooth, 'hard', sound-reflecting surfaces, and by the use of sound-absorbing material. Another design tool for creating quiet is spatial separation of quiet places from busy places. A ring main for people wearing hearing aids can be useful in a room where use is made of radio, television or film apparatus or microphones.

But a sound level that is too low can also create problems. In offices where several people work in the same room a certain level of background noise is desirable to ensure auditory privacy. For example, background noise can avoid a conversation being followed word for word by someone for whom it is not intended.

The Dutch Working Conditions Act also lays down a number of requirements relating to noise and acoustics. For example, the following figures show the maximum recommended noise levels for offices:

- conference room   35 dB
- small office   40 dB
- large office/drawing office   45 dB
- landscaped office   50 dB
- computer room   55 dB

Noise above 45 dB is distracting, causing loss of concentration and reduced intelligibility of speech. Ways of avoiding this include insulating the sound source (boxing it in, moving it to another room where people are not working all the time) and using sound-absorbent material. Noise above 80 dB is harmful and starts to become painful at 140 dB, a kind of level that can be found in workshops and factories but hardly ever in offices. High dB levels make it desirable to follow some kind of noise prevention plan, giving people information and instruction, providing ear protectors and taking other technical or organisational measures.

Interior climate

The physiological well-being of people who use or visit a building is affected by air temperature, the amount of radiant heat, the presence or absence of draughts and the relative humidity. Taken together, these variables determine the level of 'thermal comfort'. An attractive interior climate demands careful adjustment of the inside temperature to suit the activities which are taking place in the space in question (walking round, sitting still, coming in and going out), a satisfactory level of air humidity (ventilation), prevention of draughts and damp and the avoidance of cooling produced by excessively cold walls and floors in places where people spend a significant amount of time. Criteria to be used when developing or checking plans can be found in the Dutch NEN standards and the Dutch Working Conditions Act previously mentioned. For example, the following requirements have been laid down for the ventilation of rooms in use as offices:

- office already in use before 1 October 1990 $9 \times 10^{-3}\,m^3/sec\ per\,m^2$
- office that came into use after 1 October 1990 $1.2 \times 10^{-3}\,m^3/sec\ per\,m^2$

- office which is only used occasionally and which contains no equipment 10.0×10^{-3} m³/sec per room

The amount of fresh air required depends on the equipment in the room. Fax machines, laser printers, photocopiers, etc., can generate heat and harmful emissions. The level of emission is an important criterion when purchasing or replacing this kind of equipment. Another factor to be taken into account is the nature of the activities carried out and whether people smoke. The following guidelines apply:

- light work   at least 30 m³ fresh air per hour per person
- heavy work   at least 50 m³ fresh air per hour per person
- smoking areas   at least 10 m³ extra fresh air per hour per person

Relative humidity should preferably be in the range 30–70% (or better still 40–60%) to discourage the growth of microorganisms. Employees wearing contact lenses often have trouble if the air is too dry.

I. Sustainability

Apart from using flexibility as a means of anticipating future change, sustainability is another important aspect of future value. Sustainability is a prerequisite for future usability and quality of life. In the last decades there has been a growing awareness that ever-expanding economic growth cannot be sustained with the finite resources of planet earth. Human activities may lead to all kinds of environmental problems, such as air pollution, exhaustion of raw materials, global warming, acid rain and, in the long run, ecological disasters. In the early 1970s, three landmark publications came out: *The limits to growth* (Meadows et al., 1972), *Blueprint for survival* (Goldsmith, 1972) and *Small is beautiful* (Schumacher, 1973). In 1972 the United Nations organised its first conference on the human environment in Stockholm. In 1987 the World Commission on Environment and Development (WCED) published a report on *Our common future*, the so-called Brundtland Report. This report defined sustainable development as development that meets the needs of the present without compromising the ability of future generations to meet their own needs. The resolutions of the United Nations conference in Rio de Janeiro (1992) were collected in the so-called *Agenda 21*, which was signed by all participating nations. Nowadays there seems to be a widespread consensus of the need for long-term environmental strategies to achieve sustainable development.

In a narrow sense, sustainability focuses on environmental quality, i.e. energy, water, material, mobility and waste. In a wider sense, it's focus is on the three P's of Planet (environmental quality), Prosperity (economic quality, including profit, transparency, payability and honesty) and People (social quality, including health, safety, freedom, participation and livability) (see for instance Figure 6.11).

(a)

Figure 6.11   Commerzbank, Frankfurt, Germany. Design by Norman Foster
(1991–1997). (a–c) Norman Foster's Commerzbank is an example of
a sustainable, energy conscious design on the scale of a skyscraper.
At different levels of the buildings, winter gardens are situated,
which allow vast amounts of light to enter deep into the building
and also provide pleasant views to those working deeper within the
building. These gardens have different functions that contribute to
the well-being of the users. Operable facades create natural ventilation
throughout the entire structure.

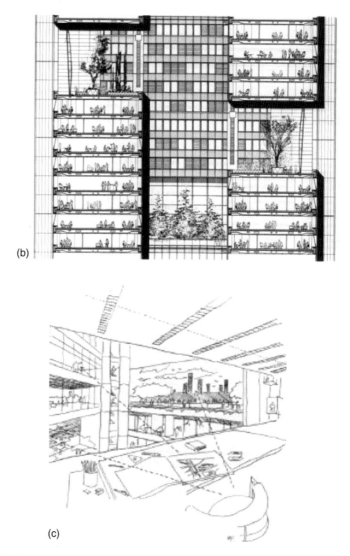

(b)

(c)

Figure 6.11 Continued.

According to Kees Duijvestein, a lecturer in sustainable building at the Delft Faculty of Architecture, sustainable building should take into account a fourth P, Project, with a focus on design quality (including issues such as beauty, biodiversity, robustness and relation through scales). In Delft, people from different disciplines work together in the Delft Interfaculty Research Centre 'The Ecological City', which is recently followed-up by an interfaculty research programme on sustainable urban transformations. Interesting deliverables from Delft are the manual 'Materials for Sustainable Urban Design' and the 'Environmental Maximisation Method', a design tool for town planners to take into account in a long-term ecological approach.

6.2 Methods of measurement

a. Questionnaires

A questionnaire is particularly suitable when a large and varied group of people are involved in the evaluation, since it provides a relatively cheap way of collecting a lot of information from a large number of people. Other advantages include the possibility of statistical analysis by computer, and anonymity, which means a reduction in the likelihood of bias (e.g. because certain answers are seen as socially desirable). Disadvantages include the limited opportunity for explanation and asking supplementary questions, and the chance of a low response. Attention points when preparing a questionnaire include logical construction, matching the questions to the level of knowledge of potential respondents, avoiding leading questions and internal checks on consistency and reliability.

b. Individual interviews

The special thing about an interview is that there is direct contact between the investigator and the respondent, which makes it is possible to clarify questions and answers and ask supplementary questions. Another advantage is the availability of non-verbal information, e.g. an irritated expression or a raised voice. Disadvantages include the increased chance of leading questions and evasive answers and the fact that the need for preparation, travelling time, administration and analysis makes interviews extremely labour-intensive and expensive. In most cases the answers received will not readily lend themselves to quantitative analysis.

c. Group interviews

This type of interviewing can save a good deal of time, because several people are spoken to at the same time. The opportunity that people have to react to one another can result in stimulating discussion, rich in information. As against this, group dynamics, – e.g. the presence of one or more dominant individuals, – can prevent every interviewee being given the same amount of attention, and conflicting opinions and interests can be suppressed. Thus, a good deal of attention needs to be paid to the size and composition of the group. Pitfalls include the chance of socially desirable answers and 'cognitive dissonance reduction', the phenomenon that people rationalise their opinions and behaviour to reduce the internally perceived conflict between the actual situation and the situation desired.

d. Observation

Observation is a good way of checking the reality of data derived from documents and discussions, getting one's own impression of the characteristics of the location and the building and collecting data about actual behaviour in a 'natural' setting or a more experimental situation. Examples include measurement of occupancy in office buildings, observation of pedestrian flows in shopping centres and analysis of activities by place and time (who does what, where and when – 'behavioural mapping'). Where necessary, observation can be supported by the use of measuring equipment, e.g. a measuring tape, photometer, hygrometer or sound-level meter. Observation, too, is expensive in time and money, and people's behaviour can be influenced by the presence of an observer. Another disadvantage is that it is generally impossible to see the motivation underlying the observed behaviour and the feelings that accompany it.

e. Documentation study

Interesting material will often be available in the form of a written programme of requirements, floor layouts, reports of site meetings, cost summaries and policy papers. A good deal of information can be derived from such documents without having to bother people with all sorts of questions. This method is relatively cheap and simple to organise. A possible disadvantage is that documents are not always readily accessible. A particular application of documentation study is the comparative floor plan analysis method (Van Hoogdalem et al., 1985). Comparison of a large number of floor plans of buildings with more or less the same function makes it possible to develop a typology of solution variants. Discussion of solution variants with users and others involved can provide an insight into the advantages and disadvantages for use and management. A combination of comparative floor plan analysis and the evaluation of a few representative cases is an excellent way of developing materials for programming and design (Van der Voordt et al., 1998).

f. Workshops

Workshops are in fact a type of group discussion with the important advantage of intensive interaction between researchers and researched. Workshops can use small tasks, brainstorming sessions, roll play, etc., and are well suited to ex ante valuation, generating ideas for the programme and design and spotting potential bottlenecks in good time. Workshops can be supported by modern audiovisual techniques, such as 'decision rooms', in which computers are used to create digital inventories of anonymous opinions and ideas, allowing participants to react to one another's positions or statements.

g. Field trips

Field trips can be excellent for ex ante evaluations, as a way of generating ideas and comparing one's own (provisional) decisions with reference projects. Field trips are also often used in preparation for the choice of architect. Although it is less usual, field trips can equally well be used for ex post evaluation, e.g. to get a better understanding of other solution variants with which to compare one's own situation.

h. Virtual reality

In addition to the huge variety of response methods to measure perception and use of buildings, there are also a number of methods to present the stimulus, i.e. the building in question, to the respondents: directly, on site, or indirectly, by means of drawings, pictures, photos, full-scale mock-ups, small-scale models, computer models and so on. Particularly in ex ante research, the use of virtual reality techniques may be helpful. Of course there is always the question as to what extent responses to representations of the real world are valid and reliable indicators of responses to the real world itself. Psychological research has shown that spatial information through three-dimensional visualisation and animations can be investigated in desktop environments. The research of Jansen-Osmann and Berendt (2002) into distance knowledge is noteworthy. They compared the response to computer-simulated three-dimensional environments with experimental results obtained in physical spaces. The computer simulation confirmed the data of an earlier field test, showing that a higher number of turns along a route increased the estimated length of that route. In this case, desktop virtual environments were shown to be a valid and economic research tool. As a consequence, researchers can use these virtual environments to investigate spatial processes in *evaluation ex ante.*

Instead of virtual reality, also the term 'cyberspace' can be used. The *Cyberspace Lexicon* defines cyberspace as a virtual reality that constitutes a new space for human communication and action. Myron Krueger, a pioneer of virtual reality, developed a series of interactive environments emphasising physical and multisensory participation in computer events. Pressure-sensitive floor pads, infrared light beams, lasers and other computer-linked feedback and control mechanisms were used by him to investigate human movement and activity in an existing space, as a kind of ex post evaluation. Recent advances in electronic techniques for creating and presenting visual information will soon enable high-resolution computer-generated images to be viewed on the inside surface of specially designed glasses. Further development should make it possible for such images to be projected directly onto the viewer's retina (www.arcspace.com/studio/jantzen/index.htm).

6.3 Checklists and assessment scales

The methods surveyed in Section 6.2 are in principle all suitable for determining whether a building achieves its aims and expectations and has any other special qualities. Instruments have also been developed which are specifically aimed at a number of criteria of architectural quality and utility value. This section discusses a number of accepted measuring instruments, international and Dutch oriented. Some are intended for general use, whereas others are intended for a single aspect, a particular building type or a special target group. Table 6.4 gives a summary of the instruments described, indicating for each where a fuller description can be found and the quality criteria for which the instrument is intended.

A. REN and REN Quick Scan

At the beginning of the 1990s a number of real estate companies (Zadelhoff, Jones Lang Wootton and Starke Diekstra) developed the *Real Estate Norm* (REN). The REN was intended to support the analysis of existing housing situations and to allow somebody to familiarise himself with office locations and buildings on the market. The emphasis is on functional quality (efficiency). The method can be used both for preparing and checking programmes of requirements and for analysing a portfolio. The instrument is also intended as an aid to communication between clients and consultants. It distinguishes two main headings: location and building. Location is subdivided into environment and site, and building into the building as a whole, the workplace and service areas. These components are examined from three different points of view – use, comfort and safety. The assessment also looks at legislation and regulations, economic aspects and (briefly) a few visual aspects. The method distinguishes a total of 40 aspects relating to the location and 94 relating to the building itself. Each aspect is rated on a five-point scale. The method is made more visual by taking a photograph of each item to represent one of the quality classes. The assessor (the user or his adviser) then gives his own weighting – A, B or C – to each heading, where A = critically important, B = moderately important and C = relatively unimportant. The different primary and secondary aspects can be used to set up a profile for both supply and demand. Matching these two profiles enables a judgement to be made of the extent to which an existing building and the available alternatives are suitable for office accommodation or perhaps more eligible for alternative use or demolition. The REN was originally intended for office buildings, but a second REN has been developed for industrial buildings, which divides aspects of functional quality under three main headings (location, plot and building). The industrial REN distinguishes 50 aspects of the location and 63 aspects of the building.

The REN makes it possible to do a thorough assessment, but is rather labour-intensive. For this reason a simplified method, *REN Quick Scan*, was developed on the initiative of the Dutch Government Building Agency, Nationale Nederlanden Real Estate and the REN Foundation. REN Quick Scan reduces the number of performance aspects to about 50 aspects of quality and a few pieces of general information, the whole being divided into five modules:

1. General information, e.g. information about the user, floor area and financial data.
2. Functional quality (utility value) of the location, building and workplaces.
3. Visual spatial quality (experiential value) of the location, building and workspace.
4. Technical quality, i.e. the general condition of the property and its plant.
5. Environmental quality, e.g. energy use, use of materials and the use made of sustainable sources of energy.

The '*Vastgoed Kwaliteitsanalyse* (VAK)' or 'Real estate quality analysis' combines a REN-based functional survey with a technical survey. This method was developed by Damen Consultants, for the Dutch Ministry of Defence in the mid 1990s. The addition of the technical survey makes it possible to carry out financial analyses to obtain a reliable idea of the costs involved in adjusting buildings in response to changes in the army. The method uses reference projects to show building-related exploitation costs over a period of 25 years and allows comparisons to be made between the required alterations and alternative options such as replacement by a new building.

B.   Building Quality Assessment method (BQA)

The New Zeeland Centre developed the Building Quality Assessment method for Building Performance Research. Its aim and general organisation are comparable with those of the REN. Like the REN, the BQA was set up to assist in evaluating one's own accommodation and comparing it with alternatives as a way of determining its relative suitability as office accommodation. The method distinguishes six headings: the company and its requirements, location, construction, space, interior climate and plant. Attention is given to features such as the presentation of the building, space, access, supporting services, staff facilities, working environment, safety and health, technical aspects and management aspects. The six headings are subdivided into a number of factors, almost 60 in all, each of which is given a brief definition. Examples are given of items relevant to each factor. Each item is rated on a 10-point scale. The assessor can either assign his own weight (0–100) to each category and each factor within that category or use weights based on user investigations carried out by the original research workers. Use of this method allows buildings to be compared in a standardised manner, while taking one's own priorities into account in the assessment. The method is quite detailed. Its advantage is that it allows subtle judgements and brings out both strong and weak points. Its disadvantage is that it is extremely labour-intensive and inflexible in the way it deals with specific organisational characteristics. It also pays little attention to fixed and variable building costs (Vijverberg, 1999).

C. Serviceability Tools and Methods (STM)

In 1993 Gerald Davis and Françoise Szigetti developed a set of 'Serviceability Tools and Methods' at Canada's International Centre for Facilities. The method was devised to improve communication about workspaces and supporting facilities and builds on the ORBIT (Organisations, Buildings and Information Technology) studies carried out by Francklin Becker and co-workers (Becker et al., 1985; Becker and Sims, 1990). An attempt was made to set up a systematic method for evaluating buildings based on these studies into the relationships between organisational characteristics and housing requirements. STM starts by establishing the organisation profile (tasks, mission, organisation structure and work processes). For each profile, requirements are formulated for the building and its facilities. Buildings are then judged on their suitability to the organisation involved by comparing the user profile and the building profile. The method distinguishes three headings:

- workspaces and rooms
- real estate and its management
- legislation and regulations.

Within these three sections, the method distinguishes 19 main aspects and 108 subsidiary aspects. A series of multiple choice questions enables each subsidiary aspect to be rated on a nine-point scale, so making possible a detailed assessment tailored to the specific needs of the particular organisation. The disadvantages of the method are complexity and the need for support by experts (Government Buildings Agency, 1994).

D. Achieving Excellence Design Evaluation Toolkit (AEDET)

In the United Kingdom, the NHS Estates Centre of Healthcare Architecture and Design developed a toolkit for evaluating the design of healthcare buildings from initial proposals through to post-project evaluation. The toolkit aims to help make better decisions. It provides support for developing design specifications and evaluating and assessing the design of healthcare building proposals. It may help to develop a national benchmarking system of design quality for healthcare buildings. The set of design evaluation criteria have been synthesised from a

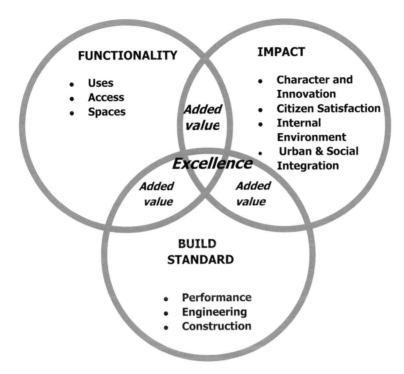

Figure 6.12 Ten criteria of the Achieving Excellence Design Evaluation Toolkit.

number of sources, which include The Patient Journey Model, Better By Design, the NHS Design Quality Portfolio technical and user criteria, the PFI Design Development Protocol and the Model Design Quality Specification. Figure 6.12 shows the basic framework and criteria.

The toolkit is to be used at various key stages in the design development process and to support the non-financial assessments required in business cases. The toolkit comprises a series of key questions supported by lists of related issues that need to be considered. The questions are answered by entering a numerical score (between 1 and 6) into an Excel spreadsheet. The spreadsheet automatically averages out the answers in each of the 10 sections and enters them in a table and a radar chart: the 'Design Evaluation Profile' (Fig. 6.13).

In the Netherlands the *College Bouw Ziekenhuisvoorzieningen* [College for Building Healthcare Facilities] also uses the AEDET toolkit. This governmental organisation is responsible for cost and quality assessments of healthcare buildings. The AEDET questionnaires have been slightly adapted. The average value of all 10 items of AEDET are included in a Quality Index (QIND), together with a test on cost standards and policy issues, flexibility, sustainability and future value (College Bouw Ziekenhuisvoorzieningen, 2003).

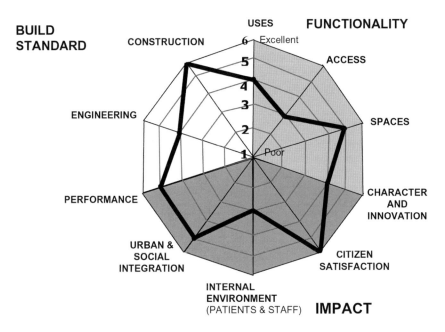

Figure 6.13 A radar chart with a Design Evaluation Profile. The example shows notional scores. Source: www.chad.nhsestates.gov.uk

E. School Building Assessment Methods

Sanoff et al. (2001) developed a number of methods to assess the quality of school buildings, including a six-factor school building checklist (as a means for a well-structured walking tour), a school building observation form, a school building rating scale and a photo enquiry. The six factors include context, massing, interface, wayfinding, social space and comfort. By using a series of checklist questions and a numerical rating scale, one can assign a score to each factor being assessed. For example: 'Does the scale of the building suit the scale of the surrounding buildings?' 'Are all the circulation routes understandable and convenient?'. The rating scale is a six-point scale and scores from very unsatisfactory to very satisfactory. The observation form includes a number of questions that should be answered with yes or no, for instance: 'The building itself is flexible, including some open large spaces, some small rooms and some multifunctional spaces'. The rating scale includes nine items, such as physical features, outdoor areas, learning environments, social areas, media access, safety and security, each subdivided in a number of sub-items such as 'control of internal and external noise level' or size of the learning groups in classrooms. For each sub-item, individuals should rate their overall satisfaction with its quality on a six-point scale. For example, the photo inquiry includes a number of photographs of the exterior and spaces such as social space and dining space: assessments are rated on bipolar scales such as interesting versus boring or novel versus common.

F. Healthy building quality (HBQ)

The end of the 1980s saw a growing concern about the sick building syndrome. To find out the extent to which complaints about ill health were totally or partially caused by the characteristics of the building, the Dutch Government Buildings Agency (GBA) developed the 'healthy building quality' method (Bergs, 1993), which built on Jaqueline Vischer's 'building-in-use' method, developed in Canada (Vischer, 1989). Vischer distinguished seven parameters for measuring the quality of workspaces: air quality, temperature control, available space, privacy, light and noise (subdivided into problem noise and differences in sound level between different workspaces). The GBA adjusted her method to suit the Dutch situation and later extended it by adding a section on work perception. A related method is the 'office health check' developed by the Dutch organisations TNO and SBR for scientific and professional research (Rolloos et al., 1999).

G. Certification system for office buildings

At the beginning of the 1990s, Centraal Beheer (1993), a Dutch insurance company based in Apeldoorn, set up a system for certifying office buildings. The system distinguishes four main groups of factors – economic, technical, commercial and social. These factors are broken down into 138 characteristics, each of which is given its own weighting. The weighted scores for each characteristic are totalled in a score per aspect group, e.g. life expectancy. Each total is multiplied by a further weighting factor. Finally, the weighted scores for each aspect group are added to give a total score for each group of factors. This method makes it possible to detect a building's strong and weak points at the level of individual characteristics, factors and groups of factors. Centraal Beheer, itself, applies its method to planning building maintenance and future investment in its buildings.

H. Evaluations by a firm of architects

Evaluations are usually undertaken by research workers or consultants. Only rarely is a building subjected to systematic evaluation by the firm of architects involved in its construction. Some firms see this as a failing, particularly when the building falls in a relatively new category. This prompted the Dordrecht firm of EGM Onderzoek to develop a method of evaluating different ways of combining housing and health care for the elderly (Leenheer, 1997). The method uses an extensive questionnaire, divided into sections covering general matters, user safety, orientation, social interaction, and ease of use, public safety and view. Two lists of questions are prepared, one for document analysis and an on-site survey of the building, and one for interviews with users of various combinations of housing and health care. The tools the method uses were mainly developed earlier, e.g. models derived from research into the functional suitability of hospitals for the elderly (Lüthi et al., 1994) and the Delft Checklist – *Sociaal veilig ontwerpen* (Van der Voordt and van Wegen, 1990). The method was not primarily intended to establish a total quality score and so does not use multiple-point scales or weighting factors. It allows a diagnosis to be made reasonably quickly, enabling bottlenecks to be detected quickly and lessons to be drawn for future projects.

I. Manual for Accessibility

The beginning of the 1970s saw the publication of the first edition of *Geboden toegang* [Call for admittance], a Dutch manual for designing and building to ensure accessibility and usability by people with handicaps. The manual, which was exclusively concerned with the handicapped, was badly needed at a time when little if any attention was being paid to accessibility by people with functional disorders, an area in which there has been much improvement in recent decades, so that today the approach is much more professional and much more integrated. Accessibility by everyone, including people with a handicap, is now seen as a basic quality requirement. The first edition of the Handboek voor toegankelijkheid [Accessibility manual] (Wijk et al.) appeared in 1995. In this manual the integrated approach was translated into a set of dimensional criteria, performance requirements and design recommendations, making it extremely suitable for use in checking a design or building for universal accessibility. Buildings that satisfy the criteria can be considered for the award of the international accessibility symbol, a seal of approval for universal accessibility. The fifth edition (2003) also pays a good deal of attention to ergonomic guidelines. In other countries, similar manuals have been published nowadays.

J. Checklist Public Safety

Although the idea that characteristics of the built environment influence public safety dates back to antiquity, the exploration of links between the two developed rapidly in the 1970s and 1980s in parallel with scores of studies, policy proposals and concrete measures. The beginning of 1990 saw the publication of the Delft 'Checklist – Designing for public safety', which summarised the insights gained in such a way as to make them accessible to planners, designers and others responsible for checking plans. The checklist developed eight important criteria for checking the public safety of a built environment, actual or planned, both objective (the likelihood of a criminal offence taking place) and subjective (perceived insecurity). The eight criteria were:

1. Presence of potential offenders
2. Attractiveness of potential targets or victims
3. Vulnerability of those victims
4. Presence of protective eyes (social control)
5. Visibility
6. Involvement of residents and passers-by in 'their' environment
7. Attractiveness of the environment
8. Presence of entrances and escape routes.

For each criterion, indicators were given for potentially risky situations, illustrated with practical examples. The checklist has been used by the *Stuurgroep Experimenten Volkshuisvesting (SEV)* [Dutch Public Housing Experiments steering group], in cooperation with other organisations, to develop a '*Politiekenmerk Veilig Wonen*' [Police Mark of Approval Safe Housing, comparable to the English mark 'Secured by Design'. This seal of approval covers a large number of items, which are divided into basic requirements and supplementary requirements. Points can be earned for each item. To be considered for the seal of approval a building must satisfy all the basic requirements and gain more than a minimum number of points on the supplementary requirements. The seal comes in two versions: one for new buildings and one for existing buildings. At present, the seal is only awarded for housing and residential environments. Both the Delft Checklist and the Police Mark contain a good deal of useful material for evaluating a building for public safety.

K.   VAC quality indicator

For many years now, local *Vrouwen Advies Commissies* (VACs) [women's advisory committees] have been publishing recommendations, asked or unasked, about the user quality of housing. To support these voluntary efforts and increase the level of professionalism, the VAC at national level has developed the VAC quality indicator (Hilhorst, 1997), which brings together a large number of points relating to the user and experiential quality of housing and residential environments.

L.   Housing approval

Although checklists and seals of approval are important aids to quality assurance and increased professionalism generally, they also face a good deal of opposition. Designers feel that their freedom is being restricted, partly because the multiplicity of rules and guidelines means that they are still not very usable, if only because of occasional inconsistencies, often minor. For this reason, in the Netherlands, a start has been made on harmonising and integrating the large number of rules and guidelines with respect to accessibility, *Seniorenlabel* and *Seniorenscore,* the *Politiekeurmerk Veilig Wonen* ('Police Mark on Safe Housing') and various NEN standards. The *Seniorenlabel* or Senior Citizen's Label is a seal of approval for the suitability of housing for use by all ages, with a focus on accessibility and safety of new buildings (Van de Donk, 1994). The *Seniorenscore* or Senior Citizen's Score is a similar seal for existing buildings (Scherpenisse et al., 1997). This harmonisation developed into the *Keurmerk integrale woningkwaliteit* [Integral housing quality seal of approval], which in turn was recently reworked into the *Woonkeur* seal of approval (SKW Certification, 2000). The requirements for this seal of approval can be used for both the development of drawings (including drawings for housing) and for checking a design or drawing as realised.

Table 6.4 summarises the checklists mentioned.

Table 6.4 Instruments for measuring building quality

Method	Sources	Aspects considered	Notes
A.1 Real Estate Norm (REN)	Stichting REN, 1992, 1993	Functionality, comfort, safety; 140 subheadings	Focus on office buildings: another REN is available for industrial buildings
A.2 Real Estate Norm Quick Scan (REN QS)	Stichting REN, 1994	Functionality, spatial and visual quality, technical quality, environment; 50 subheadings	Focus on office buildings
A.3 *Vastgoed Kwaliteitsanalyse* (VAK) [Real estate quality analysis]	Feld and Huffmeijer, 1997	Functional quality, technical quality, cost	Combination of REN and technical aspects
B. Building Quality Assessment (BQA)	Baird and Isaacs, 1994; Bruhns and Isaacs, 1996	Company, location, construction, space, interior climate, plant; about 60 subheadings	Focus on office buildings

(Continued)

Table 6.4 Continued

Method	Sources	Aspects considered	Notes
C. Serviceability Tools and Methods (STM)	Davis and Szigetti, 1996	Workplaces and workspaces, real estate and management, legislation and regulations; 108 subheadings	Builds on the ORBIT studies of Becker and Sims, 1990
D. Achieving Excellence Design Evaluation Toolkit (AEDET)	NHS Estates, 2002	Functionality (uses, access, spaces), impact and build standard, including 10 main items and 65 sub-items	Focus on healthcare buildings
E. School Building Assessment Methods	Sanoff et al., 2001	Context, massing, interface, wayfinding, social space, comfort, media access, visual appearance, safety and security, overall impression	Focus on school buildings, i.e. the whole building and areas such as learning environments, social areas, outdoor areas
F.1 Healthy Building Quality (HBQ)	Vischer, 1989; Bergs, 1993	Air quality, temperature control, available space, privacy, light, noise, work perception	Builds on the building-in-use method of Jaqueline Vischer
F.2 *Toets gezond kantoor* [Office health check]	Rolloos et al., 1999	Same as above	Same as above
G. *Certificatie systeem kantoor gebouwen* [Certification system for office buildings]	Centraal Beheer, 1993	Economic, technical, commercial and social factors; 138 subheadings	Developed for office buildings
H. *Evalueren bij een architecten-bureau* [Evaluation by architects]	Leenheer, 1997	User safety, orientation, social interaction, convenience, public safety, outlook	Focus on assisted living for the elderly

(*Continued*)

Table 6.4 Continued

Method	Sources	Aspects considered	Notes
I. *Handboek voor toegankelijkheid* [Accessibility manual]	Wijk et al., 2003 (5th edn)	Universal accessibility	Formerly *Geboden Toegang*; applicable to buildings, housing and outside spaces
J. Checklist – *Sociaal Veilig Ontwerpen* [Designing for public safety]	Van der Voordt and Van Wegen, 1990	Public safety (objective and subjective)	Used as a basis for the Police Mark of Approval Safe Housing
K. *VAC-Kwaliteitswijzer* [quality indicator]	Hilhorst, 1997	Usability, accessibility, safety, comfort	Developed for housing and residential environments
L. *Woonkeur* [checklist on user quality of housing]	SKW Certification, 2000	Usability, accessibility, safety, comfort	Integration of Senior Citizen's Label, Senior Citizen's Score, Accessibility Manual and VAC quality indicator

Other instruments

Many other sources are available besides the instruments mentioned above. In North Carolina, Henry and Joan Sanoff developed a manual containing guidelines for designing educational environments for children. The manual discusses various activity areas, investigates educational approaches and translates goals into spatial solutions. Various publications appeared that give a clear summary of key figures and guidelines for a child-friendly residential environment. Special assessment scales have been developed on hospitals, hotels, theatres and so on, and also on special themes such as testing building plans on flexibility, saving energy, application of sustainable energy sources and environmentally friendly materials, ergonomics, etc. A recent development is a series of evaluations of innovative offices, for which building performance methods have been developed (Vos and Dewulf, 1999; Preiser and Vischer, 2004). Despite the many differences in approach, there are certain recurring themes, indicating a degree of consensus about what aspects are relevant to the measurement of a building's quality.

Bibliography

6.1 Criteria for functional quality

A. Reachability and parking facilities

Chrest, A.P., M.S. Smith, S. Bhuyan (1996), *Parking structures: planning, design, construction, maintenance and repair.* Chapman and Hall, New York.

CROW (1994–1996), *Parkeren bij bedrijven* [Company parking arrangements]. A series of publications about parking, dealing with different locations and building functions. Ede.

Dutch Standards Institution (2000), *NVN 2443, Parkeren en stallen van personenauto's op terreinen en in garages.* [Parking and garaging private cars on-site and in garages]. Delft.

Kuzmyak, R. (2003), Traveler response to transportation system changes. In: *Parking management and supply.* Transportation Research Board, Washington.

Stichting REN (1992), *Real Estate Norm. Methode voor de advisering en beoordeling van kantoorlocaties en kantoorgebouwen* [Method for advising on and assessing office locations and office buildings]. Nieuwegein.

B. Accessibility

American National Standards Institute (1992), *A117.1, Specifications for making buildings and facilities accessible to, and usable by, physically handicapped people.* New York.

Dutch Standards Institution (2000), *NEN 1814, Toegankelijkheid van gebouwen en buitenruimten* [Accessibility of buildings and outside areas], 2nd edn. Delft.

Imrie, R., P. Hall (2001), *Inclusive Design. Designing and Developing Accessible Environments.* Spon Press, London.

Lidwell, W., K. Holden, J. Butler (2003), *Universal principles of design.* Rockport, Gloucester.

Preiser, W., E. Ostroff (eds) (2001), *Universal design handbook.* McGraw-Hill, New York.

Steinfeld, E., G.S. Danford (1999), *Enabling environments.* Plenum Publishers, New York.

Wijk, M., J.J. Drenth, J. van Ditmarsch (2003), *Handboek voor toegankelijkheid* [Accessibility manual], 5th edn. Elsevier Bedrijfsinformatie, Doetinchem.

Zajicek, M., A. Edwards (2003), *Proceedings of the 2003 Conference on Universal Usability.* ACM, New York.

For psychological accessibility see journals such as the *Journal of Environmental Psychology and Environment and Behaviour.*

C. Efficiency

Benes, J, J.K. Vrijling (1990), *Voldoet dit gebouw? Het bepalen van functionele kwaliteit.* [Is this building satisfactory? The determination of functional quality]. SBR Rapport 222. Building Research Foundation, Rotterdam.

Duin, L. van, J. Zeinstra (eds) (1989), *Functioneel ontwerpen. Ontwikkeling en toepassing van het doelmatigheidsbeginsel in de architectuur* [Functional design. Development and application of the efficiency principle in architecture]. Publications Office (Architecture), Delft University of Technology.

Kroemer, K.H.E., H.B. Kroemer, K. Kroemer-Elbert (2002), *Ergonomics: how to design for ease and efficiency.* Prentice Hall, Upper Saddle River, New Jersey.

Kubba, S. (2003), *Space planning for commercial and residential interiors.* McGraw-Hill, New York.

Marmot, A., E. Joanna (2000), *Office space planning: designing for tomorrow's workplace.* McGraw-Hill, New York.

Polak, B.M. (1973), *Functioneel ontwerpen* [Functional design]. Amsterdam/Brussel.

Apart from this general literature on efficient and functional design, there are countless publications dealing with specific types of buildings such as childcare centres, school buildings, health centres, assisted living for the elderly, nursing homes, hospitals, hotels, etc., and a number of checklists on these building types (see Section 6.3).

D.   Flexibility

Boerman, J., W. Lans, A. Thomsen, D.J.M. van der Voordt (1992), *Veranderbaar gebruik* [Changeable use]. Internal report, Faculty of Architecture, Delft University of Technology.

Brand, S. (1994), *How buildings learn: What happens after they are built.* Viking, New York.

Building Research Foundation, Rotterdam (1985), *Verkavelbare dragers* [Divisible load bearers]. Rotterdam.

Eldonk, J., H. Fassbinder (1990), *Flexible fixation.* Van Gorcum, Maastricht/Assen.

Geraedts, R., Y. Cuperus (1999), *Flexibiliteit en kantoorhuisvesting.* [Flexibility and office accommodation] Internal report, Faculty of Architecture, Delft University of Technology and ABN AMRO, Amsterdam.

Helm, J.J., van der, R.P. Geraedts (1996), *Flexis. Communicatie over en beoordeling van flexibiliteit tussen gebouwen en installaties* [Communication and assessment of flexibility between buildings and plant]. SBR 375, Building Research Foundation, Rotterdam.

Nicolai, R., K.H. Dekker (1991), *Flexibiliteit als bouwstrategie* [Flexibility as a building strategy]. Nationaal Ziekenhuis Instituut, Utrecht.

Proveniers, A., H. Fassbinder (1992), *New wave in building: a flexible way of design, construction and real estate management.* Department of Building and Architecture, Eindhoven University of Technology.

Vreedenburgh, E. (ed.) (1992), *De bouw uit de knoop* [Building untangled]. Faculty of Architecture, Delft University of Technology

E.   Safety

Barling, J., M.R. Frone (eds) (2004), *The psychology of workplace safety.* American Psychological Association, Washington.

Dutch Standards Institution (1983), *NEN 5088 and NEN 5089, Inbraakveiligheid van gebouwen* [Burglar protection for buildings]. Delft.

Perry, P. (2003), *Health and safety: questions and answers.* Telford, London.

Poyner, B. (1983), *Design against crime. Beyond defensible space.* Butterworths, London.

Ridley, J., J. Channing (2003), *Safety at work.* Butterworth-Heinemann, Amsterdam.

Servicepunt Veilig Wonen (1997), *Politiekeurmerk Veilig Wonen* [Police safe housing seal of approval]. Public Housing Experiments Steering Group, Rotterdam.

Soomeren, P. van, H. Stienstra (1987/1989), *Beveiliging van gebouwen* [Protection of buildings]. A series of publications on the protection of houses, shops, offices, industrial buildings and school buildings. Building Research Foundation, Rotterdam.

Voordt, D.J.M. van der, H.B.R. van Wegen (1990), *Sociaal veilig ontwerpen* [Designing for public safety]. Faculty of Architecture, Delft University of Technology.

Voordt, D.J.M. van der, H.B.R. van Wegen (1993), The Delft checklist on safe neighborhoods. *Journal of Architectural and Planning Research* 10(4), 341–356.

Voskamp, P. (1995), *Handboek gezondheid en veiligheid in kantoren* [Manual for health and safety in offices]. Recommendations, guidelines, standards and regulations. SDU Uitgevers, The Hague.

F. Spatial orientation

Lynch, K. (1960), *The image of the city.* MIT Press, Cambridge, Massachusetts.

Paul, A., R. Passini (1992), *Wayfinding; people, signs and architecture.* McGraw-Hill Ryerson, Toronto.

Passini, R. (1984), *Wayfinding in architecture.* Van Nostrand Reinhold, New York.

Voordt, D.J.M. van der (2001), Lost in a nursing home. IAPS Bulletin for People-Environment Studies No. 18 (spring 2001). Special issue on *Environmental Cognition* 19–21.

Various checklists are given in Section 6.3.

G. Privacy, territoriality and social contact

Altman, I. (1975), *The environment and social behavior.* Brooks/Cole, Monterey, California.

Cammock, R. (1979), Confidentiality in health centres and group practices, the implications for design. *Journal of Architectural Research* 4(1), 5–17.

Deasy, C.M., T.E. Lasswell (1985), Designing places for people. *A handbook on human behavior for architects, designers, and facility managers.* Whitney Library of Design, New York.

Gifford, R. (1997), *Environmental psychology, principles and practice.* 2dn edn. Allyn and Bacon, Boston.

Hall, E.T. (1966), *The hidden dimension.* Doubleday, New York.

Hoogdalem, H. van, D.J.M. van der Voordt, H.B.R. van Wegen (1985), *Bouwen aan gezondheidscentra. Functionele grondslagen voor programma en ontwerp* [Building health centres. Functional principles for programming and design]. Delft University Press.

Kupritz, V.W. (2000), Privacy management at work. A conceptual model. *Journal of Architectural and Planning Research* 17(1), 47–63.

Lang, J. (1987), *Creating architectural theory. The role of the behavioral sciences in environmental design.* Van Nostrand Reinhold, New York.

Osmond, H. (1966), Some psychiatric aspects of design. In: L.B. Holland (ed.), *Who designs America?* Doubleday, New York, 281–318.

Sommer, R. (1969), *Personal space: the behavioral basis of design.* Prentice Hall, Englewood Cliffs, New Jersey.

Voordt, D.J.M. van der (2003), *Costs and benefits of innovative workplace design.* Center for People and Buildings, Delft.

Westin, A. (1970), *Privacy and freedom.* Ballantine, New York.

Various checklists are given in Section 6.3.

H. Health and physical well-being

Boo, H. de (1990), *Ziekmakende gebouwen.* [Sick making buildings]. Faculty of Architecture, Delft University of Technology.

Burge, P.S., A. Hedge, S. Wilson, J. Harris-Bass, A.S. Robertson (1987), Sick building syndrome. A study of 4373 office workers. *Annals Occupational Hygiene* 31, 493–504.

Clements-Croome, D. (2000), *Creating the productive workplace.* E&EF Spon, New York.

College Bouw Ziekenhuisvoorzieningen (2002), *Heilzaam bouwen,* Healing environment. Bijlage bij Signaleringsrapport Integraal Evaluatiesysteem. Utrecht.

Devlin, A.S., A.B. Arneill (2003), Health care environments and patient outcomes. A review of the literature. *Environment and Behavior* 35(2), 665–694.

Evans, G.W., J. Mitchell McCox (1998), When buildings don't work: the role of architecture in human health. *Journal of Environmental Psychology* 18(1).

Hasking, S., L. Haggard (2001), *Healing the hospital environment.* Spon Press, London.

Hedge, A., E.M. Sterling, T.D. Sterling (1986), Building illness indices based on questionnaire responses. *Proceeding IAQ/86, Managing Indoor Air for Health and Energy conservation* 32–43.

Lip, E. (1997), *What is feng shui?* Academy Editions, London.

Lüthi, P., M.N. Niclaes, D.J.M. van der Voordt (1994), *Ouderen in ziekenhuizen. Problemen en oplossingen voor de bouw.* [Elderly in hospitals. Spatial problems and solutions]. Stichting Architektenonderzoek Gebouwen Gezondheidszorg, Amsterdam.

Malkin, J. (1992), *Hospital interior architecture. Creating healing environments for special patient populations.* Van Nostrand Reinhold, New York.

Molhave, L. (1987), The Sick Buildings. *Proceedings of the 4th International Conference on Indoor Air Quality and Climate, Berlin* 2, 469–473.

Norback, D., I. Michel, U. Widstrom (1990), Indoor air quality and personal factors related to the sick building syndrome. *Scandinavian Journal of Work, Environment and Health* 16, 121–128.

Ryan, C.M., L.A. Morrow (1992), Dysfunctional buildings or dysfunctional people. *Journal of Clinical and Consulting Psychology* 60, 220–224.

Seppänen, O., M. Tuomainen, J. Säteri (eds) (2000), *Healthy Buildings 2000.* Workshop summaries. SIY Indoor Air Information, Helsinki.

Sterling, E.M. (1986), Indoor air quality – Total environment performance. *Canadian Journal of Real Estate* 21–25.

Ulrich, R.S. (1984), View from a window may influence recovery. *Science* 224, 42–421.

Ulrich, R.S. (1991), Effects of health facility interior design on wellness. *Journal of Health Care Design* 3, 97–109. Reprinted in S.O. Marberry (1995), *Innovations in healthcare design.* Van Nostrand Reinhold, New York.

Ulrich, R.S. (2000), Evidence based environmental design for improving medical outcomes. *Proceedings of the Conference Healing by Design.* McGill University Health Centre, Montreal.

Valjborn, O. (1989), Building sickness syndrome. A guide to approach a complaint building. *NIVA Course on Sick Building Syndrome.* Copenhagen.

Versteege, S., L. van Heel (2004), Healing environment. *Een fundament voor veilig, duurzaam en gezond ontwikkelen.* [A basis for safe, sustainable and healthy development] In: P.G. Luscuere (ed.), *Evidence based design for healing environments.* Faculty of Architecture, Delft University of Technology.

Voskamp, P. (ed.) (2000), *Handboek ergonomie* [Ergonomics manual]. Samsom Bedrijfsinformatie, Alphen a/d Rijn.

Wijk, M., I. Luten (2001), *Tussen mens en plek. Over de ergonomie van de fysieke omgeving* [People and place]. DUP blueprint, Delft.

Various checklists are given in Section 6.3.

I. Sustainability

Birkeland, J. (2002), *Design for sustainability.* A source book of integrated ecological solutions. Earthscan Publications, London.

Duijvestein, K. (2002), The environmental maximisation method. In: T.M. de Jong and D.J.M. van der Voordt (eds), *Ways to study architectural, urban and technical design.* Delft University Press, Delft, 313–318.

Goldsmith, E. (1972), *Blueprint for survival.* Houghton Mifflin, Boston.

Graham, P. (2003), *Building ecology: first principles for a sustainable built environment.* Blackwell Science, Oxford.

Guy, S., S. Moore (ed.) (2004), *Sustainable architecture.* Spon Press, London.

Hyde, R., S. Watson, W. Cheshire, M. Thompson (2004), *The environmental brief.* Spon Press, London.

Meadows, D.H., D.L. Meadows, J. Randers (1972), *The limits to growth.* Universe Books, New York.

Priemus, H. (ed.) (1999), Environmental sustainability. *International Planning Studies* 4(2), 173–280. Special issue.

Reid, D. (1995), *Sustainable development.* Earthscan, London.

Schumacher, E.F. (1973), *Small is beautiful.* Blond & Briggs, London.

Sunnika, M., G.A.M. Vijverberg (2002), Sustainable buildings in Europe–government policies and regulations. *Open House International* 27(2), 30–37.

Williamson, T., A. Radford, H. Bennetts (2002), *Understanding sustainable architecture.* Spon Press, London.

Wooley, T., S. Kimmins, P. Harrison (1997/2000), *Green building handbook, Vols. 1 and 2. Guides to building products and their impact on the environment.* Spon Press, London.

World Commission on Environment and Development (1987), *Our common future.* Oxford University Press, Oxford.

6.2 Methods of measurement

Baird, G., J. Gray, N. Isaacs, D. Kernohan, G. McIndoe (1996), *Building evaluation techniques.* McGraw-Hill, New York.

Bechtel, R., R. Marans, E. Michelson (1987), *Methods in environmental and behavioral research.* Van Nostrand Reinhold, New York.

Hoogdalem, H. van, D.J.M. van der Voordt, H.B.R. van Wegen (1985), Comparative floorplan-analysis as a means to develop design guidelines. *Journal of Environmental Psychology* 5, 153–179.

Jansen-Osmann, P., B. Berendt (2002), Investigating distance knowledge using virtual environments. *Environment and Behavior* 34(2), 178–193.

Jong, T.M. de, D.J.M. van der Voordt (eds) (2002), *Ways to study and research architectural, urban and technical design.* Delft University Press, Delft.

Preiser, W.F.E., H.Z. Rabinowitz, E.T. White (1988), *Post-occupancy evaluation.* Van Nostrand Reinhold, New York.

Sanoff, H., C. Pasalar, Hashas (2001), *School building assessment methods.* North Carolina State University, USA.

Voordt, D.J.M. van der, D. Vrielink, H.B.R. van Wegen (1998), Comparative floorplan-analysis in programming and architectural design. *Design Studies* 18, 67–88.

Yin, R.K. (1994), *Case study research. Design and methods*, 2nd edn. Sage. Thousand Oaks, California.

Zeisel, J. (1981), *Inquiry by design. Tools for environment-behavior research.* Brooks/Cole, Monterey, California.

6.3 Checklists and assessment scales

Baird, G., J. Gray, N. Isaacs, D. Kernohan, G. McIndoe (1996), *Building evaluation techniques.* McGraw-Hill, New York.

Baird, G., N. Isaacs (1994), A checklist for the performance evaluation of buildings and building services. In: *Engineering for better building performance.* CIBSE Australia and N.Z. Third Regional Conference, Melbourne, Australia.

Becker, F.D., G. Davis, F. Duffy, W. Sims (1985), *ORBIT-2: organizations, buildings and information technology.* The Harbinger, Norwalk, Connecticut.

Becker, F.D., W.R. Sims (1990), *Matching building performance to organizational needs in performance of buildings and serviceability of facilities.* American Society for Testing and Materials, Philadelphia.

Bergs, J.A. (1993), *Evaluatie-onderzoek kantoorgebouwen. Handleiding voor onderzoek met de GBK-methode* [Evaluative research into office buildings. Guide to research using the GBK method. DHV Bouw, Amersfoort.

Bruhns, H., N. Isaacs (1996), Building quality assessment. In: G. Baird, J. Gray, N. Isaacs, D. Kernohan, G. McIndoe, *Building evaluation techniques.* McGraw-Hill, New York, 53–58.

Centraal Beheer (1993), *Certificatiesysteem voor kantoorgebouwen* [Certification system for office buildings]. Apeldoorn.

College Bouw Ziekenhuisvoorzieningen (CBZ) (2003), *Quality Index to Uitvoeringstoets inzake. (QIND)* [Test on quality]. Utrecht.

Davis, G., F. Szigetti (1996), Serviceability tools and methods. In: G. Baird et al. (eds). *Building evaluation techniques.* McGraw-Hill, New York, 58–68.

Donk, B. van de (1994), *Seniorenlabel. A seal of approval as suitable for all ages.* Stuurgroep Experimenten Volkshuisvesting, Rotterdam.

Government Buildings Agency (1994), *Comparative study REN – STM – BQA.* The Hague.

Hilhorst, H.L.C. (1997), *VAC-Kwaliteitswijzer.* An integrated view of the user quality of housing and residential environments. National Contact of the VACs, Utrecht.

Leenheer, R. (1997), *Evalueren bij een architectenbureau* [Evaluation by a firm of architects]. Faculty of Architecture, Delft University of Technology.

NHS Estates (2002), *Achieving excellence design evaluation toolkit.* United Kingdom.

Preiser, W.F.E., J.C. Vischer (eds) (2004), *Assessing building performance.* Elsevier, Oxon.

Rolloos, M., C. Cox, R.H. de Gans (1999), *Toets gezond kantoor* [Office health check]. *Facility Management Magazine* February, 35–38.

Sanoff, H., J. Sanoff (1981), *Learning environments for children.* Humanics, Atlanta, Georgia.

Sanoff, H., C. Pasalar, M. Hashas (2001), *School building assessment methods.* North Carolina State University, USA.

Scherpenisse, R., J. Singelenberg, E. Nolte, J. Drenth (1997), *Opplussen.* Adjusting existing housing. Stuurgroep Experimenten Volkshuisvesting, Rotterdam.

SKW Certification (2000), *Handboek woonkeur* [Housing approval manual]. Almere.

Stichting REN (1992), *Real Estate Norm. Methode voor de advisering en beoordeling van kantoorlocaties en kantoorgebouwen* [Real estate norm. Method for advising on and assessing office locations and office buildings], second version. Nieuwegein.

Stichting REN (1993), *Real Estate Norm Bedrijfsgebouwen* [Industrial buildings]. Nieuwegein.

Stichting REN (1994), *Real Estate Norm Quick Scan Kantoorgebouwen* [Office buildings]. Nieuwegein.

Vijverberg, G. (1999), Methoden voor kwaliteitsmeting. [Quality assessment methods]. *Facility Management Magazine* 12, March, 42–45.

Vischer, J.C. (1989), *Environmental quality in offices.* Van Nostrand Reinhold, New York.

Voordt, D.J.M. van der, H.B.R. van Wegen (1990), *Sociaal veilig ontwerpen* [Designing for public safety]. Checklist for the development and checking of the built environment. Faculty of Architecture, Delft University of Technology.

Vos, P., G.R.R.M. Dewulf (1999), *Searching for data.* A method to evaluate the effects of working in an innovative office. Delft University Press.

Wijk, M., J. Drenth, M. van Ditmarsch (2003), *Handboek voor toegankelijkheid* [Accessibility manual], 5th edn. Elsevier Bedrijfsinformatie, Doetinchem.

Zeisel, J. (1981), *Inquiry by design. Tools for environment-behavior research.* Brooks/Cole, Monterey, California.

Name index

Aalto 54
Alberts 54, 55
Alexander 113, 114, 115, 125, 135
Altman 114, 135, 188, 189, 190, 221
American National Standards Institute
    173, 219
Anderzhon 166
Ang 80, 105
Anna 18, 68
Archer 111, 118, 135
Argan 131, 135
Arneill 199
Arnheim 25, 68
Augenbroe 133, 135
Aymonino 132, 135

Baiche 106, 138
Baird 151, 159, 166, 216, 224
Bakema 14, 27
Barbieri 15, 50, 68
Barling 220
Barrett 101, 105
Barrie 47, 68
Bax 116, 135
Bechtel 159, 166, 224
Becker 157, 166, 210, 224, 225
Benes 151, 166, 219

Bennetts 224
Benthem 17
Benthem Crouwel Architects 20
Benton 68
Berendt 207, 224
Bergs 213, 217, 225
Bhuyan 219
Bijvoet 15, 17
Birkeland 223
Blyth 72, 92, 93, 97, 101, 105
Boekholt 118, 120, 135
Boer de 33
Boerman 180, 182, 220
Bofill 50
Bolle 59, 60, 68
Bonnema 18
Boo de 195, 222
Bordas 157, 166
Bosma 35, 68
Brand 179, 220
Brinkman 15, 25
Broadbent 114, 118, 135
Broek van den 14, 27
Brown 58
Bruhns 216, 225
Bruijn de 97, 98, 105, 107, 126, 136
Building Research Foundation 72, 74, 77,
    80, 81, 83, 101, 102, 105, 220

Burt 149, 166
Burge 195, 222
Burgee 58
Burgh Leever van der 99, 101, 106
Burie 114, 136
Butler 219

Calatrava 18, 23
Cammock 191, 221
Canter 114, 136
Carmann 166
Casciato 15, 69
Centraal Beheer 213, 217, 225
Channing 221
Charles Prince of Wales 49, 68
Cheshire 223
Chrest 219
Clements-Croome 195, 222
Cold 7, 11
College Bouw Ziekenhuisvoorzieningen 211, 222, 225
Colquhoun 131, 136
Cooper 114, 133, 136
Corbusier le 26, 29, 54, 55, 57, 128, 129
Cotton 116, 136
Cox 225
Craik 114, 136
Cross 118, 136
Crouwel 17
CROW 219
Cuperus 182, 220

Daish 167
Dam 46, 47
Danford 219
Darke 122, 136
Davis 217, 224, 225
Deasy 221
Deen 69
Dekker 181, 220
Deleuze 62, 68,
Delft University of Technology 89
Derrida 59
Descartes 19
Devlin 199, 222
Derwig 69
Dewulf 157, 218, 226
DHV AIB 87, 88, 90, 94
Dijk van 4, 11, 16, 51, 68
Dijkstra 5, 11
Dirken 3
Ditmarsch van 102, 107, 168, 219, 226

Doesburg van 55
Donk van de 225
Doorn van 133, 134, 136
Downing 120, 122, 130, 136
Drenth 102, 107, 168, 219, 225, 226
Duerk 101, 106
Duffy 224
Duiker 15, 17, 25
Duin van 31, 68, 97, 105, 114, 126, 136, 220
Duijvestein 204, 223
Durand 20, 130, 131
Dutch Standards Institution 72, 84, 85, 106, 219, 221

Edwards 219
Eekels 111 118, 119, 121, 124, 127, 138
Eekhout 111, 116, 124, 136
Egeraat, van 117
Eisenman 59, 60, 62, 63, 64
Ekambi-Schmidt 3, 11
Eldonk 220
Emmitt 133, 136
Ener 150
Engel 114, 136
Evans 137, 222
Eyck van 28, 29, 33, 34, 68

Fang 130, 137
Fassbinder 220
Feld 216
Fielden 111, 137
Floet 68
Foqué 110, 116, 122, 124, 137
Foster 17, 21, 203
Foucault 59
Fraley 144, 166
Frampton 68
Franck 29, 68, 131, 137
Friedman 33, 150, 166

Gans de 225
Gaudí 53, 54
Gehry 59, 60, 62, 63, 117
Geraedts 182, 220
Gero 127, 128, 138
Ghirardo 60, 68
Giddings 149, 166
Gifford 221
Goldfinger 57
Goldsmith 202, 223

Gössel 14, 69
Government Buildings Agency 210, 225
Graaf de 4, 11
Grafe 69
Graham 223
Grassi 39, 40
Graves 58, 59
Gray 133, 137, 166, 224
Greenhough 20
Groot de 123
Gropius 25, 26
Gunsteren van 117, 118, 137
Guy 223

Haak 99, 101, 106
Haaksma 166
Haan 69
Habraken 34, 35, 68
Hadid 63
Haggard 195, 222
Hall 137, 188, 219
Hamel 116, 119, 137
Handler 67, 68
Häring 25, 57, 58
Harris-Bass 222
Harrison 224
Hashas 224, 225
Hasking 195, 222
Hedge 195, 222
Heel van 199
Heintz 117, 137
Helm 220
Herzberger 33, 35, 114
Heuvel van 17, 20, 33, 47, 68
Hilhorst 218, 225
Hill 47, 68
Hillier 2, 11, 121, 137
Himmelblau 60, 62, 64
Hitchcock 69
Holden 219
Holness 149, 166
Hoogstraten van 68
Hooftman 146, 166
Hoogdalem van 95, 105, 150, 157, 162,
    163, 166, 191, 206, 221, 224
Houben 157
Hughes 133
Huijbrechts 83, 106
Huijgen 103
Hume 24
Huut van 54, 55
Hyde 223

Ibelings 14, 42, 61, 69
Imrie 219
Isaacs 216, 224, 225
Ishikawa 135

Jacobs 61
Jahn 18
Jansen-Osmann 207, 224
Jencks 47, 53, 58, 61, 62, 63, 64, 69
Joanna 220
Jodidio 69
Johnson 58, 59, 69
Joiner 167
Jones 113, 118, 125, 137
Jonge de 114, 137
Jong de 68, 113, 114, 123, 137, 224
Jongert 39, 69

Kahn 33
Kasteel van 33
Kelbaugh 38, 69
Kernohan 141, 145, 166, 224
Keys 150, 167
Kimmins 224
Kipnis 63
Klerk 51
Koolhaas 29, 60
Kopp 17, 69
Korfker 97, 98, 105, 126, 136
Körning 69
Koutamanis 132, 137
Kramer 51
Krier 58
Kroll 114
Kroemer 220
Kroemer-Elbert 220
Krueger 207
Kubba 220
Kupritz 222
Kuzmyak 219

Laarschot van de 79, 82, 83, 106
Labrouste 49
Lampe 69
Lang 222
Langdon 113, 137
Langenhuizen 113, 137
Lans 220
Lasswell 221
Lawrence 138

Lawson 113, 118, 120, 138
Leaman 2, 11, 157, 166
Leenheer 214, 217, 225
Lefaivre 38, 69
Lepori 29
Leupen 31, 47, 69, 130, 138
Leusen van 130, 138
Leuthäuser 14, 69
Lévi-Strauss 59
Libeskind 29, 60
Lidwell 219
Lip 195, 222
Lissitzky El 17
Loghum van 25
Loon van 117, 118, 138
Loos 24
Lotze 181
Luchi de 62
Luckman 111, 113, 118, 126, 138
Luten 223
Lüthi 214, 222
Lynch 186, 221
Lynn 63

Macel 49, 69
Mackertich 58, 69
Malkin 195, 222
Marans 150, 166, 167
Marmot 220
Mattie 25, 55, 69
McIndoe 224
McLuhan 116
Meadows 202, 223
Mecanoo Architects 32
Meel van 41, 42, 69
Mees 24, 49, 57, 69
Mendelssohn 51
Mendini 62
Mey van der 51
Meyer-Ehlers 114, 138
Michel 222
Michelson 166
Ming 61
Ministerie van WVC 12
Miralles 64
Mitchell McCox 222
Molema 15, 69
Molhave 195, 222
Moliére 37, 38
Morrow 195, 223
Mumford 25, 69

Neufert 106, 132, 138
NHS Estates 225
Niclaes 222
Nicolai 181, 220
Noever 60, 70
Nolte 225
Norback 195, 222
Norberg-Schulz 2, 11
Nox 64

Oliver 116, 136
Oosterhuis 65, 70, 117
Osmond 188, 222
Ostroff 173, 219
Oud 25, 27, 28, 55, 57
Ouwerkerk 69, 137

Panero 101, 106
Parvin 33
Pasalar 224, 225
Passini 186, 221
Paul 186, 221
Pearson Clifford 42, 70
Pevsner 70
Pelli 43
Perry 221
Poe 157, 166
Polak 97, 106, 126, 138, 220
Pos 134, 138
Powell 137
Poyner 221
Preiser 101, 106, 145, 150, 151, 164, 167,
    173, 218, 219, 224, 225
Priemus 114, 138, 223
Prigogine 118, 138
Prins 133
Proshansky 114, 138
Proveniers 220
Puglisi 116, 138

Rabinowitz 167, 224
Radford 224
Randers 223
Reid 223
Reijnhoudt 146, 166, 167
Reitzenstein 150, 168
Renzo Piano 17, 19
Reijenga 33
Ridder de 118, 138
Ridley 221
Rijksgebouwendienst 106

Rietveld 25, 55, 56
Risselada 151, 167
Robinson 130, 138
Rogers 17, 19, 22, 40, 70
Rohe van der 26
Rolloos 213, 217, 225
Roozenburg 111, 118, 119, 121, 124,
    127, 138
Rosdorff 36
Rosemann 113, 137, 138
Rosenman 127, 128, 138
Rossi 40, 41, 58, 70, 132, 138
Rossum van 4, 6
Ryan 195, 223

Sanoff 72, 97, 101, 106, 157, 167,
    212, 217, 224, 225
Säteri 223
Scharoun 54
Scherpenisse 146, 166, 167, 216, 225
Schneekloth 131
Schön 113, 124, 130, 138, 139
Schramm 151, 164, 167
Schumacher 202, 223
Scott Brown 70
Semper 12
Seppänen 223
Servicepunt Veilig Wonen 221
Shepley 144, 145, 167
Silverstein 135
Sims 210, 224, 225
Singelenberg 225
SKW Certification 225
Smith 47, 57, 70, 219
Sobek 18
Soeters 58, 59
Sommer 114, 139, 193, 222
Speaks 38, 70
Spreckelmeyer 150, 167
Spuybroek 65, 117
Stam 25
Stanley 101
Stark 62
Steiner 53, 54
Steinfeld 219
Sterling 222, 223
Stichting 151, 159, 161, 167, 216,
    219, 225
Stigt van 33
Stijl De 17, 28, 55, 56
Sullivan 15, 70, 125
Summerson 57, 70

Sunnika 224
Symes 130, 139
Szigetti 217, 225

Talbot 137
Tatlin 16
Taylor 25
Teikari 145, 150, 167
Thomsen 220
Thompson 223
Thornley 113, 137
Tijen van 25
Toumainen 223
Tunstall 133, 139
Turpijn 139
Tzonis 38, 69, 128, 139

Uhl 33
Ulrich 195, 223
Ungers 61
Utzon 55

Valjborn 195, 223
Venema 139
Venturi 58, 61, 70
Verbrugge 17, 47, 68
Versteege 199, 223
Vesnin 17
Vidler 139
Viera 39
Vijverberg 210, 224, 225
Viollet-le-Duc 20
Vischer 145, 150, 167, 213, 217, 218, 225
Vlugt van der 15, 25
Vollers 117, 139
Voordt van der 10, 11, 72, 96, 104, 106,
    107, 113, 137, 146, 147, 149, 157, 166,
    167, 168, 184, 186, 206, 214, 218, 220,
    221, 222, 224, 226
Vos 68, 157, 218, 168, 226
Voskamp 221, 223
Vreedenburgh 220
Vrielink 10, 11, 75, 81, 106, 107, 149, 168
Vrijling 151, 166, 219

Waalwijk 92, 107
Walliman 106, 138
Ward 118, 135
Watson 223
WCED 202

Name index

Weber 33
Weeber 29, 30, 35, 114
Wegen van 106, 107, 146, 147, 166, 168, 184, 214, 218, 221, 224
Wener 150, 167, 168
Wesemael 68
Westin 189, 222
White 167, 224
Whittick 14, 70
Widstrom 222
Wigley 59, 69, 70
Wijk 102, 107, 146, 168, 173, 214, 218, 219, 223, 226
Wildt de 4, 6, 11
Williamson 224
Wilson 222
Wooley 224
World Commission on Environment and Development 224

Worthington 72, 92, 93, 97, 101
Wright 24, 52, 53

Yeomans 133, 136
Yin 224

Zajicek 219
Zeeman 1, 12
Zeeuw 69
Zeinstra 106, 136, 220
Zeisel 159, 168, 224, 226
Zelnik 101, 106
Zimring 145, 150, 166, 168
Zube 166
Zwam van 166
Zweers 97, 107

Subject index

Accessibility 85, 90, 100, 101, 146, 156,
    170–178, 183, 184, 214, 216, 218
Acoustics 88, 201
ADA (Americans with Disabilities Act) 173
ADM (Architectural Design Management)
    133
AEDET (Achieving Excellence Design
    Evaluation Toolkit) 210, 211, 217
Aesthetics 14, 47
Affordability 14
Air quality 195, 213, 217
Amsterdam School 17, 51
Analogy 128
Analysis 114, 119–126
ANSI standards 104
Anthroposophy 51
Appropriation of Space 33
Archigram 17
Archi-Neering 18
Architectonic quality 4, 7
Assessment scales 208–204
Association of Dutch Architects 111

Baroque 48
Bauhaus 25, 131
Beauty 15, 19, 24, 26, 31, 40, 46, 47,
    48, 67, 156

Behavioural mapping 206
Bidder 81
Blob architecture 62, 117
Blobism 61, 63
Blobitecture 62
BOT (Built Operate Transfer) 76, 79, 83
BPE (Building Performance Evaluation)
    104, 151, 164
BQA (Building Quality Assessment)
    209, 216
Brainstorming 127
Brief 8, 71–79, 81, 87, 89–90, 101,
    109, 143
    basic 90
    definitive 90
    fit-out 92, 93
    global 90
    operating 93
    project 92, 93
    strategic 92, 93
Briefing 71, 72–76, 92, 116
Brochure plan 79, 83
Brutalism 57
Building process 8, 75, 76, 79, 82, 83,
    144, 145
Building Research Foundation (SBR)
    72–74, 80, 81, 83, 92,
    101, 105

CAD (Computer Aided Design) 64, 116, 132
Car parks 147
CEN standards 104
Checklist(s) 212, 216, 218
Chicago School 15
CIAM 27, 29
Clarity 5, 85, 187
Classicism 58
Client 71, 73–83, 86, 93, 100, 105, 109, 134, 143, 144, 148, 149, 208
Climate 2, 3, 177, 198, 201, 209, 216
Cognition 47
College Bouw Ziekenhuisvoorzieningen (CBZ) 195, 211
Comfort 85, 101, 201, 208, 212, 216, 217, 218
Complexity 5, 112, 152, 156
Composition 47
Concession 83
Condition(s) 86, 87, 92, 99, 169, 177, 178, 188, 191, 194
Conjecture 120–122
Constraint 111
Construction 10, 165
Constructional efficiency 14–18, 19, 20, 31, 37, 46
Constructivism 16
Consultant 77, 79, 80, 82, 134, 149
Context 5, 9, 13, 37–45, 46, 66
Contract 73, 75, 79–83, 134
Contractor 8, 9, 79–83
Convenience 15, 20, 24
Cost(s) 73, 74, 83, 84, 104, 151, 152, 153, 156, 161
Creative methods 127
Critical regionalism 37, 38, 39
Cyberspace 63, 207

Database 144, 148
Decision support 116
Decision tree 126
Decision-making 143, 144
Decomposition 119, 125
Deconstructivism 59–61, 62, 131
Delft School 37
Demand 14, 155
Design 71–82, 109–113, 118–135, 165, 169, 210, 211, 212, 214 and Build 76, 79, 82, 83 for All 101, 173
    concept 151
    guidelines 144, 146–148

methodology 112–118, 133
methods 110, 113–115, 118, 124, 129, 133
principles 186, 194
process 73, 109, 110, 114–119, 145
strategies 113, 114
team 93
tool 200, 204
Designer 73–82, 86, 94, 109, 119, 133, 144, 148
DHV/AIB 88, 90, 94
DIN standards 104
Dutch Practice Guidelines 85, 106
Dutch Working Conditions Act, 200, 201

Echo times 88
Eclecticism 59
Ecole des Beaux Arts 20
Ecole Polytechnique 20
Ecology 53, 202, 204
Efficiency 14, 16, 18, 19, 20, 24, 32, 37, 42, 46, 47, 112, 152, 156, 170–178, 277, 278
Egressability 175
E-Motive architecture 64
Empirical cycle 123
Enlightment 19
Environmental psychology 151
Ergonomic(s) 94, 182, 196, 199, 214, 218
Evaluation 8, 114, 118, 121, 123, 125, 141–166, 194, 205, 206, 207, 210, 214, 217, 218
    ex ante 142, 144, 145, 164, 206, 207
    ex post 105, 142, 144, 164, 207
    process 141, 142
    product 141, 142
Expansion 87
Expressionism 17, 50

Fantasy Analogy 88
Feasibility 8, 72, 74, 91, 112, 117
Flexibility 42, 87, 101, 152, 158, 170, 178–180, 182, 202, 211, 218
Floor plan 179, 181, 187, 191
Floor plan analysis 206
Form 4, 6, 13–68, 114, 123, 129, 131, 132, 142, 151
Formal Architecture 41
Forum 28, 29

Function 1, 6, 10, 13–68, 74, 86, 87, 114, 123, 129–132, 142, 151, 160
  aesthetic 3
  climatologic 3
  cultural 2
  economic 2, 3
  protective 1
  social 2
  symbolic 2
  territorial 1
  utility 2
Function analysis 97, 99, 126, 131
Functional 10, 151, 169
  analysis 9, 35, 37, 97
  design 3, 31, 97
  efficiency 14, 19, 21, 32, 37, 57, 177
  quality 3, 10, 11
  requirements 94, 95, 97
Functionalism 14, 15, 16, 18, 25, 27, 28, 29, 31, 32, 33, 57
Functionality 3, 47, 48, 58, 67, 68, 178, 216, 217
Function-neutral 35

General contracting 76, 79, 82
Genius loci 38
Gestalt 25, 187
Globalisation 42

HBQ (Healthy Building Quality) 213, 217
Healing environment 195
Health 85, 142, 195, 196, 197, 199, 202, 209, 213, 214
High Tech 17, 86
Humanist Architecture 29
Humidity 178, 201, 202
Hyperbodies 64

Identity 161, 178, 186, 187, 196
Image 161
International Style 26, 56
Interview 158, 205, 214

Legibility 177, 186
Leningrad-Pravda 17
Light 178, 183, 185, 186, 195, 196, 200, 202, 203, 207, 213, 217
Liquid architecture 64

Management 9, 73, 76, 80, 82, 93, 104, 141
Meaning 6, 11, 14, 46, 47, 48, 51, 52, 53, 58–60, 186
Mission statement 91
Modern movement 25, 54, 55–58, 131
Modernism 58
Morphological 126, 132
Multifunctionality 32, 180

NEN standards 76, 83–85, 94, 104, 106, 153, 200, 201, 216
Neo-rationalism 37, 39
Neo-styles 47, 49
NHS Estates 210, 217
Nieuwe Bouwen 28, 55, 57
Nieuwe Zakelijkheid 55
Noise 178, 190, 195, 197, 200, 201, 212, 213, 217
Non-territorial office 193
Normalisation 26

Observation 206, 212
Occupancy 85, 101, 164, 165, 206
Opbouw de 25
ORBIT (Organisation, Building, and Information Technology) 210, 217
Organic Architecture 24, 54, 62
Orientation 85, 150, 152, 157, 179, 200, 214, 217
Over-dimensioning 87

Parking 154, 170, 172, 176, 178
Participation 114
Pattern language 115–116
Perception 42, 47, 64
Performance 72, 73, 76, 80–83, 86, 94–97, 111, 118, 125, 134, 164, 173, 195, 209, 214, 218
Personal space 188, 192, 193
Personalisation 192, 193, 194
POE (Post Occupancy Evaluation) 8, 9, 104, 142, 150, 162, 164
Polar scales 165
Police Mark 215, 216, 218
Postmodern 114
Postmodernism 58, 59, 131
Praxis 122
Precedents 9, 31, 104, 122, 129–132
Pre-design research 142

Prefabrication 25
Prerequisites 84
Primary generator 120, 122
Privacy 1, 151, 170, 188–194, 196, 197,
    199, 201, 213, 217
    auditory 190, 201
    territorial 190
    visual 189, 191
Productivity 195, 196, 197,
    198, 199
Programme of requirements 8, 72–79, 83,
    84, 88–92, 96, 97,100, 109, 118,
    123, 132, 142, 169, 206
Programming 8, 71–73, 99, 130, 142, 143,
    169, 206
Project procedure 84
Prototype 122, 132
Proxemics 188

QIND (Quality Index) 211
Quality 7, 10, 11, 14, 72, 74, 86, 89, 92,
    132, 142, 143, 149–153, 156, 158,
    159, 164, 165, 169–218
    architectonic 4, 7, 10, 81, 142, 143,
        150, 165
    aesthetic 7, 10
    cultural 7
    economic 10, 11, 151, 202
    environmental 202, 209
    functional 3, 10, 11, 165, 169–204
    physical 11
    representational 152
    social 202
    spatial 209
    technical 11, 14, 151, 165, 209, 216
    user 133, 158
    visual 14, 86, 89, 92, 142, 143, 152,
        156, 209, 216
Questionnaire 158, 205, 211, 214
Quincy, Quatremére de 130, 131

Rating scale 212
Rationalism 19
Rationalistic 114
Reachability 152, 156, 160, 170–172, 173,
    174, 178
Regionalism 37, 38
Reliability 112, 159
REN (Real Estate Norm) 1, 171,
    208, 216
REN Quick Scan 171, 208, 209
Reverberation time 88, 200

Safety 1, 101, 146, 152, 156, 160, 170,
    177, 178, 182–185, 202, 208, 209,
    214–215, 216, 217, 218
SBR see Building Research
    Foundation
SBS see Sick Building Syndrome
Seal of approval 214, 215, 216
Secured by Design 215
Security 1, 85, 101, 185, 196, 199, 212,
    215, 217
Semantic 122
Semiotic 152
Senior citizen's label 216, 218
Senior citizen's score 216, 218
Sick Building Syndrome (SBS) 101,
    195, 213
Significance 26
Simulation 118, 207
SKW Certification 216, 218
Social contact 170, 188, 190
Social interaction 188, 194, 197
Sociofugal 188, 189
Sociopetal 188
Socio-prevention 185
Sound 170, 173, 182, 200, 201,
    206, 213
Space book 92
Spatial organisation 2, 6
Spatial orientation 170, 177, 178,
    185, 186
Specification 8, 9, 80
Spiritual 7, 53
Stakeholders 117
Standardisation 26, 27
STM (Serviceability Tools and Methods)
    210, 217
Structuralism 33–35
Supply 14, 155
Sustainable/sustainability 11, 38, 85, 101,
    152, 156, 170, 202, 203, 204, 209,
    211, 218
SWOT (strengths, weaknesses,
    opportunities, threads) 145
Symbolic 47, 51, 91, 152
Symbolism 14, 44, 47, 61
Synectics 127
Syntax 122
Synthesis 114, 119, 122–125
System analysis 120

Taller de Arquitectura 50
Team X 29

Technology 3, 26, 28, 35, 47, 142
Techno-prevention 185
Tendenza 39
Tenderer 78, 81–83
Territoriality 152, 170, 188, 189,
    192, 193
TOTE model 120
Tradition, 28, 37
Traditionalism 37
Turnkey 83
Type 129–131
Typology 6, 31, 58, 113,
    129–131, 163

Usability 112, 156, 173, 174, 202, 214,
    218
User 74, 76, 79, 86, 96, 109, 142, 148, 149
Utility 7, 10, 14, 15, 24, 29, 47, 58, 67, 73,
    85, 112, 208, 209

Validity 112, 159
Value 14, 29, 31, 37, 141, 159
    cultural 7, 47
    experiential 14, 47, 151
    future 7, 179, 202, 211
    historical 47
    symbolic 91
    utility 7, 10, 14, 29, 47, 85, 132,
        208, 209
Ventilation 201, 203
Virtual reality 207
Visual scope 187

Wayfinding 212, 217
Well-being 195–202
    physical 170, 194, 195
Workbook 92
Workshops 201, 206